THE MODERNIZATION OF EASTER ISLAND

J. DOUGLAS PORTEOUS

Western Geographical Series Volume 19

Department of Geography, University of Victoria
Victoria, British Columbia
Canada

1981 University of Victoria

Western Geographical Series, Volume 19

editorial address

Harold D. Foster, Ph.D.
Department of Geography
University of Victoria
Victoria, British Columbia
Canada

Publication of the Western Geographical Series has been generously supported by the Leon and Thea Koerner Foundation, the Social Science Federation of Canada, the National Centre for Atmospheric Research, the International Geographical Union Congress, the University of Victoria and the National Research Council of Canada.

THE MODERNIZATION OF EASTER ISLAND

(Western geographical series; v. 19 ISSN 0315-2022)
Bibliography: p.
Includes index.
ISBN 0-919838-09-X

1. Easter Island—History. I. University of Victoria (B.C.). Dept. of Geography. II. Title. III. Series.
F3169.P67 996'.18 C80-091102-4

THE MODERNIZATION OF EASTER ISLAND

For
Tofino Porteous

who sat on the manuscript less than anyone

ACKNOWLEDGEMENTS

My thanks go to the people of Easter Island for their interest and help during my fieldwork on the island in 1974, 1975-6, and 1978. Especial thanks are due to Juan Haoa, Nicolas Haoa and family, Victoria Rapahango, Antonio Tepano, and Leon Tuki. I am also grateful for the support and cooperation of Chilean officials and other residents, notably the parish priest Father David, two successive governors, Mayor de Carabineros Omar Fuenzalida and Capitán Arnt Arentsen, the staff of the gobernación, especially practicante Barros, the carabineros of comisería no. 9, judge Orasmin Gillies, and hotel managers Pedro Alfonso and señor Pick.

In Santiago help was provided by Gerald Cooper, Reginald Stockins, and Renato Valenzuela of the Compañía de Inversiones "La Escocesa" Limitada, Joe Calvo of the Canadian Embassy, Carlos Browne of the Comisión Nacional Isla de Pascua, and Gonzalo Figueroa of the Fundación Pacífico. Dr. Sergio Sepúlveda of the Department of Geography, University of Chile at Santiago, helped me find two research assistants, Veronica Riquelme and José Abalos, who searched Easter Island data in the newspaper library of the Biblioteca Nacional. Professor Otto Klein and Mrs. Marta Klein of Viña del Mar provided encouragement and hospitality on several occasions. Dr. and Mrs. Bengt Danielson, Tahiti, and Dr. Thor Heyerdahl, Kon-Tiki Museet, Oslo, also provided assistance, as did Dr. Georges Nogrady, Montreal. Welcome companionship in the field was given by Enrique Klein and Gerry Bernard. My thanks are due also to two anthropologists, Drs. Grant McCall (Australia) and Bernardo Berdichewsky (Chile) who read the manuscript with a critical eye for problems of anthropology and Chilean history. Their comments proved most useful. John Flenley provided some details of his ongoing work on Easter Island vegetation history.

Renee Stovold efficiently typed me yet another book manuscript, and retyped the many changes that were made with commendable patience. Brian Turnbull assisted in finding maps of the Pacific, and Jon Turlock helped organize the index. Ole Heggen produced the excellent drawings (some of them copies of Kon-Tiki Museet artifacts, by kind permission of Dr. Thor Heyerdahl), and both he and Ken Quan worked with my lamentably rough sketches to produce the maps and diagrams. Diane Brazier typeset the manuscript with precision. Ian Norie supervised the mapping, the photographic work, and the overall production of the book. To all these my thanks. Thanks also to Alastair Pitty for rescuing the proofs of this book from an East Yorkshire road into which they had fallen from the roof of my car.

Grants for Easter Island research 1974-9 were provided by the following Canadian agencies: the Canada Council/Social Sciences & Humanities Research Council; the International Development Research Centre; the Social Science & Humanities Research Council's Leave Fellowship Division; and the University of Victoria Faculty Research Fund. I was also fortunate in obtaining publication grants. This book has been published with the help of a grant from the Social Science Federation of Canada, using funds provided by the Social Sciences & Humanities Research Council of Canada. A supplementary grant was provided by the University of Victoria to assist with the cost of illustrative material. I am most grateful for the support of all these agencies. Señora Carmen Balcells kindly gave me permission to quote two extracts from Pablo Neruda's poem *La Rosa Separada*. All plates are from photographs taken by the author, except half-tones 2-7, 10, 21, 22, 29, 30, and 37 (the latter courtesy G. McCall), and colour plates 11 and 15 (courtesy G. Bernard).

Last, but most, I thank my family: Carol Porteous for walking many miles in blazing heat over lava fields and through craters during fieldwork, for unfailing encouragement, for research assistance, and for patiently bearing with me during the prolonged labour which brought forth this book; Jonathan Gavin Mell Porteous, for his contribution to the lore of family planning in that he was conceived on Easter Island on or about Christmas Day 1978; and Tofino Porteous, cat, for his silent companionship during the long hours of writing. Without the help of Tofo this book could have been completed much earlier; to him the book is dedicated.

J. Douglas Porteous

PREFACE

This book provides an historico-geographical account of the economic, political, and social development of Easter Island since the 1860s, together with a discussion of the resulting transformation of the island's cultural landscape. Externally-induced modernization began in earnest in 1862 when the island, previously rarely visited, was raided for slaves. This brief but violent external impact involved the transportation of many islanders to foreign mines and plantations, the assaults of previously-unknown diseases, emigration induced by missionaries, and a significant disintegration of the indigenous Polynesian culture. The first white resident, a sheeprancher, took up residence in the late 1860s. By the 1870s a population estimated to have been in the order of 3-4,000 persons was reduced to a mere 110.

At this point a Tahiti-based Scots-French partnership purchased most of the island from the surviving indigenes and established Easter Island as a sheepranch. The collapse of this partnership facilitated annexation by the Republic of Chile in 1888, and the subsequent control of the island by a Scots-Chilean firm which dominated the sheeprearing operation until the 1950s. Only since the 1960s has the island experienced the full effects of twentieth-century modernization through tourism and government intervention. Weekly scheduled airflights between Chile, Easter Island and Tahiti replaced, from 1967, the island's reliance upon a single boat per year.

In analyzing the above sequence of events this book seeks to fill a void. The literature on Easter Island is dominated by popular works which emphasize the island's "mystery", "secrets", or "enigma".[1] Content analysis of the subject matter of a score of popular works in English (8), Spanish (6), and French (6) reveals an overwhelming emphasis on the problems of prehistory.[2] Great attention is given to the megalithic ceremonial centres, the great statues, and speculations on the cultural origins of the group responsible for these works. Published scientific research has been addressed to a similar range of problems. A single major work has emerged in each of the fields of archaeology,[3] art,[4] ethnology,[5] ethnomusicology,[6] linguistics,[7] microbiology,[8] politico-administrative history,[9] and prehistory.[10] This emphasis on archaeology and anthropology is confirmed in several doctoral theses.[11]

These problems are important and exciting, but the single-minded pursuit of Easter Island prehistory has resulted in an almost total neglect of the island's modern development. Few general works highlight a South American phase of colonial expansion in the Pacific. Specifically, little scholarly effort has been devoted to an analysis of the modernization of Easter Island after it first became part of a colonial sphere of influence in the second half of the nineteenth century. Little attention has been paid to the social, political, and economic changes which followed the disaster of 1862, or to the resultant landscape transformations. Few efforts have been made to consider the development issues and other problems which face the island's population today.

Perhaps the real "mystery" of Easter Island is the story of its historical development. By supplying such an account, this book seeks to remedy the existing informational imbalance. It does so by placing island development within the context of Chilean, rather than Pacific Island, development. Few works have attempted to consider Easter Island within a non-Polynesian historical or geographical context.

Easter Island illustrates, in microcosm, the impact of external modernizing forces on small traditional societies.[12] Two very different external influences have transformed the island since the 1860s; profit-oriented foreign business corporations were followed by a series of paternalist Chilean state agencies. Viewed in the context of an analysis of centre-periphery relations, the island's development could well be divided into: (i) a colonial period, up to 1888; (ii) a neocolonial period, 1888-1952; and (iii) a period of internal colonialism, which began in 1952 and has yet to terminate.

In a modification of this framework, however, I have chosen to emphasize four major themes. Easter Island's geopolitical history, culminating in the annexation by Chile in 1888, is considered in Chapter 2. The assumption of effective control by foreign entrepreneurs, and the relationships between these *de facto* rulers and the *de jure* sovereign, the Republic of Chile, are explored in Chapters 3 and 4. Chapters 5-7 are devoted to an analysis of the socioeconomic and cultural landscape transformations resulting from the conversion of an autarkic subtropical island into an externally-oriented wool-exporting estate. Finally, the recent impact of government agencies engaged in deliberate modernization policies, together with the effects of air transportation and tourism since 1967, are considered in Chapters 8-10.

These emphases are predicated upon the availability of field evidence in the Easter Island landscape and of documentary evidence, which was gathered from archives in Britain, Chile, Tahiti, the United States, and Easter Island itself. Many of the documents are in nineteenth-century French or Spanish; all quotations are my own translations.

In the nineteenth century Easter Island was a remote place. Even its name and location were in dispute. Known to the original inhabitants as Te Pito o Te Henua (the navel of the world), the island was variously referred to by Europeans as Davis' Land, San Carlos, Teapy, and variants of Vaihu. As late as the 1870s vessels called at Easter Island in search of the island of Wahou which, although nonexistent, was nevertheless to be found on contemporary European maps (Figure 1,0). Today's indigenes refer to the island, to themselves, and to their language as Rapanui. In this book the term Rapanui is used to refer to both language and inhabitants. To avoid

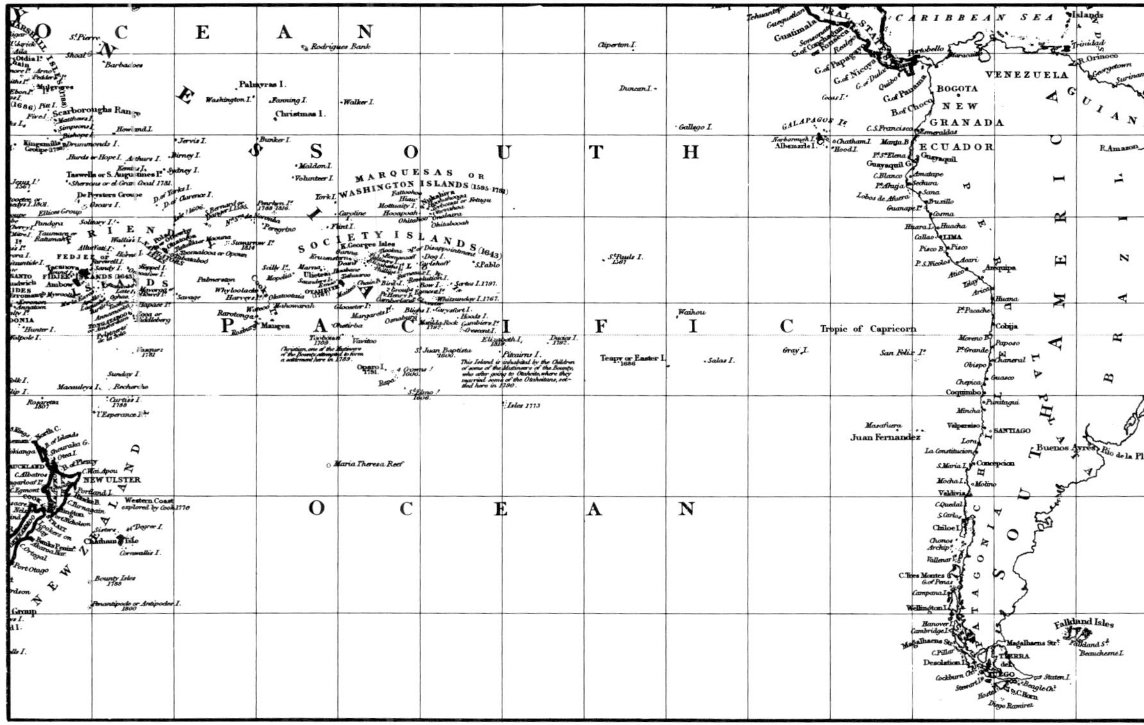

FIGURE 1,0 A nineteenth century map of the Pacific (c. 1842) indicating the locational confusion regarding "Easter Island" and "Wahou".

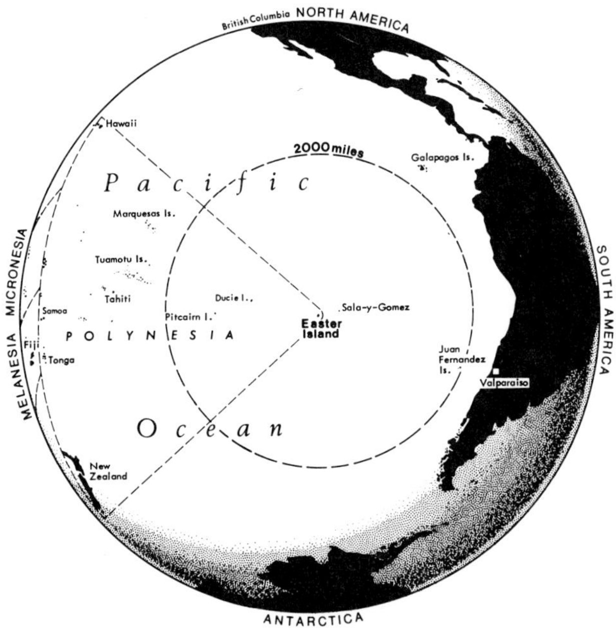

FIGURE 2,0 The location of Easter Island (Te Pito o Te Henua, the Navel of the World).

confusion, and because it is the name most frequently used by non-Rapanui (with the exception of Polynesian specialists), the name of the island appears throughout as Easter Island.

Despite modern airline connections, Easter Island remains remote in the 1980s. Physically, it is over 3,000 kilometres (2,000 miles) from a major city (Figure 2,0). From official reports of the 1880s to the Ministry of Education in 1969, Chileans habitually refer to "this far-flung possession of Chile"[13] . . . "lost in the immensity of the Pacific Ocean".[14] Metaphorically, Easter Island has remained remote because of our ignorance of anything beyond its prehistory. It is significant that a Rapanui, commenting in 1975 upon the proposal of the Rolling Stones rock group to hold a festival on the island, should remark that such an event would "put Easter Island on the map, so that people abroad will at least know something of us beyond the statues."[15]

This book attempts to provide such information with less trauma to the island. As an historico-geographical overview based largely on primary sources, it may provide a context for more detailed research on the modernization of Easter Island during the last one hundred and twenty years.

TABLE OF CONTENTS

SECTION THREE

LIST OF TABLES

LIST OF FIGURES

LIST OF HALFTONE PLATES

LIST OF COLOUR PLATES

1

2

3

4

5

6

7

8

9

10

11

12

13

14

15

16

17

18

21

22

23

24

25

26

27

28

29

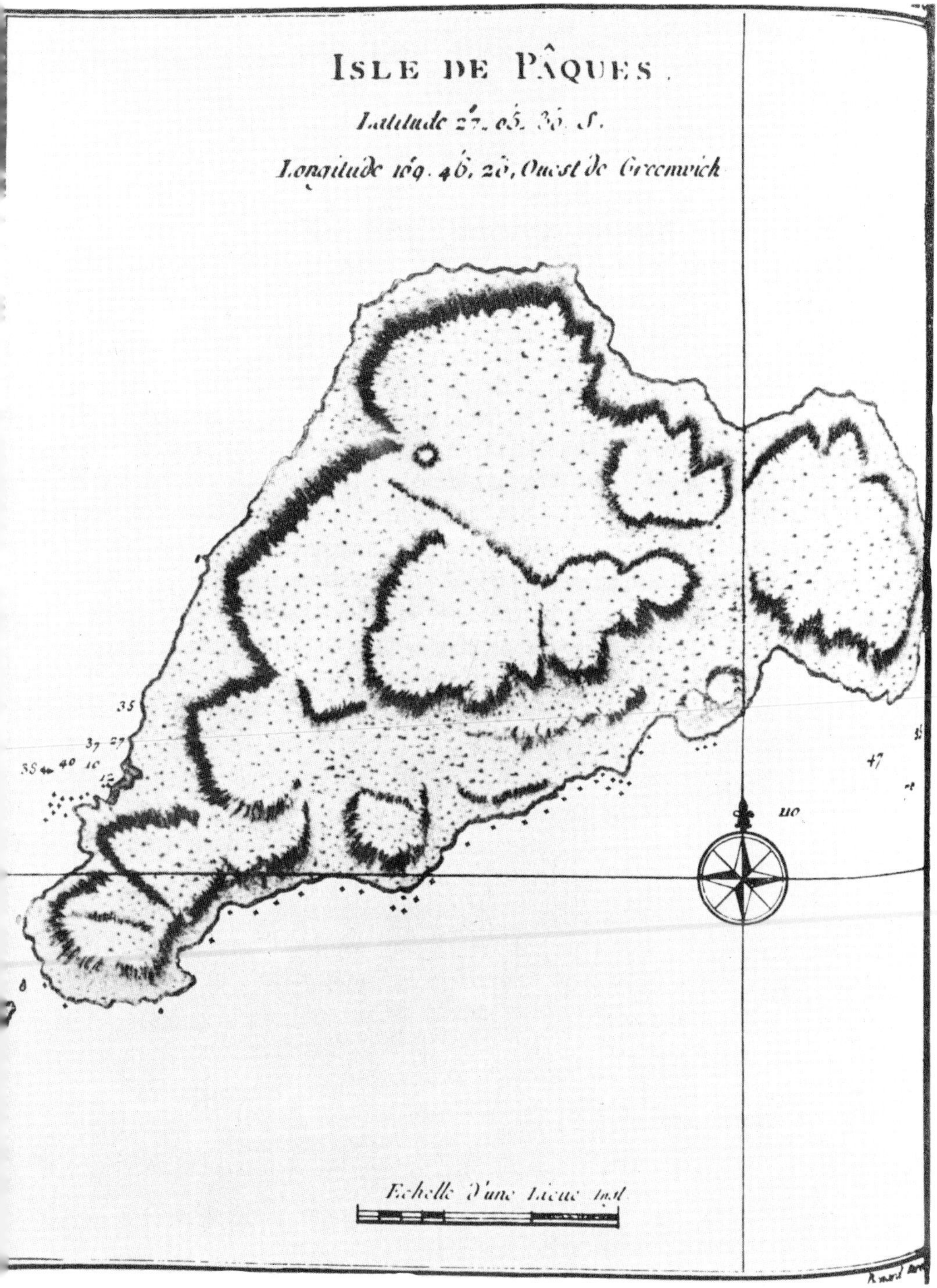
ISLE DE PÂQUES.
Latitude 27. 05. 30. S.
Longitude 109. 46. 20. Ouest de Greenwich
Echelle d'une Lieue Angl.

si navegáramos en tropel hacia la Isla,
si todos fueran sabios de golpe y acudiéramos
a Rapa Nui, la mataríamos,
la mataríamos con inmensas pisadas, con dialectos,
escupos, batallas, religiones,
y allí también se acabaría el aire,
caerían al suelo las estatuas,
se harían palos sucios las narices de piedra
y todo moriría amargamente.

Pablo Neruda
La Rosa Separada (1973)

◀ **PLATE 1** The first European map of Easter Island, Captain James Cook, 1774

◀ **PLATE 2** The statue quarry at Rano Raraku

PLATE 3 Rapanui male, drawn by Hodges, artist on Cook's voyage, 1774 ▶

SECTION ONE

FORCES FOR CHANGE

What is civilisation?

Mr Skionar

It is just respect for property:
a state in which no man takes wrongfully
what belongs to another, is a perfectly
civilised state.

Mr MacQuedy

Thomas Love Peacock, *Crochet Castle* (1831)

PLATE 4 Rapanui-European contact, voyage of La Pérouse, 1786 ▸

2

1 EXTERNAL IMPACT

> It is a sad fact that in these islands, as in North America, wherever the white man establishes himself the aborigines perish.
>
> Commander, H.M.S. *Topaze*, 1868

As the European expanded the horizons of his known world after the fifteenth century, he inevitably came into contact with human groups whose ways were strange. Mutual astonishment was expressed, and each learned from the other. Inevitably, because European technology and institutions proved more powerful, many traditional political, economic, and social systems were undermined. In extreme cases whole racial groups were obliterated, occasionally through a deliberate policy of genocide, as in Tasmania. More frequently, indigenous groups were simply cleared from the land coveted by Europeans.

Almost everywhere the homeostatic population balance frequently achieved by indigenous societies was destroyed by European diseases, medicines, alcohol, and firearms, or the imposition of codes of conduct which illegitimized traditional ways of life. As Captain James Cook so trenchantly observed in his Pacific journals, the introduction of new wants among peoples formerly oblivious of the dubious blessings of European technology was often sufficient to permanently disrupt existing social and environmental equilibria.[1]

The destruction of a society was not normally accomplished at a single blow. Locational and attitudinal differences, the unevenness of diffusion, and the restricted numbers and only temporary visits of the first Europeans ensured that societal transformation was a lengthy and discontinuous process. Yet it may be possible to identify a relatively short period during which the impact of European power on any traditional society was so overwhelming that the radical changes which followed may be traced directly from that traumatic epoch. Such confrontations would be most likely to occur where traditional societies, small in absolute numbers, inhabited small or fragile ecosystems such as minor islands or deserts. Moorehead has termed an intense, devastating experience of this type a "fatal impact . . . that fateful moment when a social capsule is broken open, when primitive creatures . . . are confronted for the first time with civilization."[2]

THE EXTERNAL IMPACT IN THE PACIFIC

It is possible to treat the impact of the white man upon the Pacific islands historically, in terms of roughly homogeneous periods of influence, or geographically, in terms of the experiences of selected subregions. For example, Moorehead gives an historical account of the initial effects of Europeans upon Australia, Tahiti, and Antarctica.[3] The varied influences of the French, British, Americans, Germans, and other colonizers could also be traced.

During the initial impact period, however, the impacted territory is generally treated as a frontier by those responsible for the impact. The "frontier thesis" has been well documented by North American historians.[4] One of its tenets is that frontier development often proceeds in stages, the initial work of explorers being followed by the invasions of small entrepreneurs, whose uncoordinated attempts at resource exploitation are finally consolidated by well-organized corporate enterprises. From this emerges a view of frontier development as progressing through a series of phases, each characterized by a particular type of non-native who penetrates the frontier for motives peculiar to his type. In this way a common result, the incorporation of a new region into the interdependent global economic system, is achieved by a variety of groups operating through radically different means and with varying goals.

The following analysis of the Pacific frontier is predicated upon the semi-independent operation of a variety of actors whose initial goals were often in disharmony and who frequently came into conflict with each other. Sweeping views of Pacific history, as well as careful analyses of specific regions, suggest that the major types of actors involved in the Pacific frontier can be identified as explorers, commercial entrepreneurs, slavers, planters, and missionaries.[5]

Explorers

These were, by definition, the first group to appear in the Pacific Islands. From the sixteenth to the early nineteenth century small fleets of Spanish, Dutch, British, French, and other vessels quartered the Pacific, charting its myriad islands. The impact of these explorers was brief, discontinuous, and uneven. By nature peripatetic, they rarely remained long in a single location. Curiosity was tempered by caution, for many islanders resented such intrusions and were prepared to defend themselves.

The explorers had two radical effects upon the islands. One involved a considerable time-lag. The reports and journals they carried back to

Europe were in the nature of time bombs set to explode years later when traders, missionaries, and planters, their appetites whetted, began to flow into the new frontier. The other impact was more immediate, but had the far-reaching consequence of paving the way for future invaders. By introducing the islanders to alcohol, firearms, metal tools, and European clothing, the explorers not only disturbed existing social and environmental equilibria but also induced feelings of relative deprivation which could be assuaged only by the importation of more European artifacts.

James Cook saw this clearly, reporting with strong guilt feelings that the growing use of iron tools in Polynesia would inevitably lead to an inability to produce indigenous tools of wood, bone, and stone. Although they also introduced European diseases, with devastating results, the chief effect of the explorers was to tie the first cord of the many which were soon to bind the island peoples into the web of external dependence. After the era of explorers the course, for many island societies, was set: ". . . once having entered into the coil of civilization you cannot go back; you must go on whatever the dangers may be."[6]

Commercial entrepreneurs

Entrepreneurs began to appear very shortly after the wave of British and French exploration which swept across the late-eighteenth century Pacific. The first major group were the whalers, who ranged the entire Pacific from the coasts of Chile to Australia. As whaling reached its peak towards the 1850s, hundreds of vessels, many of them American, were involved. Calling at island harbours to effect repairs and to take on water and fresh provisions, the crews of these vessels continued the transformation of island society begun by the explorers.

To the eighteenth century transPacific trade in American furs and Chinese luxury goods were added the indigenous products of Oceania: trepang, coconut products, sandalwood, shells, and pearls. With the traders came beachcombers, often the flotsam of Euramerican society. Although regulated trading centres appeared on some of the larger islands, the history of the early traders, whalers, and beachcombers is often one of injustice and violence. Despite the efforts of missionaries and government commissions, only with the appearance of large organized merchant companies in the second half of the nineteenth century did some semblance of order and fair dealing appear in entrepreneurial operations. Even then justice could not be assured, for the far-flung agents of the major companies were often free to act as semi-independent operators.

Planters

This was the first group to regard the Pacific as something more than a resource frontier from which to extract loot for European markets. Unlike the whalers and traders, the planter was less concerned with making fast profits than with building up a fairly long-term source of income from supplying the growing world demand for tropical agricultural products. Of the many tropical plants transplanted to Oceania, sugar, coffee, copra, cotton, vanilla, and rubber achieved significance in terms of economic and social change.[7] In general, terrain and climate made pastoral pursuits impossible or unprofitable. One exception to this rule, as we shall see, was Easter Island.

One of the chief results of the expansion of plantation agriculture, and to some extent of the mining enterprises which came later, was the alienation of land. Many planters and land speculators succeeded in duping indigenous rulers into selling large tracts of land for derisory prices. In many cases the traditional users of the land, to their bewilderment, found that they had suddenly become mere wage labourers upon it. Where an island's labour was insufficient, inefficient, or protected, other labour was imported, resulting in ethnic imbalances which are still major sources of conflict in Oceania. As the plantocracy developed corporate structure, so some indigenes developed the characteristics of a proletariat or peonage. A docile labour force was most easily assured by transporting island labour to a new environment in which they were compelled to become totally dependent upon their employer.

Slavers

Blackbirders, otherwise known as kidnappers or slavers, were an indispensable adjunct to the mining and plantation economies developing within the Pacific and on its margins. Demands for labour for ships' crews and from enterprises as various as stockranching in Australia, island plantation agriculture, and guano mining in South America were the motive force behind the slave ships which despoiled the Pacific after the 1840s. To give the trade an aura of legality, islanders were often compelled or otherwise induced to sign contracts committing themselves to work long hours in distant regions. The dividing line between properly contracted labour and outright kidnapping is very difficult to draw.

Island labour was indifferently treated. Unaccustomed to the unvarying routines of the mine or plantation, islanders were inefficient and prone to succumb to disease and death under a regime of overstrenuous work, poor diet, inadequate accommodation, and ill-treatment. When returned to Oceania, they were frequently dumped on any suitable island, and many underwent lengthy delays in their attempts to reach their former home islands. Although the British were the chief blackbirders, their kidnapping Act of 1872 made some attempt to regulate the worst outrages of this traffic in human beings. It was impossible to kill the trade, however, and the transportation of island labour continued, particularly to Queensland, into the early twentieth century.

Missionaries

Ostensibly involved only in converting the heathen and supplying supplementary medical and educational benefits, missionaries were a major factor in the undermining of indigenous ways of life. Gaining considerable political power, they frequently came into conflict with traders, beachcombers, whalers, and planters. They also came into conflict with each other. The most notable rivalry emerged between the largely British and American protestants and the catholics, some of whom were supported by the French government as effective agents in the dissemination of French culture, language, and power.

Whereas the work of the individual protestant missions, although well-organized, was on the whole uncoordinated, the early nineteenth century witnessed a papal strategy which, like the Treaty of Tordesillas three centuries before it, divided the conquerable world in twain. In this case the Pacific was divided between two French religious orders. Responsibility for missionary work in Western Oceania was granted to the Société de Marie. The conversion of the Eastern Pacific was to be brought about by missionaries of the Société de Picpus. The latter, already established in Chile and the Gambier Islands, ousted the protestants from Tahiti and from this headquarters spread the Catholic faith eastwards into the Marquesas and Tuamotus.[8]

It is clear that, although the different actor groups occupied fairly distinct phases of Pacific history, there was considerable overlap in their periods of operation (Figure 1,1). Their combined effect upon any particular island was frequently deleterious. As early as the eighteenth century Diderot had warned the Tahitians that Christians would arrive

> with crucifix in one hand and the dagger in the other to cut your throats or force you to accept their customs and opinions; one day under their rule you will be almost as unhappy as they are.[9]

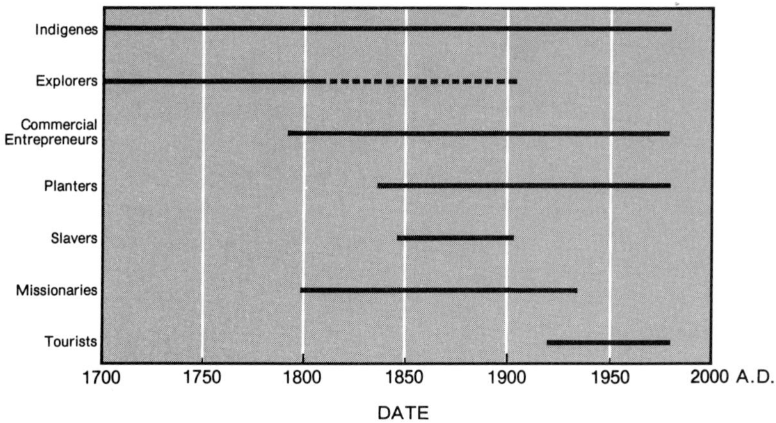

FIGURE 1,1 A general historical model of Pacific Island development impacts.

Loss of their land, degradation of their culture, acceptance of Euramerican technology and its accompanying values, the importation of alien labour, the substitution of white leaders for indigenous rule, the promotion of warfare between rival native groups, the conversion of their souls, and the kidnapping and transportation of their bodies, all served to destroy the indigenous way of life on those islands which were unable to absorb such multidimensional assaults. The effects of slaving, disease, and warfare are nowhere more apparent than in population crashes. In Tahiti, for example, Cook allegedly found about 40,000 inhabitants in the 1770s. At the turn of the century the first missionaries found only about 15,000 islanders to convert, and by the mid-nineteenth century the population had fallen to 6,000.[10] It has taken a century for the Tahitian population to regain the level of the 1770s. Similar decimations took place throughout Oceania. Although wide-ranging indigenous groups had had similar effects upon each other for aeons of time, the European impact was more profound because of its universality.

THE EXTERNAL IMPACT ON EASTER ISLAND

Heyerdahl notwithstanding, the bulk of the evidence points to a Polynesian origin for the Easter Islanders.[11] The island's prehistory, known largely through legends and some meagre archaeological work, suggests an island divided among several clans or tribes, whose continuous rivalries frequently flared into war.[12] Isolated from their Polynesian origins, the islanders developed elaborate autochthonous rituals, the physical expressions of which are the statues, ceremonial areas, and ritual buildings still evident in the landscape. Although the climate was too extreme for breadfruit and coconut, the usual Polynesian staples were grown. Sugar cane, bananas, taro, ti, sweet potatoes (*kumara*), and fruits were supplemented by fish, crustaceans, chickens, and the edible Polynesian rat.

Not all the actors who were responsible for the general transformation of the Pacific are represented in the demonology of Easter Island. Commercial entrepreneurs, whether private traders or large companies, found nothing worth removing from this resource-poor, volcanic island. There was nothing to mine. Even plantation agriculture seemed impossible to European minds which associated it with the luxuriant vegetation and climatic benevolence of central Polynesia. Windswept and bleak, almost wholly grass-covered and with very few trees, the remote island appeared more suitable for stock rearing. Given the apparent lack of normal Oceanic commercial opportunities, Easter Island received its initial impact from four major types of actor. The explorers and slavers were followed by missionaries and commercial freebooters, who, because they engaged in a form of agrarian production, will be dignified with the term planter (Figure 2,1).

The Explorers

If the Spanish pioneers of the sixteenth century ever put in at Easter Island they did not broadcast their discovery. The first indication of such an island was the legendary "Davis's Land" sighted by the English privateer Edward Davis in 1687. In their search for Terra Australis Incognita, later explorers were unable to find Davis Land. It was not until Easter Sunday, 5 April 1722, that Jacob Roggeveen of the Dutch East India Company hove to off the isolated speck of land he named Easter Island (Paasch Eylandt, Osterinsel). Roggeveen's visit set the style for subsequent European appearances over the next century. During this period Easter Island was rarely the goal of Pacific explorers, but was usually accorded merely a brief visit by explorers anxious to encounter more productive isles in balmier climes.

Easter Island's initial explorers were those who sailed with Roggeveen (1722), González (1770), Cook (1774), and La Pérouse (1786). In each

---

PLATE 5 Rapanui ceremonial as interpreted by Pierre Loti, 1872 ▶

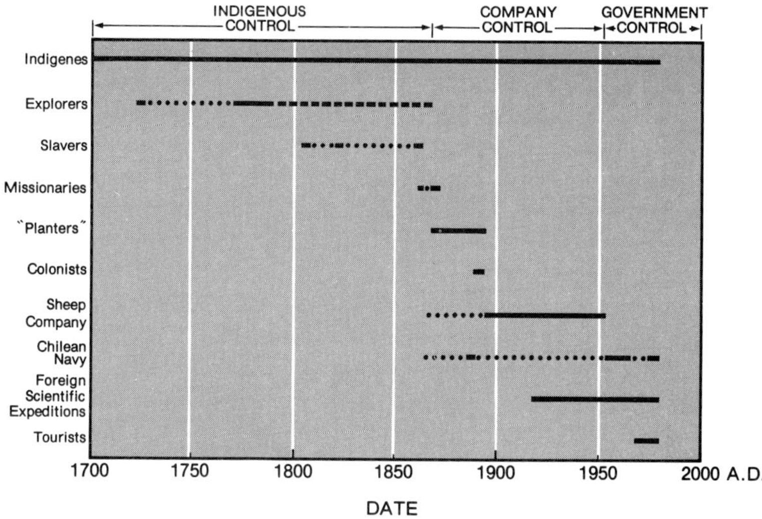

FIGURE 2,1 An historical model of Easter Island development impacts (compare Figure 1,1).

case the encounter between Europeans and indigenes took a more or less similar form. Natives and visitors expressed mutual astonishment. The whites disembarked to make cursory investigations of landscape, agriculture, vegetation, and inhabitants. Visitors were impressed by the numerous statues and other major artifacts, by the sexual freedom of the women, and by the "thievery" of the men. Local products were traded for European goods, but the latter were also stolen in great quantity. Only the Spanish refrained from retaliation. Members of the other three expeditions fired on the Rapanui wounding or killing several individuals. Not one of these expeditions stayed as much as one week. The island's productivity was not impressive, it lacked good fresh water, and sheltered anchorages were absent. Cook's remarks will serve to summarize the perceptions of the first explorers:

> They saw not an animal of any sort, and but few birds; nor indeed anything which can induce ships that are not in the utmost distress to touch at this island.[13]

The reports and narratives of these explorers, and notably those of Roggeveen, Behrens, Cook, and the Forsters, were responsible for giving Easter Island a place in the Euramerican world view. The more exaggerated accounts, such as that of Behrens, provoked much interest in the island. After the turn of the eighteenth century the island's position became more generally known and alien visits increased. The depredations of whalers and sealers, however, quickly rendered the inhabitants hostile to white visitors. Poor sea conditions and Rapanui hostility were responsible for the failure of four vessels to effect a landing in the period 1804-9.[14] When landings were made, as in the subsequent visits of the Russians (1818) and British (1825), initially peaceful transactions soon gave way to hostile demonstrations and the rapid retreat of the visitors to their boats.

It is probable that several whalers made unrecorded visits to the island in the early part of the nineteenth century.[15] From these, and from the explorers who preceded them, the islanders acquired a taste for European clothing and artifacts, were infected with venereal disease, and learned to fear and mistrust European power as manifested in firearms. Their hostility and fear were amply justified by their experiences at the hands of the slaving expeditions which climaxed in the early 1860s.

The Slavers

Rapanui mistrust of white visitors during the first half of the nineteenth century is readily attributable to the work of American slavers. During the eighteenth century the visits of explorers were regarded as strange but providential windfalls of valuable clothing and goods. This perception of the outside world was rudely dispelled on the arrival in 1805 of the schooner *Nancy*. A seal-hunting colony was then being established on the Chilean island of Mas Afuera in the Juan Fernández group. To provide labour for this venture the *Nancy*'s crew kidnapped 22 islanders. Other attempts were made, and it is probable that whalers also resorted to kidnapping when requiring replacement crew members or women; one such incident occurred in 1822.[16]

These raids were minor in comparison with what followed some forty years later. By the 1850s the Peruvian economy was in an expansive phase, with coastal plantations, domestic establishments, and offshore guano deposits all experiencing severe labour shortages. To solve this problem it was merely necessary to regard the Pacific as a vast reservoir of free labour, the only requirement being to round it up and convey it to Peru. Blackbirders began to scour the islands. "Shiploads of Micronesians and Polynesians were taken to Peru and sold off at so much a head . . .".[17]

Easter Island, the closest Polynesian island to the Peruvian coast, was a prime target. The systematic kidnapping of islanders possibly began earlier, but the fatal blow came in 1862.[18] In December of that year some eight Peruvian vessels landed their crewmen. With a mixture of blandishments and violence they managed to transfer several hundred islanders to the ships, and thence to Peru. Although the evidence is not unequivocal, it appears that perhaps 1000 islanders were transported to Peru in the early 1860s.[19] Labour conditions were poor, especially for those islanders put to work on the shelterless guano deposits of the Chincha Islands. All were exposed to diseases and climatic conditions never before experienced. It is generally believed that about ninety per cent of the transported Rapanui died within one or two years of their capture.

Despite the continued depredations of their countrymen in the Western Pacific, French and British governments were scandalized by the conditions to which Polynesians were subjected in Peru. The expostulations of Mons. Tepano Jaussen, Bishop of Axieri and Vicar Apostolic of Eastern Oceania, were in great part responsible for this official attitude. Given the strong representations of the French and British, the Peruvian authorities assembled the survivors at Callao and shipped them back to Polynesia. Little consideration was given to the precise repatriation of the islanders. Few vessels passed Easter Island, and thus several Easter Islanders found themselves deposited not on their home island but in Tahiti.

The number of Easter Islanders who managed to return, directly or indirectly, to their home island was probably less than a score, at most a mere two per cent of those kidnapped. The two thousand or so inhabitants who greeted them were met by carriers of contagious civilized diseases, notably tuberculosis and smallpox. Previously unexposed to these scourges, the Rapanui suffered the full ravages of a pandemic. Casualties are said to have risen well above one thousand.[20] The bodies of the victims accumulated so rapidly that the survivors were unable to dispose of them.

The Missionaries

There are unconfirmed reports of missionaries touching at Easter Island in the middle decades of the nineteenth century. The first attested visits, however, came within a year of the slavers' ravages of 1862. Having passed by the island in 1862 in the *Cassini*, one Captain Lejeune reached Valparaiso and brought the plight of the island to the attention of the Chilean branch of the Société de Picpus, who were charged with the Christianization of the Eastern Pacific.

Several missionaries, mainly French in nationality, then left Chile for Tahiti, where they were regaled with facts and fictions concerning recent events on Easter Island. The picture painted must have been grim, for only brother Eugene Eyraud landed on the island in the first attempt at Christianization. Eyraud appears to have been badly treated by the islanders, and in 1864 was prevailed upon to leave by a visiting ship. By 1865 Eyraud's reports, the successful efforts of Bishop Jaussen to free the Easter Islanders in Peru, and the arrival of some of them in Tahiti, had considerably increased French missionary interest in the island. In 1866 Eyraud returned, accompanied by father Roussel and several native assistants from French Polynesia. Two more missionaries arrived later in the same year.[21]

Land in the Hangaroa area was purchased from the indigenes in 1868 and subsequent years. The missionaries built churches, erected housing, and planted gardens. New species of fruit trees, vegetables, and animals were introduced, and some stockrearing was practised. From their headquarters in Hangaroa the missionaries gradually extended their influence over the several hundred remaining inhabitants. Besides converting them to Christianity, the missionaries introduced the islanders to crafts such as large-scale woodworking and home-building skills. More importantly, they played a major role in the conversion of the islanders to a more European mode of living and thinking.[22] They introduced and explained such awesome unknowns as the horse and the wheelbarrow. In their five years of residence, 1865-71, the missionaries accomplished a great deal, according to their lights. But in the latter year their work was rudely terminated by Captain Dutrou-Bornier.

The Planters

Jean-Baptiste Onéxime Dutrou-Bornier, "capitaine au long cours," probably saw Easter Island for the first time in the 1860s.[23] A French sea captain of some years standing, he was employed on the Tahiti-Valparaiso route. In 1866, as captain of the *Tampico*, he landed two of the French missionaries on the island.[24] Keenly aware of the opportunities available on a partially depopulated island lacking effective European jurisdiction, Bornier returned with the intent of taking command of the island's population and resources. In conjunction with his business associates, the Catholic mission and the Brander family of Tahiti, his goals were to find plantation workers for Tahiti and to convert most of their grassy island into a sheepranch.[25]

In 1868 Bornier purchased a tract of land a little to the south of the missionary estate at Hangaroa. From this headquarters, known as Mataveri, he arranged a series of further land purchases which continued into the early 1870s. Finding the purchase of land from the inhabitants both easy and cheap, Bornier had two major obstacles to the attainment of his goals of ultimate control and the establishment of a ranch.

The Taking of Control

Bornier's initial relationship with his compatriots, the missionaries, was apparently friendly.[26] Their initial purchase of land in Hangaroa was witnessed and approved by Bornier. In letters dating from the late 1860s he commends their work and their civilizing influence upon the island.[27] There is some evidence that the missionaries cooperated with Bornier when, having pretensions to grandeur, he proclaimed himself the representative of France.[28] Above his dwelling in Mataveri he flew the French flag; gradually, more indigenes came to settle in the Hangaroa-Mataveri area which had been renamed *Sainte-Marie de Rapanui*. Bornier established a Council of State, with four indigenous members, which regulated and witnessed land sales and stored the deeds in the town archive. Gaspar Zumbohm, a missionary, was Secretary-General, but Bornier took upon himself the title of President.

It was not long, however, before Bornier found that the missionaries posed an awkward problem for his policy of island control. Bornier's claims to ultimate authority over the indigenes resulted in conflict with the missionaries. The latter were strongly opposed to the shipment of Easter Islanders to work Brander's Tahitian plantations, for they had plans to ship the remaining Rapanui to mission lands in southern Chile or Mangareva. Quarrels flared up and a state of civil war emerged, each group having its Rapanui supporters. Arming his native followers with guns and spears, Bornier and his two European assistants led the people of Mataveri and Anakena against the missionary establishments of Hangaroa and Vaihu. His intention was to intimidate, not to kill, and this end was achieved by constant harassment, the destruction of crops, frequent assaults, and the eventual burning of some buildings belonging to the missionaries.

Bornier swept through the island with fire and gun. Missionized indigenes were intimidated, but the missionaries appealed to Bishop Jaussen. The latter protested to John Brander, Bornier's business associate, who visited the island but made no attempt to restrain his partner. Unable to defend themselves and prevented from continuing their work, the missionaries were recalled. Eyraud having died earlier, the remaining missionaries abandoned Easter Island in 1870 and 1871. "Nous avons évacué l'île de Pâques" wrote Jaussen to the Chilean brethren in September 1871.[29] The bishop then visited the island and, after conferring with both Brander and Bornier, wrote in 1872: "Il serait inutile a nous de retourner a Rapa Nui."[30] Although native catechists remained on the island, and Father Roussel returned several times for short visits, no permanent white ecclesiastical representative was to arrive until well into the twentieth century.

The Population Clearances

Free of the restraints imposed by the presence of other European authorities, Brander and Bornier were able to implement their plans for Easter Island without impediment. One of the reasons which induced Bishop Jaussen to abandon the island was its expected depopulation; deportations were a deliberate policy of both the Brander-Bornier partnership and certain of the missionaries. John Brander was probably the motive force behind Easter Island events, for Bornier, having little capital, effectively acted as his agent on Easter Island.

The Branders were a well-known Tahiti-based family of Scots provenance, and were in the process of building a fortune from their activities as shipowners, merchants, and plantation owners. Possibly the instigator of Bornier's change of attitude towards the missionaries, John Brander senior did nothing to discourage his agent. On the contrary, during the early 1870s he called at Easter Island several times to recruit islanders for plantation work elsewhere in Polynesia.

In view of their recent experiences and the situation then prevailing, the majority of the inhabitants were induced to leave. About 200 islanders were transported to Tahiti to work on plantations. A further 150 who did not choose this mode of employment were, on Jaussen's appeal to Brander, redistributed among the islands of the Gambier archipelago.[31] Only about 175 remained under the autocratic rule of Dutrou-Bornier.[32]

EASTER ISLAND AS A COMPANY ESTATE

By 1871 Easter Island had been cleared of surplus Rapanui and interfering missionaries. Having been looted of its most obvious resource, cheap labour, the island was now open to the unrestricted exploitation of its natural resources. In pursuit of this end, Brander and Bornier formed a legal partnership, the details of which were notarized in Papeete, Tahiti, in October 1871. The goal of this enterprise was:

> l'exploitation de l'île de Pâques connu aussi sous le nom de Rapanui pour l'èlevage des moutons et autres bestiaux, le commerce de laines et en général tous les produits de ladite île susceptibles d'être exportis.[33]

Originally to last five years, there was a possibility of a further five year extension of the partnership. During the whole period Bornier was to administer the island, with responsibility for sheep, employees, and bookkeeping.

John Brander was to provide the necessary shipping communications with Tahiti and Valparaiso. He was also responsible for the marketing of wool, beasts, and other products exported from the island. Should either partner die, the survivor was to inherit the entire business on payment of a half share to the deceased's heirs. Disputes were to be referred to arbitrators or courts in Papeete. Both these contingencies arose within the first five years.

From 1871 Bornier and his European lieutenants ruled Easter Island without interference. In a provisional agreement with the Catholic mission, Bornier was left in charge of its land, animals, and other goods.[34] The remaining Rapanui, reduced to little more than one hundred in number, continued their traditional cultivation methods and were employed, when needed, in sheeprearing activities. Bornier supported his local pretensions to supreme command by cohabiting with the so-called queen of the island. The intensive miscegenation so apparent today in Easter Island began in this period. Despite their conversion and demoralization, however, the surviving inhabitants still retained some spirit. In 1877 Dutrou-Bornier's reign, generally nasty and brutish, was also cut short by his murder at the hands of the indigenes.

The affairs of the partnership were now in the hands of John Brander. As a replacement for Bornier, he installed Alexander Salmon, a half-Tahitian relative, on the island.[35] But no legal settlement of the partnership had been made with Bornier's heirs when, in 1877, John Brander also died. Although the Brander heirs remained in effective control of Easter Island, the business itself was soon involved in a series of legal proceedings which, begun in 1878, were not fully resolved until 1893.

Throughout the first seven years of disputes, an incredibly tangled web of legal suits, appeals, and counterclaims was spun in the several courts of Papeete.[36] The delay occasioned by these proceedings, no less than the final outcome, was a major influence on the development of Easter Island until the 1950s. In January 1878 John Brander's widow, Tetuanuireiaiteraiatea Salmon, was made provisional administrator of the Brander-Bornier enterprise. As she had remarried, her new husband, the Scots merchant George Darsie, also had a claim on the Brander side. The Brander faction was represented by M. Goupil, who was also Chilean Consul in Tahiti. On the Bornier side the claimants included both the widow and the mother of Dutrou-Bornier as well as the Papeete merchant Van der Veene, a Bornier creditor.

In 1879 an inventory of Easter Island land, animals, and other goods was made, and in the following year the liquidation of the partnership was called for. In the same year the numerous land sale contracts made by Bornier with the Rapanui were officially registered, for the first time, in Papeete. The property of the partnership on Easter Island was declared indivisible, and was ordered to be sold as a single lot.

Bornier's widow officially opposed this unitary sale, asserting that several land parcels were the personal property of her deceased husband. Further complications arose with the entry into the fray of Bishop Jaussen. Since the abandonment of the island by the Catholic mission in 1871, the mission's stock had been run with those of the Brander-Bornier enterprise. Jaussen therefore claimed a *de facto* partnership between the mission and the company, entitling him, as the mission's representative, to one-third of all the animals on Easter Island. Despite much opposition he was eventually awarded a share in the value of the enterprise. More turmoil occurred when seven Rapanui, now residents of Tahiti and Moorea, appeared in court represented by the same lawyer who served Bishop Jaussen. They declared that the claims of the partnership to legal ownership of Easter Island land were erroneous, and depended solely upon the European misinterpretation of the place-names recorded in the sale contracts. M. Goupil managed to quash this interference on the grounds that the sale of the business would be interminably hindered by a lengthy investigation of the exact measurements of the partnership's land holdings. This omission was to have far-reaching consequences for the partnership's successors in Easter Island.

Final judgements were made in 1884, and shortly afterwards the Darsies transferred the ownership of the Easter Island lands, improvements, and animals to John Brander junior. Within a few years the mission's lands and animals were sold to Brander's relatives, the brothers Tati and Alexander Salmon. Neither the Bornier nor the ecclesiastical faction was wholly satisfied with its settlement, however, and further appeals were made. These reached the appeal court in Bordeaux, France. After due consideration of the depositions, cases, judgements, appeals, counterappeals, and interventions of the previous fifteen years, the Bordeaux judges finally decreed in 1893 that the Papeete judgements of 1884 were fundamentally sound. By this time, however, the island was beyond French jurisdiction, having been annexed by Chile five years earlier.

A *TABULA RASA*?

By the early 1880s, to contemporary entrepreneurs at least, Easter Island seemed to have become almost a *tabula rasa*, free to develop in whatever way a future owner would wish. Both its indigenous occupants and those responsible for the impact it sustained in the two decades after 1862 had

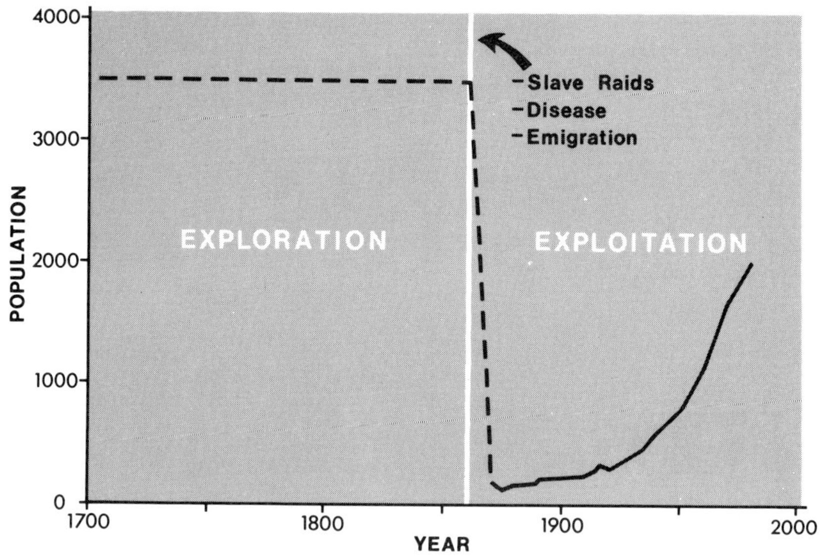

FIGURE 3,1 Population fluctuations 1800-1975 A.D. Pecked line indicates fragmentary data.

either left the island or were only slowly recovering from a state of uncertainty and disorganization. Brutal kidnappings and transportations, the ravages of disease, and induced migration to other parts of Polynesia had reduced an initial population of several thousands to significantly less than two hundred souls (Figure 3,1). Moreover, slavery, disease, the teachings of the missionaries, and the reign of Dutrou-Bornier had exacerbated already existing divisions, so that the population crash sustained by the island was partially attributable to internecine strife.

The Peruvian depredations of the early 1860s had brought about the almost total loss of the nobility and priestly class. Without guidance from these traditional leaders, the demoralized islanders were easily subdued by aliens. Fearful of further depredations, some lost the will to cultivate the soil. Former agricultural lands were increasingly given over to stockraising. After the Brander and Bornier deaths, however, social and material conditions improved somewhat under the rule of the part-Tahitian Salmons.

PLATE 6 An evocation of decline, Hodges 1774 ▸

Legal ownership of land, animals, and all improvements, however, remained in dispute between French, British, and Tahitian entrepreneurs, the Catholic mission, and the Rapanui. No nation had yet claimed the island and, though the French were most deeply involved, no nation felt responsibility for recent events there. But interest in the island was growing, especially in France, Britain, Germany, and Chile. As the ships of these and other nations made increasingly frequent calls, the geopolitical relationships of the as yet unclaimed Easter Island became subject to increasing scrutiny.

PLATE 7 Russian expedition, commander Kotzebue, attempts a landing, 1816 ▸

2 CHILEAN GEOPOLITICS

> . . . even the natives weren't unprepared for our being annexed some day by a passing man-of-war—though all hoped it would go on as it was, with nobody interfering with us nor pasting proclamations on trees. It is all very fine to see "GOD SAVE THE QUEEN" or "VIVE LA REPUBLIQUE" at the bottom of a proclamation, but . . . it meant taxes and licenses and penal servitude if you did this or failed to do that, and all those other blessings that are served out to a Pacific island when one of the great powers suddenly discovers it on the map.
>
> Beachcomber in Lloyd Osbourne's *A Son of Empire*[1]

On 9 September 1888 Captain Policarpo Toro Hurtado of the Chilean navy took formal possession of Easter Island in the name of the Republic of Chile. In a solemn exchange of documents twelve Rapanui chiefs ceded the "full and entire sovereignty" of the island to Chile "for ever and without reservation".[2] The chiefs signed the document with crosses, which were witnessed by three Europeans, John Brander junior, George Frederick, and A. Plotmer, and by the Tahitian Alexander Salmon, who also acted as interpreter. The cession was accepted by Toro in the form of a proclamation and the transfer of territorial control was confirmed in the traditional manner by the raising of the Chilean flag.[3] In his report to his naval superiors Toro commented that the Rapanui greeted this symbolic act with much enthusiasm.[4]

By this action Chile became the only Latin American nation to possess territory in Polynesia. No other Latin American country has claims, in the Atlantic or Pacific oceans, to island groups even one third the distance from the home country of the approximately 3,000 kilometres (2,000 miles) which separate Easter Island from Chile. The history of national expansion in Latin America during the nineteenth century had largely been one of struggles to control the mountains, deserts, forests, and grasslands of the continental interior. For a clearer understanding of Chile's unusual behavior, therefore, Easter Island geopolitics must be considered in the context of world, national, and regional developments during the later nineteenth century.

Thornton asserts that "the fact of empire may well prove to be the nineteenth century's most lasting contribution to world politics."[5] Indeed, the latter quarter of the nineteenth century, often termed "The Age of Imperialism", saw Belgium, Britain, France, Germany, Italy, the United States and other powers feverishly competing to build sea-based empires in those parts of the world not yet subject to imperial domination. A mythology of imperialism emerged. The prevailing ideology held that it was the duty of Europeans to unlock the slumbering resources of the savage world using local labour which would be more than compensated by the untold blessings of Christianity.[6]

In the later nineteenth century much of Oceania was involved in an immense economic and cultural upheaval, largely fostered by private traders and missionaries. The collapse of indigenous political systems, which were not immediately replaced by official colonization, created a power vacuum. On many of the remoter islands this vacuum was filled by individual European adventurers who installed themselves as feudal lords, as Lloyd Osbourne has so amusingly described in *A Son of Empire*.[7] Easter Island under Dutrou-Bornier is a typical example. Such petty fiefdoms, each dominated by the idiosyncrasies of a single alien, were not looked upon with favour by those European powers which were feeling a growing responsibility for the Pacific Islands.

By 1900 the Pacific had been effectively partitioned. A vast power vacuum in 1870, with few hindrances to movement, the region was eventually invested with the same sharp colonial boundaries which were simultaneously being etched upon the map of Africa. With this rapid assumption of European and American control the islands were inevitably bound to the wheel of modernization, some to be broken thereupon as they were inexorably drawn into the interdependent network of international trade. Indigenous control had all but disappeared, as had the backward-looking relicts of the former Spanish Empire. "About the only remnant of Hispanic memory left in Oceania was Easter Island . . . annexed by Chile in 1888."[8]

It is remarkable that, at the height of the European partition of the Pacific, a South American state less than two generations old should have been able to snatch up a possession in Oceania. A combination of European indifference and aggressive Chilean expansionism may account for this event. With the annexation of Easter Island Chile completed a decade of massive territorial gains "in an era of exuberant confidence."[9]

Chile achieved its independence from Spain in 1818. The nation that emerged was much smaller than at present, its as yet indeterminate boundaries adjoining Bolivia to the north, Argentina to the east, and the independent Araucanian Indians to the south of the river Bio-Bio (Figure 1,2). Internally, Chile swiftly achieved a degree of political stability which permitted the rapid development of agriculture, mining, industry, and com-

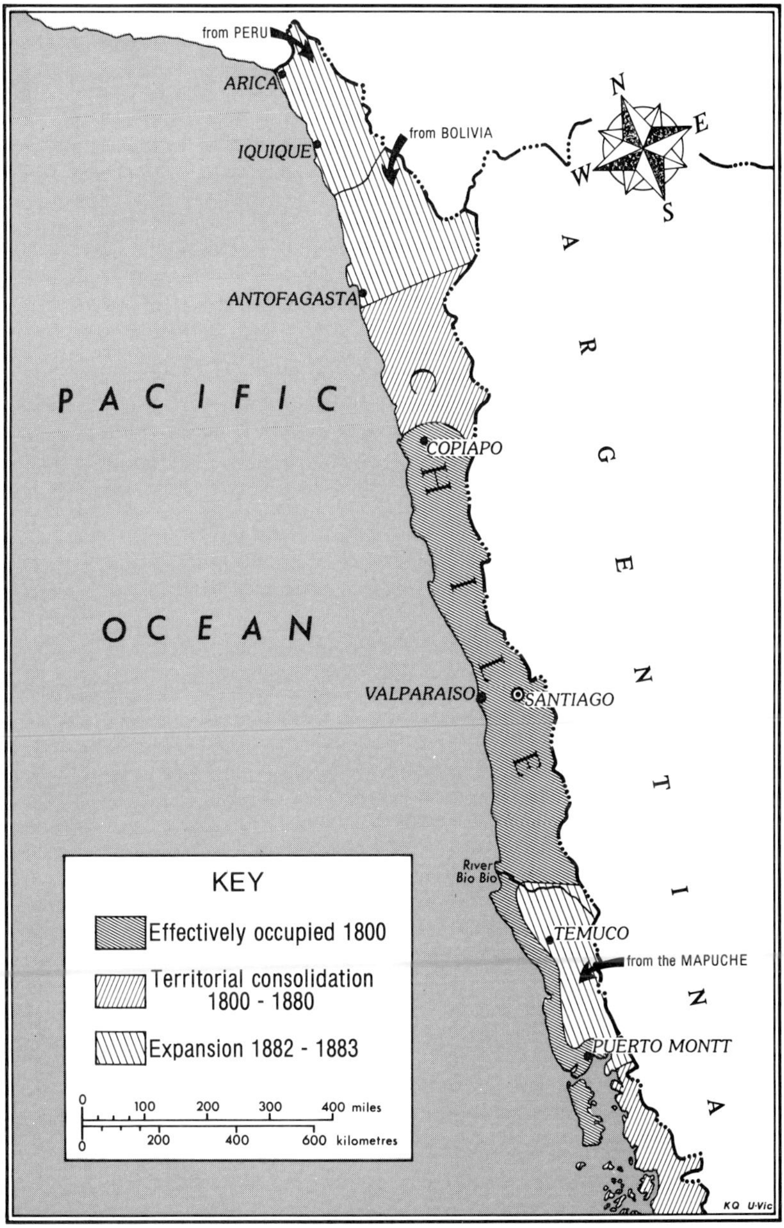

FIGURE 1,2 The expansion of mainland Chile 1800-1883.

merce. Confined within such a small territory, energetic Chilean capitalist-adventurers looked beyond national boundaries to the potential riches of what appeared to be "underdeveloped, malgoverned, and sparsely occupied" neighbour nations.[10]

Territorial ambitions on the mainland were directed towards aggrandizement on two fronts. To the south the last campaigns were fought in 1883 and the Indians, who had held out for over three hundred years, were confined to reserves. Their former lands were opened up to speculators, and in an intense wave of agricultural colonization new towns such as Temuco (1882) were founded to consolidate centralized power.

As Chile destroyed Indian power in its domestic version of the winning of the American West, a rather more formal war was fought against the mestizo nations of the north. Chilean entrepreneurs took a leading role in the development of mining in the Atacama Desert. Because of its effective occupation of the Atacama, Chile needed little excuse to extend its political control over the region. In the protracted war known as the War of the Pacific (1879-83), both Bolivia and Peru were defeated, and Chile annexed large sections of their territories.[11]

In Chilean terms such expansionism was morally justified; Chile would bring the benefits of civilization tc regions previously dominated merely by Indians. Current geopolitical thought, with Ratzel, was wholly in favour of state growth.[12] The state was considered an organism which must grow until its "natural limits" were reached. A recent work on geopolitics by General Pinochet, president and military geographer, illustrates the point:

> States with limited territory, whose populations possess great vitality, tend to extend the space initially available to them . . . the growth of the State is neither an end nor an objective, but rather a natural phenomenon.[13]

Because of these successes Chileans came to regard themselves as a Latin American master race. Bismarck considered them the "Prussians of Latin America".[14] Victory touched off a major economic boom. With less than six per cent of Latin America's population in 1887, Chile enjoyed thirteen per cent of the continent's trade and the highest per capita income of any nation south of the Rio Grande.[15] "Combined with pride in past attainments was an unbounded confidence in the future, and a conviction that Chile was well on the way to becoming one of the world's great powers. This attitude was in the 1880's as much a part of the national outlook as was ever Manifest Destiny in the United States."[16]

In this heady era of national self-congratulation only a single source of bitterness intruded. Preoccupation with the War of the Pacific had compelled Chile to sign a treaty in 1881 by which it gave up its claims to

Eastern, or transAndean, Patagonia. Loss of potential territory in the east, however, was shortly to be balanced by maritime adventures in the west. For Chile, most unusually for a Latin-American nation, was also a seapower. Successes against Spain, and the rout of Peru in the significantly-named War of the Pacific, were largely due to an effective and vigorous navy. Trained by British experts, the Chilean navy rapidly became a formidable force. Naval heroes and battles became the highlights of national history. Naval symbols took prominent places in the national iconography. Prominent sectors of Chilean society, both military and commercial, had always looked to the sea, but the naval successes of the early 1880s turned all eyes seawards.

In the late nineteenth century Chilean naval supremacy was balanced by the nation's important role in international seaborne commerce. Strategically located on the trade and emigrant route around Cape Horn, Chile was admirably placed to develop strong links with Europe and both coasts of the Americas. Before the opening of the Panama Canal Valparaiso and the nitrate ports were major havens for international trade. The gold rushes of California and Australia forged new links as the agricultural surpluses of the fertile Chilean heartland were carried to the agriculturally unproductive goldfields.

In this commercial expansion Chilean ventures were ably supported by British entrepreneurs. Like other nations of the southern cone, Chile was effectively within the British Empire at this period.[17] Valparaiso became a decidedly Anglo-Chilean port, and Chilean vessels were encouraged to visit Australia and even British Asia. In doing so, Chilean sailors and merchants became familiar with Polynesia.

As throughout the Pacific, and indeed the world, political ambitions followed trade. Chilean commercial expansion, backed by a powerful navy, inevitably led to dreams of westward expansion into the Pacific. These were, in fact, revivals of former dreams of grandeur. In the early days of independence Chilean extremists had suggested the annexation of the Galápagos and even the Philippine Islands.[18]

CHILEAN PERCEPTIONS OF EASTER ISLAND

With its expansionist successes, resulting in an enormously elongated coastline, its maritime traditions, its proven naval power, its growing Pacific trade, and its foothold in the near-continental archipelagos, Chile was indeed "a naturally oceanic country."[19] Frequent sailings through Polynesia had focussed Chilean attention on Easter Island, the nearest inhabited island west of the Juan Fernández group. Aware of what they regarded as a growing scramble for the Pacific, Chilean leaders were assessing the island's potential as national territory some twenty years before the final act of annexation. The motives which impelled Chile to annex the island were almost wholly military and commercial. As perceived by the government from the partially inaccurate reports of naval officers, Easter Island was valuable for its agricultural potential, for its strategic possibilities, for usage as a naval station, and for its location on what were believed to be the future mainstreams of seaborne commerce.

Agricultural Potential

Notwithstanding the rather meagre output of Easter Island agriculture in the mid-nineteenth century, the island was represented as having very favourable agricultural possibilities. The whole island was productive; crops would grow with hardly any effort on the part of the grower. Such statements are probably a product of mental transfer from the luxuriance of Tahiti. More important yet, extensive grasslands and the semi-tropical climate would yield large returns from all types of animal husbandry. The numerous Brander stock seen by visiting Chilean officers was in part responsible for this asseveration.[20] Contemporary developments in Patagonia had sharpened Chilean interest in pastoralism. Independent evidence of the island's fertility was available from returning missionaries.[21] Replete with rainforest, scrub, and hot and cold deserts, Chile coveted tropical terrain.

The origins of the belief in the exceptional fertility of Easter Island are to be found among the writings of the eighteenth century explorers, although their opinions varied widely on this point. Many nineteenth century explorers were more positive. Delano, who merely sailed by the island in 1805, nevertheless reported that "The greatest part of the island has the appearance of being capable of cultivation, and much of it was cultivated in beautiful plantations."[22]

Dutrou-Bornier, as quoted by the Chilean press, had great faith in Easter Island's agricultural potential. "Easter Island has, I believe, a great future. As soon as the population becomes accustomed to working, the land, which is unsurpassable, will produce all the cereals found in temperate climates."[23] As the only European with considerable experience of the island, Bornier's prognostications could not be doubted.

Final proof, for many Chileans, came with the reports emanating from the exploratory visit of the Chilean naval vessel *O'Higgins* in 1870. Members of the expedition stressed that Easter Island was more fertile than the islands of Juan Fernández, where Chilean agricultural settlement colonies had already been tried.[24] In particular, Dr. Rodolfo Philippi, a respected botanist, stated categorically that "with the exception of some very small areas, the whole island is susceptible to cultivation."[25]

Naval Station

Despite its maritime strength, Chile lacked suitable mid-Pacific stations where naval crews could disembark and ships be supplied. Ships involved in naval manoeuvres and training cruises were compelled either to sail north-south along the coast or to undertake the lengthy 6,500 kilometre (4,000 mile) voyage to French Polynesia. Easter Island, at half that distance, was seen as an excellent naval station where ships could take on meat and water, crews could recreate, and military exercises be undertaken.[26] Naval and other reports, totally ignoring the island's lack of deep, sheltered roadsteads, saw the island as a permanent base for sea exercises as well as a refuge for shipping during inclement weather.[27]

Their beliefs were supported by some independent reports. Delano, for example, although prevented from landing by rough seas, opined that the island "affords good landing for boats at least."[28] The use of the island by German squadrons in World War I suggests that it was valuable as a minimal naval base, although ship to shore connection had to be made by launch.[29] Toro believed into the 1890s that a deep harbour might be found (Chapter 3). Although four ships were wrecked on the island during the short period 1871-5, this was viewed as a blessing, as their timber was utilized for housing, for the construction of a seagoing vessel by Bornier, and for export.[30] Easter Island's notorious reputation for shipwreck had not yet emerged.[31]

Strategic Possibilities

From the Chilean point of view, Easter Island was the nearest Pacific territory likely to be occupied by a foreign power. Conscious of continuing international rivalries on the mainland, Chilean strategists were concerned to secure a strong seaward defence. The occupation of Easter Island by a hostile force would inevitably menace the coasts of Chile and adjacent republics.[32] With a Chilean naval garrison this important defensive site would not only protect the homeland in time of war but would also act as a forward position from which further commercial or territorial ventures might be launched with impunity. At the very least, a squadron stationed off the island would serve to protect Chilean transPacific commerce.[33]

Commercial Location

In the 1880s Chile was apprehensive lest it lose its focal position on world shipping lanes. With the inevitable opening of a canal across the Isthmus of Panama, vessels would no longer round Cape Horn and thus would desert Chilean coasts. Important links with Europe and Australia would be weakened, and Chile's relative position would change from that of a front-line commercial state to that of an inconsiderable backwater.[34]

The opening of the Panama Canal, however, would be likely to inaugurate a major new shipping route passing directly from Panama to Australasia. Following this route, shipping would inevitably pass through Polynesia (Figure 2,2). Both French and Chilean strategists took the view that the new mainstream of trade would pass close to Easter Island.[35] The latter was perceived as a future coaling and provisioning station of some importance, providing a convenient intermediate bunkering point on the long trip between Australia and the isthmus.[36]

Prestige

Annexation of Easter Island, coupled with the military and commercial advantages noted above, would doubtless redound to Chile's already prestigious world position. Prestige would also derive from philanthropic efforts to succour a native people so overwhelmingly devastated by the impact of Europeans. The romantic historian, journalist, and diplomat Benjamin Vicuña Mackenna was one of several distinguished Chileans who incited the oceanic adventure in patriotic prose.[37] Accepting the political expansion of civilized states as a natural process, Vicuña Mackenna drew the attention of his fellow-Chileans to the recent German, French, British, Australian, and American annexations of Pacific islands, which had taken place "under our very noses." Of Anglo-Chilean stock, this influential writer was especially aware of British expansionism:

> Great Britain, like the child-eating giants of the stories, is an insatiable island-eating nation . . . which, stimulating its appetite with an archipelago such as the Bermudas or Falkland Islands, follows by digesting the New Hebrides or some delicious morsel like Cyprus.[38]

Yet Chile, while making enormous sacrifices to maintain an expensive navy, possessed not even "one small pinnacle of rock" among the myriad islands of Oceania.

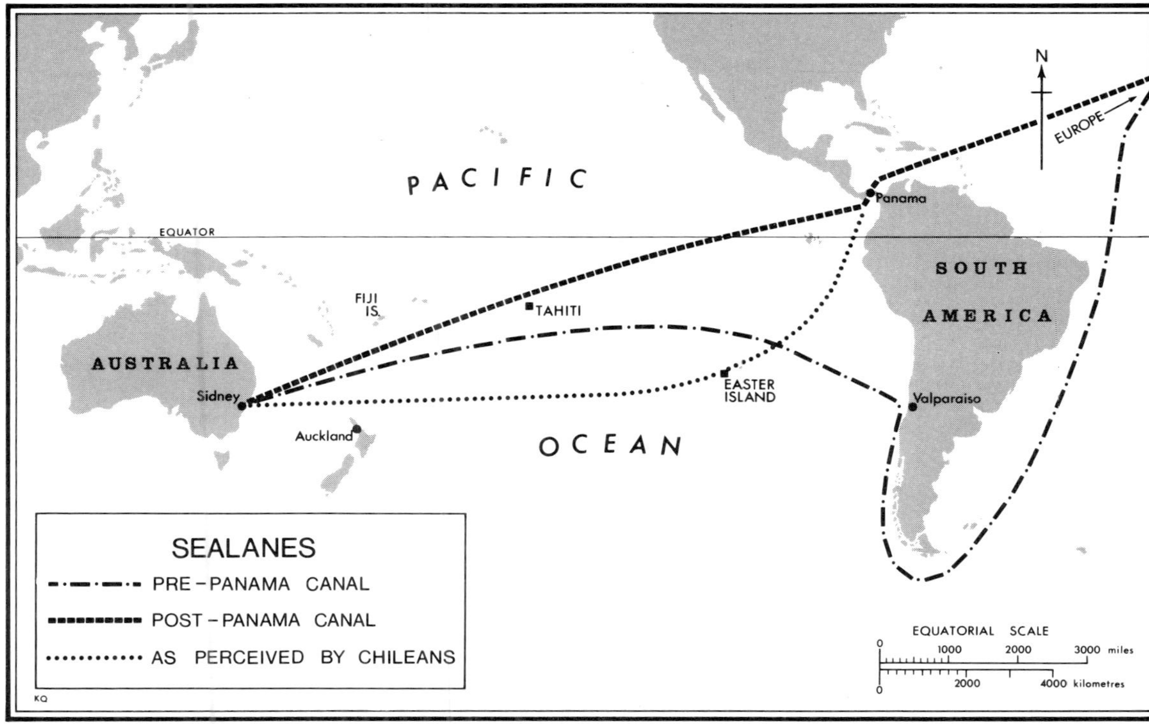

FIGURE 2,2 The relative location of Chile and Easter Island with regard to seaborne commerce before World War I.

Prestige factors were also bound up with Chile's fear that other nations, realising its future possibilities, would seek to annex Easter Island. At this time the island was becoming an international scientific cause célèbre, and in the twenty years before 1888 was visited by American, British, German, Latin American, and even Russian vessels. As early as the 1870s Bornier had told the Chileans that several warships of various nationalities had called at Easter Island in search of the island of Wahou, one of the several cases of confusion caused by the existence of a multitude of names for the same island.[39]

The traditional rivalry between Britain and France was at that time manifesting itself in what seemed, to Chileans, to be a race to annex the remaining free islands of the Eastern Pacific. While France took the Tuamotus, Britain acquired the Line Islands which, with the Pitcairn group, put that nation on an equal footing with France with respect to possible expansion towards Easter Island. These annexations were noted with alarm in the Chilean press, which reprinted reports from the London *Times* to demonstrate to its Chilean readers that the European powers regarded even the smallest Pacific islands as worthy prizes in their incessant struggle to annex yet more territory.[40] Prevailing Chilean opinion was expressed by one Jacobo Eden who asserted that even if no other advantages should accrue, the expense of annexation by Chile would be amply repaid by thus preventing the domination of Chilean waters by possible future enemies, such as Britain, the United States, or Peru.[41]

That Easter Island was to prove of equivocal value as a strategic naval station, and quite peripheral to the trade routes eventually forged between Australasia and Panama (Figure 2,2) was not apparent in the early 1880s. Although there were some outcries against the venture, the general mood of political and commercial success was in favour of further expansionism. A favourable image of Easter Island had developed from the reports of French missionaries and naval authorities. The extravagant language of the latter, notably of Policarpo Toro, further enhanced the positive image held by Chileans. Few naval officers had seen the island; even fewer knew its exact position. Yet they were able to persuade President Balmaceda that Chile's manifest destiny to rule the waves of the Pacific would best be accomplished by annexing Easter Island and developing "the fertile shores of that Oasis of the Ocean."[42]

ANNEXATION BY CHILE

Chilean decision-makers were well aware that their claims to sovereignty over the island were at best tenuous and likely to be disputed. Several potential claimants had better rights to Easter Island than had Chile. The claims of the indigenes were, as usual, easiest to dismiss. It is significant that early Chilean reports on the island speak of "Indians", who were "indolent, timorous, and servile."[43] In the 1880s Chilean popular opinion ascribed the defeat of Peru and Bolivia to the strongly Indian character of these nations.[44] More important, naval officers had portrayed Rapanui health levels as very low, and it appeared that population numbers were rapidly diminishing. The conclusion naturally drawn was that the Easter Island race was "condemned to disappear."[45]

A possible claim by Spain could have been based legitimately upon an official "act of possession" which took place in 1770.[46] But loss of the Spanish Empire in Latin America reduced considerably the value of any possible Spanish claim. The important report of Policarpo Toro to the Chilean government suggested that Peru's claim to the island was as good as that of Chile.[47] Fortunately for Chile, Peru in the 1880s had hardly recovered from the War of the Pacific, had not achieved internal stability, and was thus in no position to launch territorial annexation ventures.

British visits to Easter Island aroused suspicion among Chileans, who suggested that the island had already been placed on British admiralty charts as a British possession.[48] Add to this the British ancestry of the Branders, the recent annexation of the Line Islands, and Britain's possession of Pitcairn, Easter Island's nearest inhabited neighbour, and Chilean uneasiness concerning British intentions may well be imagined. Anglo-Chileans tactlessly attempted to allay such feelings by stating: "the island has no port nor water, and is practically valueless, or the probabilities are that the Union Jack would have waved over it long ago."[49] British attitudes to the island in the 1880s were apparently little different from those expressed so trenchantly a century before by Captain James Cook:

> No Nation will ever contend for the honour of the discovery of Easter Island as there is hardly an Island in this sea which affords less refreshments, and conveniences for Shiping than it does.[50]

Unlike the British, France could claim extensive and lengthy occupation of Easter Island by its citizens. French missionaries were responsible for Christianizing the islanders, French bishops made several visits, and there had been a semicontinuous missionary presence until 1871. Churches and other buildings had been erected. Moreover, the adventurer Dutrou-Bornier had dominated the island for almost a decade. He was responsible for the first commercial exploitation of the island, had purchased land, had erected buildings and fences, had made roads, had arrogated to himself the chieftainship of the island, and had flown the French flag. Throughout the 1880s the varied claims of the French heirs of Bornier, the half-Tahitian Salmons, and the Papeete-based Branders were being considered by courts in Papeete and Bordeaux. Moreover, Easter Islanders had petitioned France to establish a protectorate.

In contrast, Chile had little claim to the island. The prior act of possession by Spain, though more naturally devolving upon Peru, could have been used in Chile's favour, but was, in fact, rarely appealed to. Though Chile, in its Juan Fernández islands, possessed the nearest inhabited territory to the east, the French and British islands to the west were equally close. Chile's claim was perhaps strongest in the ecclesiastical area, for on quitting the island the French missionary authorities had ceded their rights to the Archbishop of Santiago.

Chile apparently felt the need to justify its annexation of Easter Island as long as fifty years after the event. In a detailed study of Chile's rights, published in 1939, V.M. Vergara expounded the means by which, under international law, a nation might legally annex non-adjacent territories.[51] According to the Berlin Conference of 1885, whereby the European powers legitimated their partition of Africa, three criteria were necessary. First, the land in question should be *res nullius*, signifying an uninhabited zone or an area occupied merely by uncivilized or un-Christian groups. Should a civilized power have evacuated such an area, it would be liable to recolonization by another power as a *res derelictus*. Second, the annexing power should exhibit *animus domini*, the will to establish permanent, definitive, and effective sovereignty over the annexed area. Third, the symbolic act of *apprehensio*, an act of taking possession, should be effected with due ceremony.

In the 1880s Easter Island might well have been considered a *res derelictus*. The Spanish were unlikely to follow up their claim of 1770. No other nation had made an official claim, and even the legal ownership of the land surface was being disputed among several private individuals. French missionaries no longer acted in an official capacity, and had, moreover, abandoned residence on the island.

The rousing of an *animus domini* in Chilean government circles was largely the work of a patriotic visionary, Policarpo Toro Hurtado. Toro had visited the island on naval training voyages, but it was not until he arrived in the corvette *Abtao* in 1886 that he finally matured his proposal for annexation by Chile. In his short but important report of October 1886 he outlined the military and commercial advantages of the island, stressed its strategic position, and alluded to its fertility.[52] In an accompanying plan he listed the numbers of cattle, sheep, and inhabitants. Noting that no major power at present exerted suzerainty over the island, Toro stressed that this situation could not be of long duration given the contemporary scramble for the Pacific. As to the final sovereign power, "Shall it be Peru? Shall it be Chile? or shall it be the French, the English or the Germans?"[53] Toro's reply to this rhetorical question is given in the title of his report: "The importance of Easter Island and the need for the Chilean government to take immediate possession thereof".

Chile had apparently been encouraged to annex the island in the early 1870s by the French missionaries ejected by Dutrou-Bornier.[54] These appeals fell on deaf ears, for Chile had more pressing concerns in its expansionist aims to north, south, and east. In the ebullient era following the victories of 1883, however, Chile was not averse to a complementary westward expansion. Accordingly, Toro was given authority to treat with the representatives of France in Tahiti, and to find the Easter Island landowners with the aim of purchasing their landholdings for the republic. While Toro sped to and fro across the Pacific in a series of arduous missions, Chilean warships were ordered to increase the frequency of visits to Easter Island. In the course of patrols which touched at Tahiti, the Galápagos, Hawaii, and California, warships such as the *Pilcomayo* and the *Lautaro* showed the flag at Easter Island.[55] When the *Pilcomayo* called at San Francisco in February 1887 Chileans were already claiming that the Easter Islanders "recognized Chile as their mother country".[56]

Chile and the French

Toro's attempt to ascertain French intentions was on the whole successful. In a letter of 25 February 1887 M. Goupil, Chilean Consul in Papeete, had assured the Chilean Foreign Ministry that despite the ongoing annexation contest between France, Britain, Germany, and the United States, France had no intention of annexing Easter Island.[57] Indeed, Goupil's impression of government thinking in the Tahitian colony was that the French would welcome Chilean control of the island. In a report made one year later (24 February 1888) Toro confirmed these assertions, telling the Chilean Minister of Finance that Easter Island was considered too far from Tahiti and that the French would prefer Chilean control to that of any other nation.[58]

French thinking in this matter is revealed in a contemporary interchange which took place in the French senate.[59] Bishop Freppel asked why France had not annexed the island, given the demands of the inhabitants, the work of the missionaries, the occupation by Dutrou-Bornier, and ongoing lawsuits in French courts. Like many contemporaries, Freppel was poorly informed about Easter Island, and perceived it to be not only a valuable way-station on the route between Tahiti and southern South America, but also as the key to the future maritime route between Panama and Australia.

He was answered by Admiral Krantz who calmly observed that France had considered the annexation since the 1860s and had decided against it. Indeed, French authorities in Tahiti had demanded in the 1870s that Dutrou-Bornier should cease to fly the French flag on the island.[60] The reasons for lack of interest were simple. Easter Island totally lacked anchorage for vessels of any size, and vessels could anchor offshore only in favourable winds. Lack of sheltered deepwater bays negated any military value the island might otherwise have had. Moreover, the population had fallen from several thousands to less than 200 within living memory, which did not indicate prosperity. For these and other reasons the French admiralty had always advised its government against annexation. In a word, the island was "worthless". That the island was worthless did not appear to Toro, who was perhaps blinded to its deficiencies by prestige considerations. Whereas France had many tropical possessions, Chile in 1887 had none.

Chile and the landowners

The second part of Toro's mission was to purchase the landholdings of Easter Island proprietors. By early 1888 Toro had established that at least six different groups of persons had rights to Easter Island real estate and movable property.[61] These were:

1. the French missionaries, although some of their land and all animals had apparently been sold to the Salmons;
2. M. Tati Salmon, who had purchased the 5,600 sheep and about 300 other animals from the mission in 1887;[62]
3. his brother, M. Alexander Salmon, who had bought land at Vaihu from the mission in 1884;
4. the heirs of John Brander, led by John Brander junior, with land and animals derived from the Brander-Bornier partnership;
5. the heirs of Dutrou-Bornier, the Brander-Bornier lawsuit being still unresolved;
6. the native inhabitants, as "primitive landowners".

The exact disposition of these various holdings was uncertain, though a general indication of the land partition prevailing in 1871 was available in the form of a crude map (Figure 3,2) based on information given by Dutrou-Bornier at that time.

After the legal decisions of 1884, however, the effective controller of the island was John Brander. The Salmons were relatives; the missionaries had left the island; Dutrou-Bornier was dead and his heirs were females and minors; the Rapanui were helpless and could be managed by the Salmons. Accordingly, Toro began detailed negotiations with the Branders in early 1887 when he sent John Brander a questionnaire regarding the land and animal holdings of the Brander clan and the Salmons.[63] Though initially "not disposed to sell", the Branders were soon willing to come to an agreement.[64]

Armed with a government authorization for land purchases, Toro left Valparaiso in the *Paloma* on 30 September 1887, reaching Tahiti after a trip of 41 days.[65] On the way he disembarked at Easter Island and concluded the purchase of A. Salmon's land and animals. On arrival in Tahiti he found to his chagrin that Salmon had not fully completed the purchase of his animals from the Catholic mission. Fortunately for Toro, Tati Salmon was authorized to act on his brother's behalf, and he ratified the land sale and completed the animal sale (5,600 sheep, 209 cattle, 40 horses, 4 burros) on 2 January 1888. The total cost to Chile of the Salmons' holdings was £2,000 sterling.[66]

By far the greater part of the island was in the hands of the Branders. The continuing litigation in French courts, however, meant that a clear title could not legally be transferred.[67] The best solution at that time was for Brander to promise to sell his holdings to Chile, for £4,000 sterling, as soon as they became free of encumbrances, although a time limit of 1 January 1890 was set.

Toro returned to Tahiti in late 1888 on his way to annex Easter Island. A number of contracts were signed in August of that year. On 7 August M. Goupil confirmed that the £2,000 sterling had arrived and Alexander Salmon, back from Easter Island, ratified in person the agreement negotiated earlier by his brother.[68] Thus the Salmon's lands, comprising at least the Vaihu area, became the legal property of the Chilean government. The following day Goupil and Toro met with Mons. Verdier, who was acting for the Catholic mission. For the sum of 5,000 francs the latter resigned all its land and other rights in the island to the Chilean government and to Mons. Casanova, Archbishop of Santiago.[69]

All the minor landowners being accounted for, Toro turned next to the Branders. Here negotiations proved more complex, for the Bordeaux court had not yet produced a decision regarding the Brander-Bornier case,

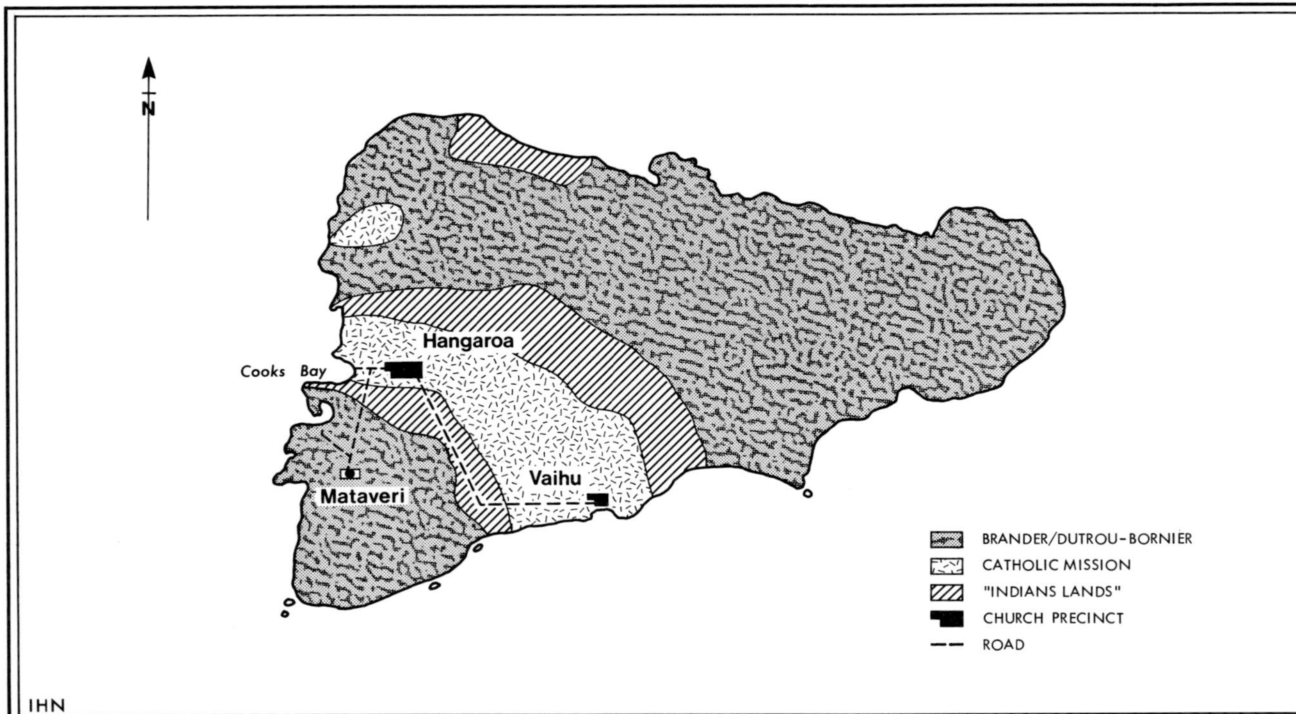

FIGURE 3,2 Dutrou-Bornier's map of Easter Island land divisions in 1871 (redrawn from Vergara).

and did not seem likely to do so in the immediate future. For this reason the contract whereby Brander had agreed to sell his property to Chile was extended to 1 January 1899.[70] Being unable to purchase an unencumbered freehold, Toro's best alternative was to rent Brander's Easter Island land, which was then believed to encompass the bulk of the island. In late August 1888, and for 1,200 Chilean pesos per year, Toro agreed to become the lessee of the Brander lands for ten years beginning on the first day of the following year.[71]

The *Apprehensio*

During 1888 Easter Island received several visitors and much attention in both Tahiti and Chile. Mons. Verdier, Vicar Apostolic of Tahiti, visited the island and exhorted the Rapanui to accept Chilean political rule and the spiritual hegemony of the Archbishop of Santiago. Toro, his Chilean assistants, the Salmons, and the Branders came and went. An independent investigation was carried out by J. Huneeus and O. Rengifo, who reported to the Chilean Naval Subsecretariat in April 1888.[72]

This report confirmed the lack of any foreign dominion over Easter Island, but the investigators deemed that it would be prudent to inform France officially of Chile's intentions. Moreover, they suggested that the mere purchase of land on Easter Island from private landowners would be insufficient evidence that Chilean sovereignty was being exercised. Rather, Chile must maintain a body of officials on the island who would act as permanent representatives of national authority. Overall, the report supported Toro's plea for annexation. For an inconsiderable financial outlay and the minimum of diplomatic effort, Chile would be able to control "an important port which dominates the coast of South America and which, in the not too distant future, will become an obligatory way-station for traffic between Europe and Oceania".[73]

Given these assurances of non-interference, and fired by erroneous but vividly optimistic evaluations of the island's potential, the Chilean government authorized Toro to annex Easter Island. After a series of false starts the cruiser *Angamos* left Valparaiso on 12 July 1888, en route for Tahiti to make the final land purchase agreements described above.[74] On his return from Tahiti, Toro claimed the island on 9 September with all due ceremony. Thus, "after a year of irresolution," what might have become the *Ile de Pâques* became *La Isla de Pascua*.

Problems emerged almost immediately. Even before the annexation there had been some opposition to Toro's aggressive pursuit of the annexation policy, opposition founded perhaps on Toro's rather rapid rise to fame.[75] After returning to Chile in his successful expedition of mid-1888, Toro was not received with universal applause. Indeed, he was censured in certain newspapers for having burdened Chile with an arid, uncultivable island lacking adequate water supplies.[76] Answering these charges, which were not wholly without foundation, Toro was at great pains to repeat earlier statements of the island's strategic and commercial value, and also suggested that it would make a good agricultural colony for Chilean settlers.[77]

Of great importance for the future was Chile's failure to obtain title to the bulk of the island's land surface, a failure attributable to Chilean unwillingness to enter into an agreement which could possibly be nullified by later legal decisions. But with Brander's promise to sell, Chile could reasonably have expected that its right to control Easter Island was now assured. On the contrary, Chile's troubles had hardly begun. The problem of sovereignty, and Chile's inability to effectively exercise it in the face of the dominion of a private landowning company, is explored in the following chapters.

PLATE 8 Mythological creature, comprising a reed boat with a whale's head (bow), ▶ a skull-like mask (stern), and a *hare paenga* reed house on deck (Kon-Tiki Museet artifact 2101)

PLATE 9 The company headquarters at Mataveri, with Rano Kao behind ▶

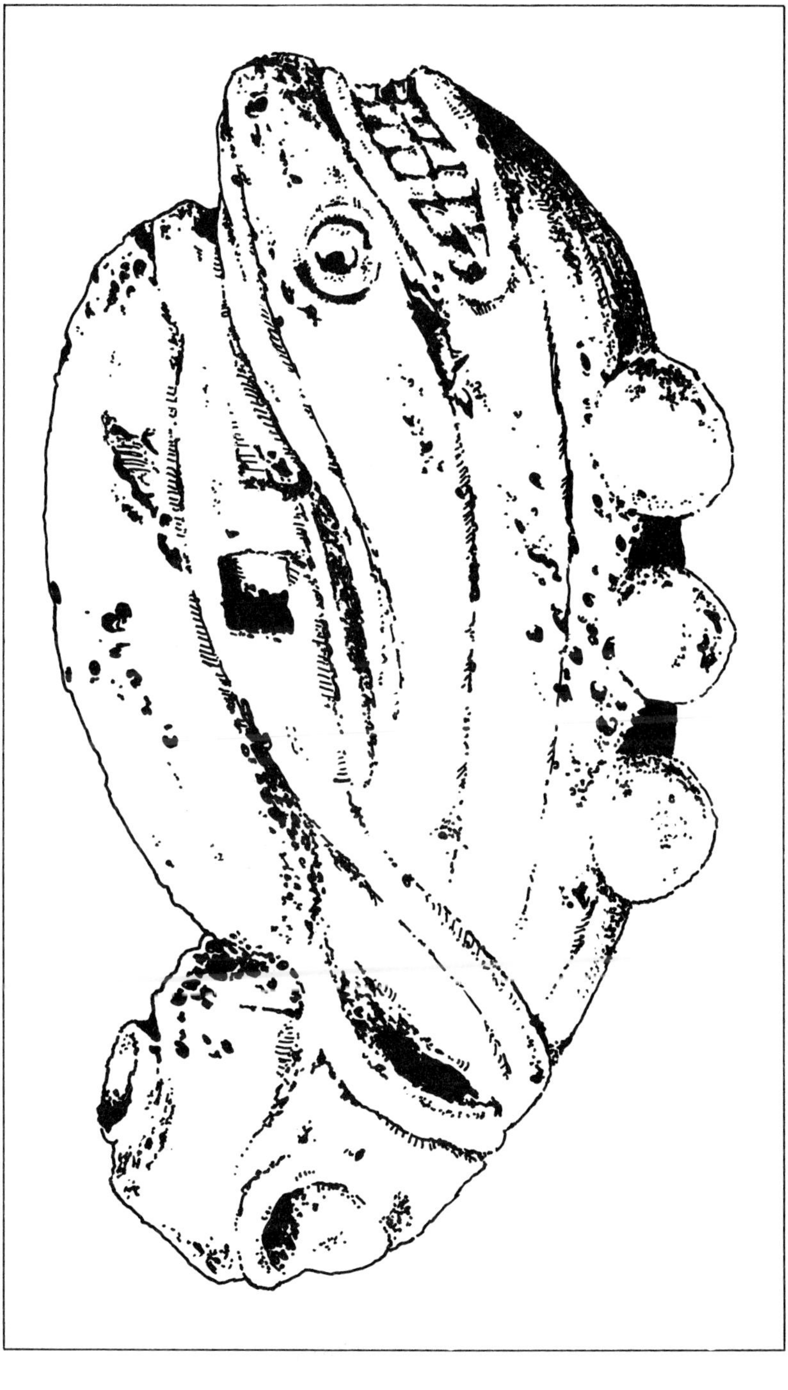

SECTION TWO

A COMPANY ISLAND

By administering the laws which he assists in making,
he disposes, at his pleasure, of the land and its live stock,
including all the two-legged varieties, with and without feathers,
in a circumference of several miles round . . .

Lady Clarinda, of Sir Simon Steeltrap

Thomas Love Peacock, *Crochet Castle* (1831)

PLATE 10 The company hacienda, c. 1917 ▶

3 THE COMPANY STATE EMERGES

> By World War I . . . companies not only dominated commerce but also . . . controlled nearly all other economic activity in Oceania . . . The most effective way to destroy natives is to take away their lands.
>
> Douglas L. Oliver

Geopolitical experience indicates that the effective political incorporation of a new region into the national territory is not accomplished merely by an act of annexation. Although its political sovereignty may be recognized by other governments, the annexing government's control becomes complete only when it is able to exert continuous police power in the area through the operation of the military, the judiciary, and other organs of establishment power. Effective control is also achieved through the settlement of the new region by national citizens and the exploitation of its resources by national companies or agencies. A communications web whose strongest strands connect the annexed territory to the heartland is also essential.

THE COMPANY STATE

The legacy of post-Industrial Revolution political and economic development has rarely enabled independent Third World countries to completely fill the political spaces legally available to them.[1] Penetration by the powerful economic forces of the developed world has frequently resulted in the heavy dependence of Third World nations on Western market forces. In spatial terms, the exploitation of resource frontiers on the peripheries of Third World states has frequently led to the effective control of such regions by a foreign enterprise. Where such an alien enterprise exerts wide-ranging economic control over a large, well-defined area, that area may be termed a functional *company region*.[2] If the company, because of remoteness or lack of indigenous enterprise, is also able to exert social and even political control through its provision of housing, social services, and its monopoly of employment and of transportation to the heartland, the region becomes a *company state*.[3] If organized and maintained by aliens, the company state's effective capital is the company headquarters, usually in another country. The citizens of the company state look to the company, rather than their legal government, for the benefits normally supplied by government agencies.[4]

Until the wave of expropriations which gathered force in the 1960s, the company state, a foreign exclave embedded within the body of another sovereign state, was a common spatial expression of the economic power of Western corporations.[5] Although the company state may constitute a sore upon the body politic in the eyes of nationalist radicals, for conservative oligarchies lacking the capital or the will to develop national resources the royalty-generating enclave is a convenient though essentially uncontrollable means to economic development.[6] But such development is spatially uneven, and modernization proceeds most rapidly within the company state. This in turn creates an indigenous labour aristocracy which prefers company rule to national control.[7] On the other hand, the company is free to impose controls upon local workers, and its abuse of their human rights may often go unremarked by a remote national government.

THE COMPANY STATE IN CHILE

In Latin America the influence of British companies, although strong in the nineteenth century, gave way in the twentieth century to company states organized by United States corporations. In Chile the operation of company states was particularly prominent in the first half of the twentieth century. After the collapse of the nitrate industry the Atacama Desert in the north was dominated by two copper-mining subsidiaries of the Anaconda Company. Until 1970 these companies operated entrenched and well-defined company states in which they controlled not only elaborate mining facilities but also a complete industrial infrastructure of roads, railways, air services, ports, and electricity, oil and water supply facilities, as well as a total social infrastructure including housing, retail, recreation, hospital, and other welfare facilities.[8]

A less well-defined company enclave, controlled by the Kennecott Corporation and again based on copper mining, was located in the Andes in the very heartland of central Chile. Until the development of oil and other mineral resources by national agencies, the remote Chilean south, including Tierra del Fuego, was dominated by enormous sheep ranches, often controlled by British companies. And in the remote west, more than 3,000 kilometres (2,000 miles) across the Pacific Ocean, an Anglo-Chilean company with a peculiarly Scottish flavour ran Easter Island as a company state until the 1950s.

So nationalistically vigorous in the 1880s, Chile lacked the will to effectively control its farflung territories after 1890. The reasons for this are complex, involving an intricate interplay of social, economic, and political forces. Soon after its decade of triumphant expansionism in 1879-88, Chile began to experience both internal and external political problems. The bloody civil war and the death of Balmaceda in 1891 provoked strong tensions within the country. Subsequent governments were unable to present a united front to national problems, and economic and political progress was paralyzed. The great strikes of 1905-6 and the Valparaiso earthquake during the latter year enhanced national dislocation. Boundary wrangles with Bolivia and Peru continued, and Argentina, a far more formidable adversary, was contesting the Andean boundary from the Puna de Atacama to Tierra del Fuego. Added to these problems was the absolute necessity to rapidly colonize the population vacua in the national territory represented by the recently-conquered territories in Araucania and the north.

Because of these mainland problems, Chilean attention was diverted from Easter Island during the decades immediately before and after the turn of the century. The nation had spatially overextended itself, and a lengthy period of readjustment was required. Lacking capital, manpower, and enterprise, Chile was unable to assert complete national control over the peripheral regions of even its mainland territory. Given the growing realisation that Easter Island was unlikely to prove useful as a naval port, a garrison, or a commercial way-station, it is not surprising that Chilean interest in the island fell to a low ebb in the period before World War I.

THE FAILURE OF COLONIZATION

The growing disregard of Easter Island by continental Chile was not reduced by the failure of an attempt to colonize the island with agricultural settlers. During the later nineteenth century a vigorous agricultural colonization process was underway in the southern heartland and Araucania. The success of this venture augured well for a similar scheme on Easter Island. The occupation of the island by a permanent body of white settlers producing agricultural exports would, moreover, functionally weld the new territory onto the national corpus.

Perceptions of agricultural possibilities on Easter Island were strongly coloured by the island's status as the only tropical region in a nation of Mediterranean, desert, steppe, and cool wet forest climates. Based on the reports of missionaries and naval officers outlined in the last chapter, an image of Easter Island as an agricultural paradise appears to have emerged. Lengthy reports in Chilean newspapers emphasized that the indigenes already produced several crops, notably sugar cane and bananas, which were impossible to produce in mainland Chile.[9] Problems of water scarcity appear to have been ignored, as was a counter-image, largely derived from foreign sources, which portrayed the island as arid, unproductive, and desolate.[10]

In a lengthy and optimistic account of the island's history and future potential the publicist Jacobo Eden discounted beliefs that the island's depopulation had been due to disease and an inclement climate. Population decline had been induced by kidnapping and internal warfare; epidemics were unknown. The climate was warmer than in the Chilean heartland, and there were no insect pests. Agricultural potential was therefore vast, as was confirmed by the size and variety of pre-European crops. The island already

> produces, with exuberant prodigality, the most exquisite bananas known, as well as sweet potatoes, sugar cane, . . . taro . . . tii. The value of tii lies in its root, an enormous fleshy bulb, with a greater sugar content than sugar cane. . . . Besides cattle and sheep, the island supports an immense quantity of chickens . . .[11]

A smooth rolling landscape with few sharp irregularities, Easter Island possessed "very few places where the ox could not pull the plough."[12]

Chouteau, another Valparaiso-based publicist of Easter Island, was in full agreement with this assessment. Relying heavily on missionary reports, this writer asserted that the fertility of the soil, the benign rainfall regime, and the mild heat of the climate all rendered the island a place "suitable for every type of product." Furthermore, the island's agricultural bounty could be tapped with relative ease, as was obvious from the work regime of the indigenes:

> These people do nothing the whole twelve months of the year. One day of work provides them with an abundant harvest . . . for the entire year. During the other 364 days they rest, sleep, stroll about, and make visits. Entertainments and festivities are continuous . . .[13]

This rather exaggerated view of the luxuriant potential of Easter Island was repeated, with variations, elsewhere.[14] It apparently took root, and the fruit was bitter.

Chile's intention to colonize the island was made before the formal annexation took place. In June 1888 Toro was ordered to deposit on Easter Island two settler families from the mainland together with his brother, army captain Pedro Pablo Toro, who was to act as a sub-Inspector of Colonization.[15] P.P. Toro's commission was to take an inventory of the island, make regular reports of occurrences thereupon, begin the instruction of the inhabitants in Spanish at the primary school level, and make preparations for the initiation of any industries which might be suggested by the nature of soil and climate.[16] In mid-1888 the *Angamos* landed three colonist families on the island, together with the materials, animals, and plants necessary for the establishment of an agrarian settlement. While Policarpo Toro sailed on to negotiate in Tahiti, and thence returned to Valparaiso, his brother remained on the island as administrator of the new settlement.[17]

The small colony was an almost immediate failure. Before a year had passed, death, illness, and dissension had reduced Toro's domain to a single settler family. The two other families returned to Chile, one because of illness, the other because of the "impossibility of (the man's) remaining on the island because of the turbulent character of his wife."[18] To the outcries against annexation, noted in the preceding chapter, were now added a series of attacks on the colonization scheme. Press reports stated that the island's climate was unhealthy and that, as medical facilities were lacking, no colony could survive. Food was scarce and lacked variety. An almost complete lack of civilized facilities made settler life wretched. Moreover, the crew of the training ship *O'Higgins* returned from Easter Island to repeat earlier statements that the island was "worthless", which accounted for its abandonment by more powerful nations. In view of this initial failure it was expected that the Chilean government would abandon the island in its turn.[19]

Policarpo Toro, however, was unwilling to abandon his enterprise. Only three families had gone to Easter Island, he noted. Although two had returned, the remaining family appeared content. Far from being worthless, the island was already producing 30 tons of wool per year from its 16,000 sheep. Chilean staples, notably beans and maize, were flourishing, and the island was already self-sufficient in grapes. Finally, Toro poured scorn on the *O'Higgins* crew who had apparently failed to carry out the hydrographic surveys necessary for the discovery of a deep anchorage close to shore.[20]

Toro immediately made a further attempt to settle the island with Chilean agriculturalists. In November 1890 the Chilean government, "not having the necessary funds to purchase the Easter Island lands belonging to third parties," arranged a contract with Toro whereby the latter added to his ten year lease of the Brander property a twenty year lease of the small government-owned area around Hangaroa.[21] Toro was given powers to represent Chile in Easter Island and Tahiti, and was to purchase, on his own account and without any obligation on the part of the Chilean state, the areas still in the hands of Brander. After reaping suitable rewards from his development of the island, Toro was to return it to Chile in 1910 at no cost, leaving intact all improvements and the same number of animals purchased by Chile from the Salmons in 1888. In addition, Toro promised to maintain, at his own cost, a minimum of three Chilean settler families on the island, and to maintain at least an annual communication by vessel with the mainland.

In return, the government promised to send at least one naval vessel per year with supplies for the colonists. If in two years Toro had failed to purchase the Brander lands, the agreement would terminate. This was the first instance in which the Chilean government sought to develop Easter Island through a private intermediary who was given almost total control. It was not to be the last, for this mode of disinvolvement remained effective Chilean policy for another 60 years.

The succeeding years saw no real amelioration of the settler situation. Agriculture soon became a secondary issue as the export of wool and animals to Tahiti, begun by the Brander-Bornier partnership, was continued by the Toro vessel *Clorinda*. But Toro's ill-luck continued; in June 1892 the *Clorinda* foundered off the island. In the same year the warship *Abtao* was sent, Captain Beaugency commander, to assess the island situation.[22] He found P.P. Toro operating a system of indirect rule, for the missionary Roussel had erected a Tahitian-style monarchy during a visit in 1882. Police control, including a curfew, was exercised through the king; religious observances were carried on by an old servant of the former French missionaries.

Easter Island is particularly prone to be forgotten during mainland upheavals, being cut off from continental communication for several days as recently as the coup of 1973. Mainland preoccupation with the civil war of 1891 ensured that the island had remained unvisited by Chilean ships for almost two years before the *Abtao* mission. During this period the Rapanui had become restless, and by 1892 had come to believe that Chile had abandoned the island. Communications from missionaries in Tahiti had apparently encouraged this belief. Unrestrained by the few resident Chileans, and thinking themselves liberated from alien domination, the inhabitants had descended upon the wrecked *Clorinda* and stripped it of all moveable goods.

An incipient independence movement on the part of the 181 Rapanui inhabitants was brought to a rapid end by the *Abtao*'s arrival. From this voyage dates the arbitration of island disputes by visiting naval officers, which became standard practice thereafter. Beaugency's arrival also ended the ordeal of the survivors of the *Clorinda* wreck, including several passengers from Tahiti, who had lived on the island as castaways for about three months. Included among the 21 adults and 4 children taken off the island were most of the remaining settlers, for whom local conditions and lack of communication with the homeland had become unbearable.[23]

The demise of the settler colony provoked further scorn on the part of certain sections of the press. Interchanges in the press during the period 1888-93 indicate the dearth of sound information on which judgements of Easter Island's worth could be made by mainlanders who had not visited the island. Interpersonal rivalries, genuine ignorance, poorly conducted surveys, sketchy reports based upon the hasty excursions of naval officers, personal biases, and political in-fighting combined to produce grossly distorted perceptions of the island. These views varied from Easter Island as a fertile paradise, at one extreme, to Easter Island as an arid wilderness at the other. Little wonder that no firm national policy for island development could be established after the failure of the colony.

In the midst of his defence of his colonization plans, during 1889, Toro identified the major problems which would beset all Chileans living on the island for the next 75 years. For Toro, the basic criteria for the creation of a "happy and prosperous colony" were: a minimum population of ten settler families; adequate medical facilities, including a paramedical functionary; and a boat to call every four or six months.[24] For the two succeeding generations these essential criteria were met only intermittently. Inadequate supplies, lack of communication with the mainland, insufficient population numbers, and a general feeling of remoteness, the perennial problems of all small, isolated islands, were all raised to a higher power on Easter Island after the settlement scheme faded away in the latter years of the nineteenth century.

THE EMERGENCE OF COMPANY CONTROL

With the failure of the colony in 1892 Toro's personal lease of the Brander lands, made so optimistically in 1888, now became a liability. In November 1892 Toro ceded all his rights in Easter Island to the Chilean state.[25] Ironically, the following year saw the final legal validation of Brander's landholdings on the island. By the agreement of 1888 the Chilean government now had the option to purchase from Brander the remaining privately-owned lands, which far exceeded in extent the government lands bought five years previously from the Salmons. With unresolved internal problems, a weak government, the return of the colonists, and the strong division of opinion concerning the value of the island, Chile was in no position to make a decision. In 1895 John Brander crossed from

Tahiti to Chile and made representations to Toro, but was still unable to complete the sale for the previously agreed sum of £4,000.

According to Toro, the government of the day refused to give him a hearing on this issue.[26] In the revolution of 1891 Toro had been expelled from the navy and was apparently *persona non grata* in government circles. On being told repeatedly to await a decision, Toro considered purchasing the Brander lands on his own account. However, having already wasted a great deal of his estate on Easter Island affairs, he was unable to afford the price. Indeed, he does not appear to have received any recompense for the 3600 pesos spent on renting the Brander lands for Chile during the years 1889-92. In a lament some 24 years later Toro exclaimed that this was

> the only case in my native land in which . . . an official has paid . . . his government, with his goods, his salary, and his mortgaged possessions, for his audacity in having taken possession of an island for Chile.[27]

Brander, ever the businessman, soon lost patience in this atmosphere of havering and delay, and began to seek a sale elsewhere. Toro asserts that after the failure of the colony in 1892 he had been repeatedly approached by a Valparaiso businessman, one Enrique Merlet, for a transfer of the Brander lease to E. Merlet and Company. In a precarious position because of his disgrace, Toro had refused to comply. Merlet, however, met with the exasperated Brander in 1895 and signed an agreement to purchase the Brander lands in Easter Island.[28] A cautious businessman, Merlet insisted that the deal could not be completed until Brander provided full documentation of his undisputed ownership of the property.

On his return to Tahiti in June, Brander informed M. Goupil, the Chilean consul, that as the stipulated price had not been forthcoming, he considered his promise to sell his property to Chile "as nul, void, and cancelled by the present letter."[29] A spate of letters followed in the short period 22-24 June 1895. Goupil regretted Brander's failure to keep him informed of events, such as the Bordeaux decree of 1893, which would be of significance to Chile.[30] Brander retorted that Toro had been informed of this over a year previously, and that the court's decision had been printed in the official colonial law journal as early as April 1895.[31] Asking Brander to await Toro's decision,[32] Goupil wrote immediately to Toro stating that he considered Chile still entitled to keep the property, as long as the agreed payment could be made before 22 February 1896.[33]

Government money was not forthcoming.[34] Toro's connection with Easter Island was severed. Unable or unwilling to pursue the plans of earlier ministries, the post-revolution government continued the policy of letting its Easter Island land to private entrepreneurs. In September 1895 Merlet's proposal for a lease of this land was agreed upon. An agreement, somewhat more elaborate than that made with Toro, was drawn up.[35]

For the small sum of 1,200 pesos per annum Merlet was able to add a twenty year lease of the government land to the extensive property which Brander had promised to sell him. In return, E. Merlet and Company was to maintain a yearly connection with Chile, maintain at least three settler families at its own cost "as a colonization base", and return the leased land to Chile in 1915. Having been unable to comply with the Toro agreement of 1890, the government felt unable to guarantee a yearly visit from a naval vessel, but stated that whenever such vessels did sail, they would transport colonists, tools, and goods without cost to Merlet.

The concept of a naval base on Easter Island was still important to Chile. To this end Merlet was to provide free medical treatment to any Chilean sailor, to provide fresh meat to naval vessels, and to create a coal depository for the use of Chilean warships. In addition, he was to build a pier to improve cargo handling and erect a house and office for one government employee. Should Chile decide to establish a population centre on the island, Merlet was to provide suitable land.

On 27 January 1896 Merlet wrote to Brander thanking him for sending most of the required documents and indicating that he had already taken possession of the Brander property on Easter Island.[36] Later in the same year an elaborate document appeared to finally confirm Brander's rights.[37] In this document the Darsies, now resident in Fife, Scotland, declared that Brander had full legal title to the Brander-Bornier property awarded to them in 1884 and confirmed in 1893. After passing through the hands of a notary in Fife and the Chilean consul in Edinburgh, as well as the Ministry of External Affairs in Santiago, the document eventually reached the expectant Merlet. In 1897 the Brander-Merlet purchase agreement was completed and Merlet became sole owner of the Brander-Bornier domain, then believed to comprise almost the entire island.[38] The whole of Easter Island was now under the control, by ownership or lease, of a single company dedicated to profitable sheep ranching. And by its failure to act, the government of the day had laid up a store of future trouble for its successors.

THE ALIENATION OF THE LAND

In view of its importance in the disputes which arose between government and company during the next half-century, an attempt must be made to ascertain exactly what Merlet actually purchased from John Brander in

1897. The general assumption made at the time was that, given a perceived island area of between 17,000 and 18,000 hectares (42,000 and 45,000 acres), Brander had owned almost the whole. The only exceptions were the government-owned area around Hangaroa, thought to be about 600-700 hectares (1,500-1,700 acres), and a few scattered pockets of poor land retained by the Rapanui. For a better comprehension of Brander's claim in 1895 to ownership of some 90 percent of the land surface of Easter Island it is necessary to trace the process of land alienation from its inception some thirty years before.

The original land base of the missionaries, later sold to the Salmons and then to the Chilean government, was approximately 635 hectares (1,570 acres) in extent. It was purchased in two pieces. On 15 October 1868 Dutrou-Bornier, as President of the Council of State of Easter Island, witnessed the purchase of 335 hectares (830 acres) by Father Roussel from five indigenes.[39] More than a year later, in December 1869, a further 300 hectares (740 acres) were purchased from one Pierre Mau, a Tahitian or Mangarevan who had previously bought the land from its native owners.[40] The ownership or extent of this core missionary property was never in serious dispute, as it was a small compact unit with fairly recognizable limits (Figure 1,3).

During the legal proceedings of 1884, however, Bishop Jaussen, with the support of several Easter Islanders then resident in Tahiti, asserted that the mission had made much more extensive purchases in 1869.[41] These purchases comprised about 40 separate parcels of land in two regions, which together made up an extensive mission-owned area. The map of 1871, based on information given by Bornier, does indeed indicate a fairly large area of "mission lands" extending from the west coast at Hangaroa to the south coast at Vaihu, and cutting the Brander-Bornier area into two sections (Figure 3,2). A further small mission-owned area appeared in the northwest, and a portion of the southeast coast at Tongariki may also have been mission-owned.

Evidence given by native witnesses provided further complications. Admitting the sale of certain land parcels in certain districts to Bornier, they denied having sold all the land in these districts. With this confusion between district names and land parcel names, it is very probably that the map of 1871 (actually drawn only in 1894) was rather inexact. It is most likely that the legally-owned Brander-Bornier and mission lands outside the Hangaroa-Mataveri area actually comprised a mosaic of parcels, intermingled with each other and with Rapanui-owned parcels, rather than large separate blocks of land.

Properties owned by the Brander-Bornier partnership were, in fact, scattered round the island.[42] The first documented land purchase by a Euro-

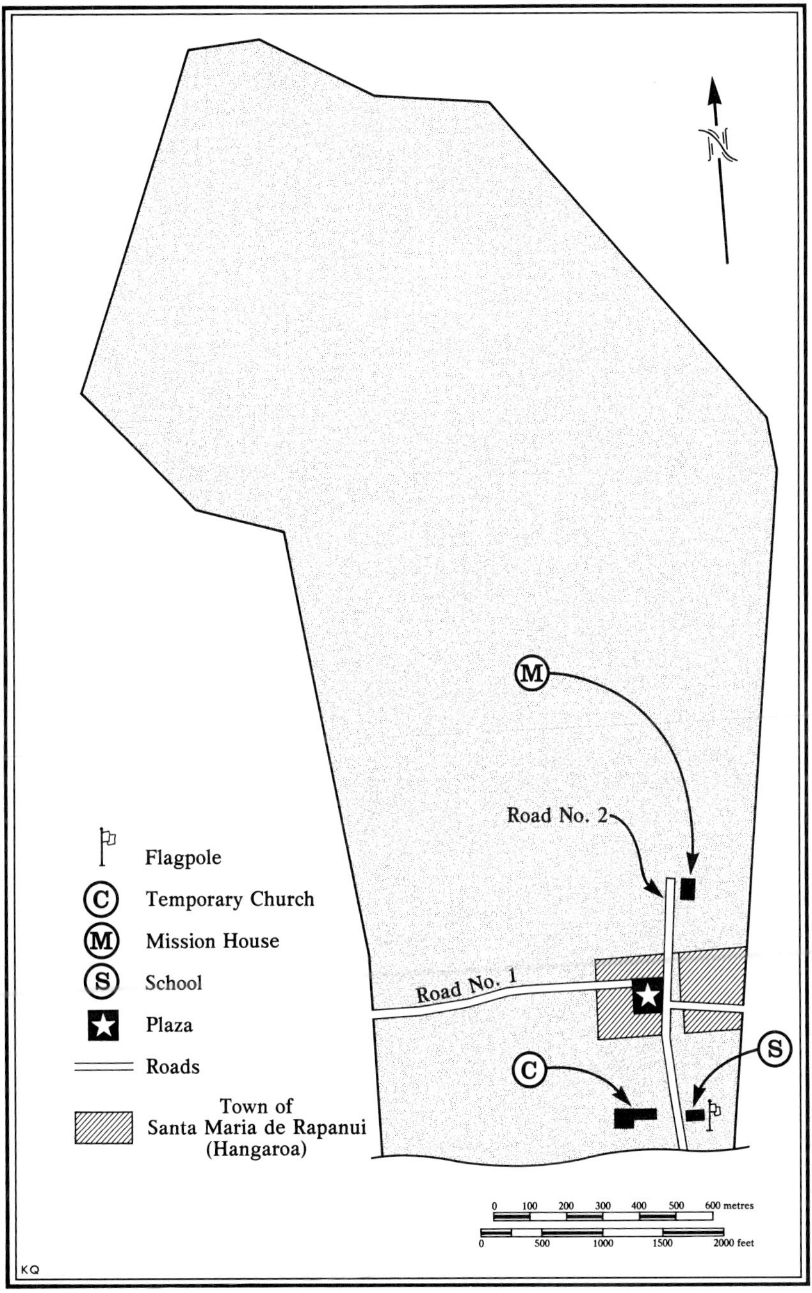

FIGURE 1,3 The first estate of the Catholic Mission, at Hangaroa, c. 1870 (redrawn from Vergara).

pean occurred on 3 August 1868 when Dutrou-Bornier, in the presence of the missionaries, bought approximately 706 hectares (1,742 acres) from seven indigenes. This first purchase had fairly well-defined limits, and contained some of the choicest land on the island. It comprised part of the crater of the Rano Kau volcano, its fertile slopes at Mataveri, and a lengthy section of coast including the cove at Hanga Piko (Figure 2,3).

This initial land sale was followed by about two dozen more in the period 1868-73. In each case a similar formula appeared in a traditional format (Figure 3,3). After the names of the local vendors and the European purchasers had been identified, the names of the land parcels were given. Type of payment varied, but was almost always converted into merchandise. Unlike the carefully organized and witnessed purchases of 1868, however, the later land sale documents recorded no witnesses, gave no measurements, omitted details of boundaries, and appended no plans. The questionable legality of such land sales was covered by a statement to the effect that no other means of recording the purchase was available, as the "Government of the island no longer exists."

This was doubtless a reference to the irreconcilable differences which by 1869 had sundered the Council of State and its attempted unification of the diverse interests of Rapanui, planters, and missionaries. With the missionaries gone, Bornier's land purchases were unrestrained, but also unwitnessed by Europeans. In their crudity, vagueness, and dubious legality, the later Easter Island land sales illustrate in microcosm the process by which Europeans the world over despoiled native peoples of their land in return for a few bolts of cloth or a handful of trinkets. It is unlikely that the Rapanui vendors were absolutely clear as to the nature of the transaction. Almost every parcel of land sold belonged to more than one person, an indication of a system of joint or clan ownership of land unknown in modern Western states except in fringe areas, such as the pre-crofting communal joint-farms of Scotland.[43]

Although the vendors probably had precise knowledge of the extent and boundaries of their joint land holdings, for boundary markers (*pipihoreko*) are an archaeological feature, these were perhaps not readily translated into the formal measurements of Western science. In most cases, then, Bornier's purchases were designated solely by a series of place-names. It is possible, however, that the recent population crash, together with the almost total loss of the upper strata of native society, had left the survivors unaware of the precise extent and boundaries of many land parcels. In such a case statements such as "the lands known as Hanga Mahiko in the Uti-iti region" needs must serve as the most precise designation possible under the prevailing circumstances.

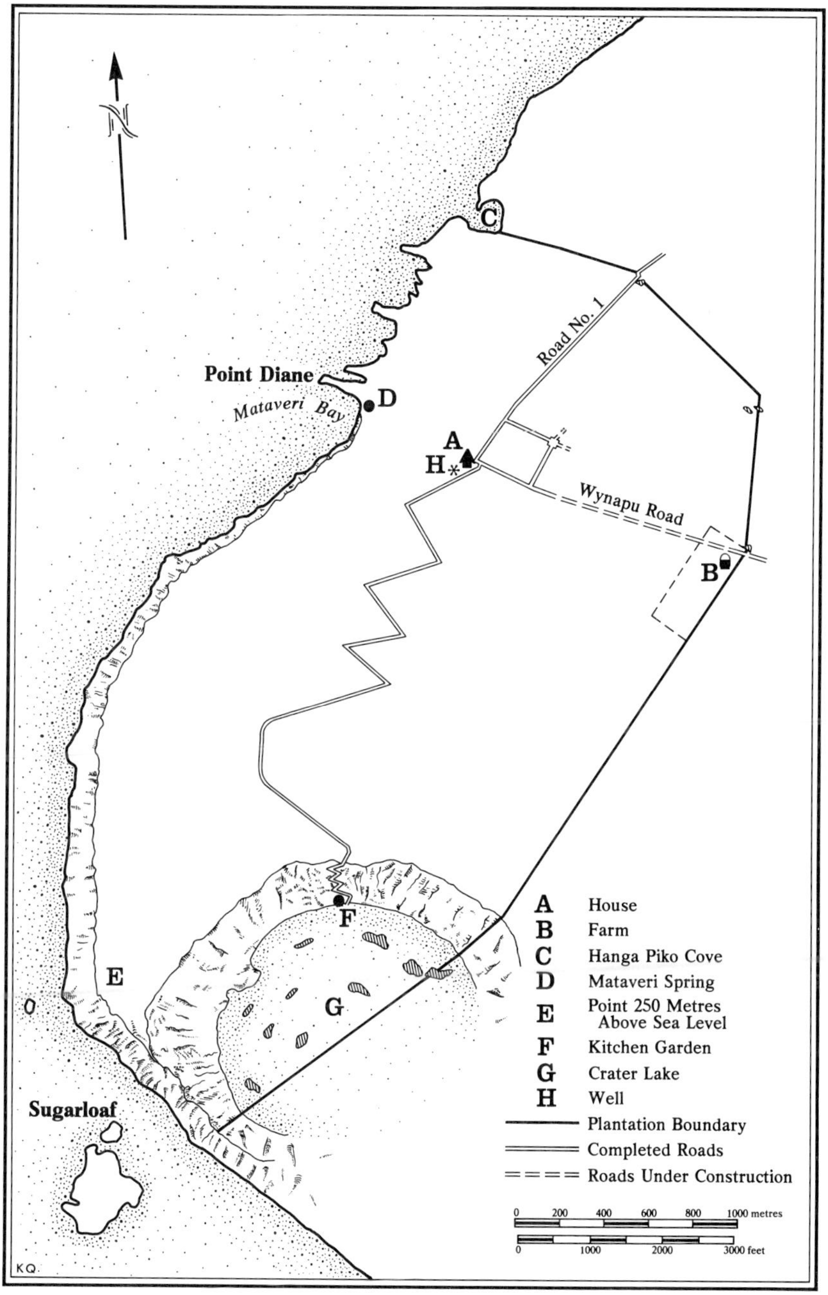

FIGURE 2,3 The first estate of Dutrou-Bornier, at Mataveri, c. 1870 (redrawn from *Documentos* LE 3).

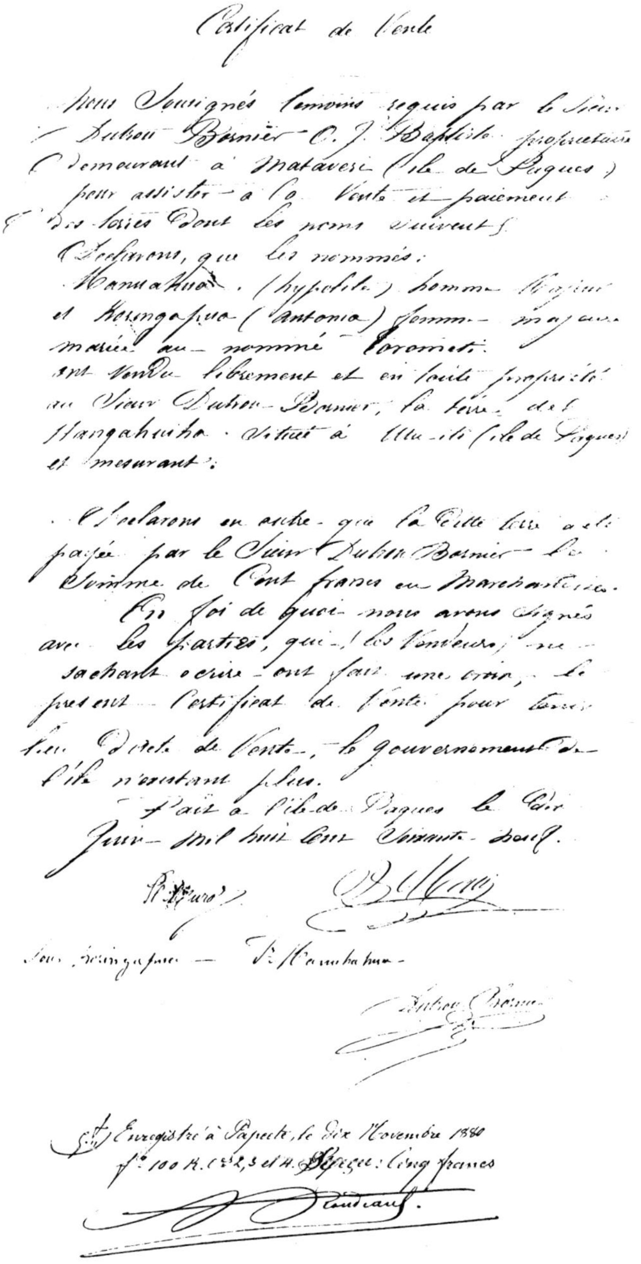
Certificat de Vente

Nous Soussignés témoins requis par le Sieur Dutrou Bornier O. J. Baptiste propriétaire demeurant à Mataveri (île de Pâques) pour assister à la vente et paiement des terres dont les noms suivent.
Déclarons, que les nommés:
Manuahua (hypolite) homme majeur et Korongapua (Antonia) femme majeure mariée au nommé Toromiti.
ont vendu librement et en toute propriété au Sieur Dutrou-Bornier, la terre de Hangahuiha situé à Uu-iti (île de Pâques) et mesurant:

Déclarons en outre que la dite terre a été payée par le Sieur Dutrou Bornier la somme de Cent francs en Marchandises.
En foi de quoi nous avons signés avec les parties, qui (les vendeurs) ne sachant écrire ont fait une croix, le présent Certificat de Vente pour tenir lieu d'acte de Vente, le gouvernement de l'île n'existant plus.
Fait à l'île de Pâques le dix Juin mil huit cent soixante-neuf.

Enregistré à Papeete, le dix Novembre 1880
f° 100 R. C. 2, 3 et 4. Reçu: Cinq francs

FIGURE 3,3 Typical land-sale contract between Dutrou-Bornier and the indigenes (source: *Documentos* LE 2).

From June 1869 to January 1870 at least 19 land purchase contracts were signed. Some omitted the names of vendors; in others, as many as 28 vendors sold Bornier a single piece of land. In only one case was a measurement of area given, and in no case was the location of the land parcel defined except by name. Many vendors were female, and others were immigrant natives of French Polynesia who sold the lands of Easter Island women with whom they were probably cohabiting.

A final spate of land purchasing occurred in the period January to August 1873. By this time Bornier was legally in partnership with Brander and had a permanent lieutenant, the Dane Christian Schmidt. It is possible that, at the instigation of the experienced businessman Brander, Bornier was persuaded to be more precise in his land purchases. The five purchases of 1873 were witnessed by Schmidt and Gure, chief of the Anakena region, and then by the notary Van der Veene in Papeete. Moreover, precise figures were given for areal extent in four cases, which accounted for 2,462 hectares (6,084 acres).

In total, Bornier is known to have purchased at least 25 properties, involving over 100 vendors. The distinction in legal ownership between the 20 pieces purchased before his partnership with Brander and the 5 pieces purchased afterwards was a major element of the appeals made by his heirs in the litigation of 1879-93. Of the 25 parcels only six had precise measurements, ranging from 9 to 1,031 hectares (24 to 2,548 acres) (Table 1,3). In the absence of further data, a very crude indication of the extent of the Brander-Bornier domain might be obtained by multiplying the total number of parcels by the mean size of the six parcels of known size. The resulting figure is 13,237.5 hectares (32,710 acres), compared with the 635 hectares (1,570 acres) of the mission's core area and total surface area then believed to be in the order of 17,000-18,000 hectares (42,000-45,000 acres).

Although transacted and recorded in a rather dubious manner, the Bornier real estate purchases were fully supported by the courts of Papeete and Bordeaux. The final Bordeaux decision of 1893 specifically stated that the Easter Island lands were "laboriously and legitimately acquired by Dutrou-Bornier."[44] In fact, throughout the lengthy lawsuit far more attention was devoted to disentangling the rights of the various parties to the approximately 10-15,000 head of stock which were roaming the island in the 1880s. Complications regarding the stock arose, of course, through the intermingling of the mission animals with those of the Brander-Bornier partnership, the continuing import and export of animals, and the propensity of animals to breed.

Legality of tenure being unquestioned, the major issue faced by all the successors to the Brander-Bornier partnership was the exact extent and

TABLE 1,3 Certain Land Purchases by Bornier

	Location of Parcel	Vendors	Date	Hectares	Price (in goods)
1.	Hanga Piko Mataveri, Rano Kau	Nicodemio Poura, Augustin Kovehu, Victorio Vaioopua, Daniel Kotupa, Komati, Gregorio, Riko, Petero Mati	3.8.1868	706	100 piastres
2.	Hanga Piko	Torometi	1.11.1869	9	100 francs
3.	Maunga teatea	(Queen) Koreta, Hurevakapito, Kote Koho, Dominique Vaka	9.5.1873	1031	300 francs
4.	Hangapiko, Apina, Vai Kapua, Vinepu	Kory, Cutano, Torometi	9.7.1873	812	100 francs each
5.	Koheky	Kotahiringa	15.8.1873	187	100 francs
6.	Promaga, in Tongariki	(Queen) Koreta	15.8.1873	432	40 dollars

location of the property. As previously noted, only 6 of the 25 parcels were measured for areal extent; even fewer had designated boundaries on the purchase agreements. A legal judgement delivered in Papeete in 1881 noted that, for most of the Brander-Bornier property, "the extent of each of these lands is presently indeterminate."[45] Comparing the place-names on the sale deeds with those of the court records one finds many errors and changes, there being no set orthography for the Easter Island language. On the ground itself these lands with largely unpronouncable names were only partially enclosed, mainly in the Hangaroa-Mataveri region. The intervention of Bishop Jaussen and several Easter Islanders in the court proceedings indicated that much confusion existed between general district names and specific land parcel designations.[46] As noted in the previous chapter, however, this call for a more exact definition of the actual extent of the Brander-Bornier properties was ignored by the courts.

Thereafter, John Brander junior was never to state explicitly his claim to ownership of the greater part of the island. On renting his Easter Island property to Toro in 1889 his description of the property was:

> an extent of land of some 700 hectares, more or less, at Mataveri, and some other pieces located in various parts of the island, which I have shown to señor Toro, though without indicating their exact boundaries . . .[47]

The 1895 contract by which Brander promised to sell the property to Merlet was equally vague. E. Merlet and Company was to accept the improvements and land "as is", the land being described as:

> that part of the island which does not belong or did not belong to Tati Salmon and the Catholic Mission . . . and which now belongs to the government of Chile.[48]

The remainder of the land surface was all Brander property

> with the possible exception of some small pieces of land which may belong to the indigenes or which are unimprovable . . . These exceptions, if they exist, represent only an insignificant value in comparison to the real estate mentioned in this contract.[49]

As Merlet apparently demurred at this vague description, Brander sent him a map, probably the only slightly less vague specimen redrawn as Figure 3,2. In an accompanying letter of 13 February 1897 Brander also dismissed any possible claims of the Rapanui to the property he hoped to sell:

> The land marked on the map, although the title deeds do not state clearly an ownership to it all, has been in the use of the property owners for running their stock, and that as the owners have been in possession for a long time back . . . it would be a very bad policy . . . to allow that the people have any claim to any portion of these lands, for should any slight claim of theirs be granted, they would after the nature of the natives at once bring forward the most absurd claims. It is my opinion Mr. Bornier got possession of all of these lands by purchase and that had he not been murdered all would have been very clear; as it is, the fact remains, that he was in possession . . .[50]

Finally, in the Brander-Merlet sale contract of 1897, the Brander property purchased by Merlet was described as the property designated in the legal judgements of 1884 and 1893, "whatever its extent or area".[51] A canny Scot, Brander was evidently able to convince a second Chilean buyer to purchase a property the exact extent and limits of which were clearly unknown to the vendor.

The problem of the exact location and extent of the Merlet lands did not become an issue in the years immediately following the purchase. In 1897 Merlet took complete control of the island by purchase, lease, and effective occupation of possible disputed areas. Their attention focussed elsewhere, the governments of the post-colonization period paid little attention to Easter Island. They ignored the recommendations of the investigators of 1888 who had explicitly warned that legal ownership of the total land surface by the government would be necessary to obviate future difficulties with private landowners.[52] The penalty for failing to heed this advice was a long series of bitter company-government wrangles which dominated the Easter Island sovereignty question throughout the first half of the twentieth century.

PLATE 11 Chicken sitting on eggs (Kon-Tiki Museet artifact 2005b) ▶

PLATE 12 Entrance to the Mataveri ranch house ▶

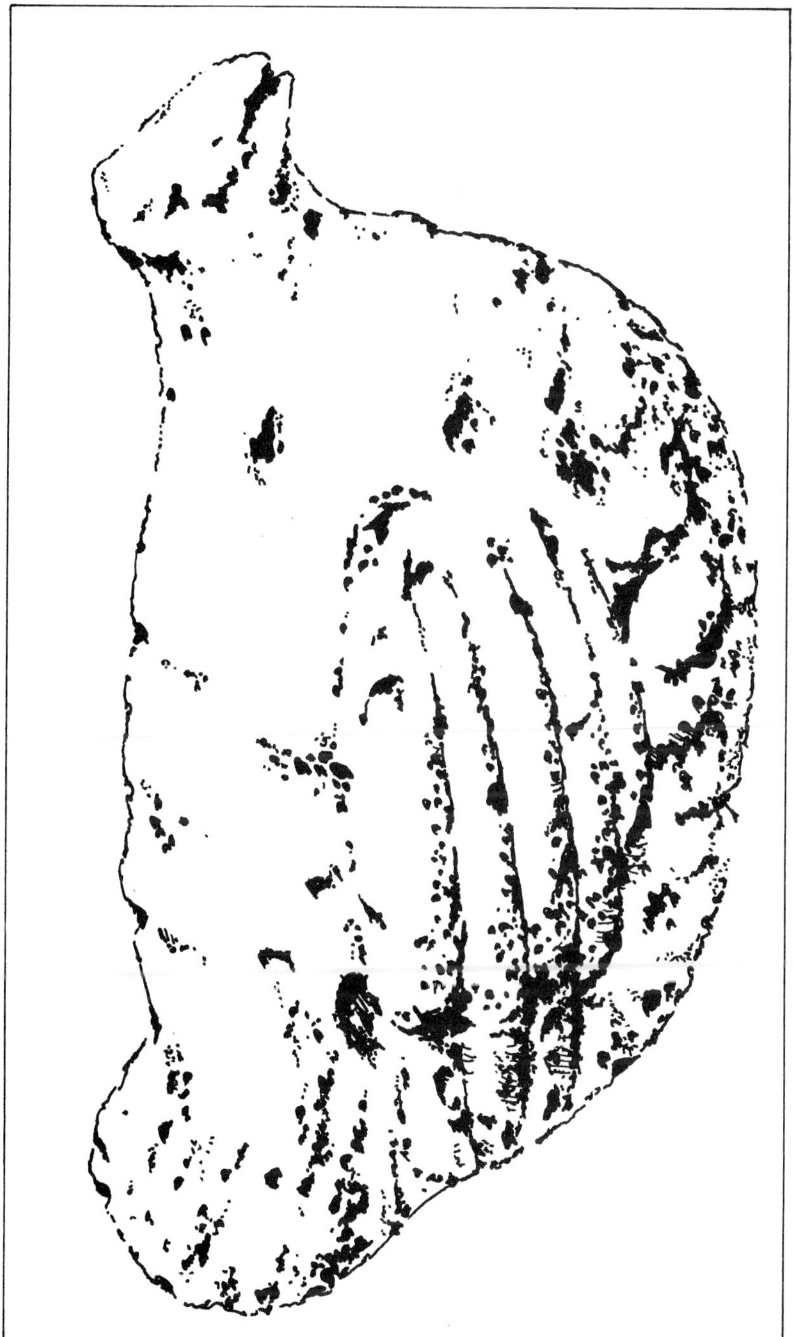

4 THE ENTREPRENEUR AS SOVEREIGN

> Did you ever expect a corporation to have a conscience, when it has no soul to be damned, and no body to be kicked?
>
> Edward, First Baron Thurlow

Having begun, with Toro, the policy of leasing the government-owned property on Easter Island to whoever controlled the former Brander lands, successive Chilean governments found themselves involved in a recurrent drama. As the term of a lease contract approached, government interest in the island would rise, frequently stimulated by intense press campaigns and the resulting surges of public opinion. After a prolonged and often vicious altercation between government, company, press, and public, a new contract would be promulgated and the company would be left to rule the whole island with little interference until the contract again ran out and the cycle was repeated.

The first cycle, or Toro colonization period, ended with the disgrace of Toro and the assumption of control by Merlet in 1895-7. The succeeding cycles, based on 20-year contracts, peaked towards the end of World War I, again in the mid-1930s, and yet again in the early 1950s. During the bulk of this period a single company, successor to Merlet, was the effective sovereign of Easter Island.

WILLIAMSON, BALFOUR AND COMPANY

The firm which was to control Easter Island's destiny for half a century was founded a decade before that island suffered its initial external impact. In 1851 three Scots businessmen from Fife founded S. Williamson and Company in Liverpool, England, their major purpose being "to ship goods to the West Coast of South America."[1] Because of local industrial expansion, the prevailing peace, abundant goodwill towards Britain, and earlier penetration by other commercial houses, Williamson chose Valparaiso as the overseas headquarters. As a British MP, Stephen Williamson was soon known as "the Member for Chile."[2] Williamson, Balfour and Company came into being officially as the Chilean branch in 1863, by which time a shipping fleet had been built up and return cargoes of wool and guano found. By the 1870s a third branch had been set up in San Francisco, and company ships such as *La Escocesa* (the Scotswoman) were trading between Europe, the River Plate, the whole west coast of the Americas, the Pacific Islands, and Australia.

At the turn of the century the company was unashamedly an "empire", as described by the official company historian.[3] Having developed a strong triangular trade between Britain, Chile, and the Pacific seaboard of the United States, the company had two offices in Britain (Liverpool and London), six in the United States, and five in Chile.

In the latter country company interests soon spread beyond the import-export business. Williamson, Balfour became involved in the commercial exploitation of the new regions opened up by the War of the Pacific and the Araucanian campaigns. Nitrates in the north and flourmilling in the south were major enterprises, but as the company grew it diversified into wheat, railways, wool, oil, tin, cocoa, cement, fruit, coffee, guano, sugar, lumber, and banking. Not all of these ventures were possible in Chile; the early part of the twentieth century saw the expansion of this early multinational into Argentina, Brazil, Peru, Ecuador, Colombia, Bolivia, the interior United States, Canada, West Africa, and the Philippines (Figure 1,4). Within Chile, the company's interest in wool and banking was most significant for the development of Easter Island.

LA COMPAÑIA EXPLOTADORA DE LA ISLA DE PASCUA

Merlet, perhaps through Brander, had links with Williamson, Balfour as early, at least, as the mid-1890s. In the tight commercial world of the late-nineteenth century Pacific, the Brander, Darsie, and Williamson families were all well-known to each other. All were Scots, or of Scottish origin. As if symbolic of the strong links between them, Stephen Williamson the younger's middle name was Anstruther, the birthplace of his father and the small town in Fife to which the Darsies retired after leaving Tahiti during the interminable Brander-Bornier lawsuit. The commercial connection is revealed in a letter from Arthur Brander to his brother John in 1897, in which he stated that "Williamson's people had told Mr. Darsie, that they had bought a lot of Easter Island wool" from Merlet.[4] It was to Williamson, Balfour that Merlet turned when trouble arose.

At first the Merlet operation on Easter Island seemed to be successful. It is probable that Merlet began to use the Brander property for sheeprearing as early as 1894, and the opinion of Arthur Brander was that "Merlet has been making a good thing out of the island."[5] By the turn of the century, however, E. Merlet and Company was in financial straits.[6] Apparently the

FIGURE 1,4 The South American commercial empire of Williamson, Balfour and Company before World War I (source: data in Hunt).

task of developing the Easter Island trade was beyond the capacity of Merlet's company.[7] Perhaps uneasy about his land titles, he wrote in 1901 to M. Goupil of Papeete for copies of the Toro-Goupil-Brander correspondence of 1895.[8] An alternative hypothesis is that Merlet was in fact acting for Williamson, Balfour, which within two years had taken effective control of the Easter Island operation.[9]

In 1898 Williamson, Balfour had advanced Merlet a loan of £4,000, upon which Merlet seemed likely to default.[10] As the Easter Island wool business seemed unlikely to succeed without further capital for improved livestock, Williamson, Balfour formed the Compañía Explotadora de la Isla de Pascua (hereafter, CEDIP) with a capital of £20,000 comprising 500 shares.[11] Of these, 375 fully paid-up shares were granted to the brothers Enrique and Numa Merlet in exchange for the cession of all their rights in Easter Island, including the government concession. Williamson, Balfour took 120 shares, and the remaining five were distributed between Williamson and his fellow partners. These partners, with the addition of Enrique Merlet, formed the board, and Numa Merlet was appointed manager.

Domiciled in Valparaiso, the company was registered on 30 July 1903 for a period of 25 years.[12] The first shareholders meeting was held in the Williamson, Balfour offices on 22 August, with Stephen Anstruther Williamson as president of the board of directors. Hunt states that one possible goal was the quick sale of the company to one of the pastoral companies of the Chilean mainland, which "might be sufficiently attracted by the undoubted excellence of the grazing to make a bid at a premium" for CEDIP.[13] Nothing transpired, however, and the company was therefore compelled to improve the island's profitability through its own efforts.

Indeed, the stated object of CEDIP was to:

> acquire the privately owned land on Easter Island, acquire or rent the state-owned land on the said island, to exploit them both, to obtain new boats and acquire any other materials necessary for the furthering of (island) development . . .[14]

The Merlets were given the task of obtaining government approval of their cession of their lease of 1895. CEDIP accepted the property "as is", but the Merlets were enjoined to legally register the Brander-Merlet land sale in Chile as soon as Easter Island was officially incorporated into a department of one of the Chilean provinces.[15]

Despite the Merlets' majority shareholding, Williamson, Balfour dominated CEDIP from its inception. The parent company became banker to CEDIP and within five years the latter's debt to Williamson, Balfour stood at £13,964 12s. 3d.[16] In 1908 further credit was extended, with the Merlet shares as security.[17] Financial collapse into the arms of Williamson, Balfour was inevitable, and with the failure of the Merlets the whole stock came under the control of the Williamsons.[18]

CHALLENGE TO THE COMPANY STATE

During the first decade of the twentieth century the government and public of Chile paid scant attention to Easter Island. In general it appeared that all was well with the island and that "the administration of Merlet and Company and the natives of the island live in complete harmony."[19] Throughout much of this period, however, the post of *subdelegado marítimo* was held by the CEDIP manager who thus represented both company and government and consequently wielded absolute power on the island.[20]

But from about 1910 government interest was engendered by the outcries of influential citizens. At this time Easter Island was, in effect, merely a Chilean colony, having not yet been incorporated into a department or province. Citizens of Valparaiso, claiming that the island had communications links, "albeit irregular," with their city, petitioned the central government to include the island in the Valparaiso *intendencia*.[21] Moreover, since the turn of the century groups of influential citizens in both Santiago and Valparaiso had become concerned with the conditions of life of the Easter Islanders, who were universally declared to be bowed beneath the yoke of the company.[22] In 1914 the islanders staged a revolt against company rule (Chapter 8).[23]

The 1916 visit of Bishop Rafael Edwards, scion of one of the first families of Chile, to Easter Island brought all these problems to a head. A persistent campaign for the liberation of the island from company rule swept through Chile in 1916-17. Opposition to the company was based on three major issues: the company's claim to ownership of the island; its treatment of the Rapanui; and a belief that the island could be better used than as a mere sheep ranch.

Ownership: Company vs. Government

Merlet's lease of the government land on Easter Island officially terminated on 29 August 1915. The Chilean state was thus entitled to take control of its land with all improvements thereon. "Because of difficulties of communication with the island," this transfer did not take place, and in

June 1916 Merlet's lease was extended under the same conditions as before.[24] The government, however, reserved the right to terminate the contract at any time.

Meanwhile, in April 1916 the president of Chile had bowed to public pressure and declared that it had become necessary to incorporate Easter Island into the judicial and administrative system of the republic.[25] Accordingly, the island became a *subdelegación* of the Department of Valparaiso. It was also to be recolonized by settlers under the aegis of the Ministry of Colonization.

As the island had now become part of an official Chilean administrative unit, E. Merlet sought to register the title of CEDIP to the former Brander landholdings. In a deposition of 27 September 1916, Merlet attempted to legalize the by now general opinion that the former Brander lands occupied almost the whole island. His description of the boundaries of the company territory was:

> to the North and South, with the property of the Government of Chile and with the Pacific Ocean; to the East with the Pacific Ocean; and to the West with the lands of the Government of Chile and with the Pacific Ocean . . . the property of the Chilean Government is that which surrounds the Port of Hangaroa and which extends in a southerly direction towards (*hacia*) Vaihu.[26]

The use of "*hacia* Vaihu" is significant. According to the Bornier map of 1871 the Mission-Salmon property, later sold to Chile, extended all the way from Hangaroa to the south coast at Vaihu, cutting the Brander-Bornier property in two (Figure 3,2). A description of such a property would require the use of the word *hasta* (up to) rather than *hacia* (towards). The revised position, which had developed in the Merlet years and was accepted even by some government advisors, was that the CEDIP lands now included Vaihu, thus encircling the government property in Hangaroa (Figure 2,4).

Once Merlet had lodged his deposition the government questioned the legality of the claim. A mere 19 years after the last rumblings of the Brander-Bornier legal proceedings which had involved action in Tahiti, France, and Scotland, a new dispute broke out in Valparaiso. By law, Merlet was obliged to publish his claim to the title in the metropolitan newspapers of October 1916.[27] The government then officially opposed the inscription of his legal right to the territory in question. Through Molina Luco, its lawyer, the government asserted that the dispositions of foreign courts were invalid and that the land claimed by Merlet for CEDIP was exclusively the property of the State by virtue of the annexation of 1888.[28]

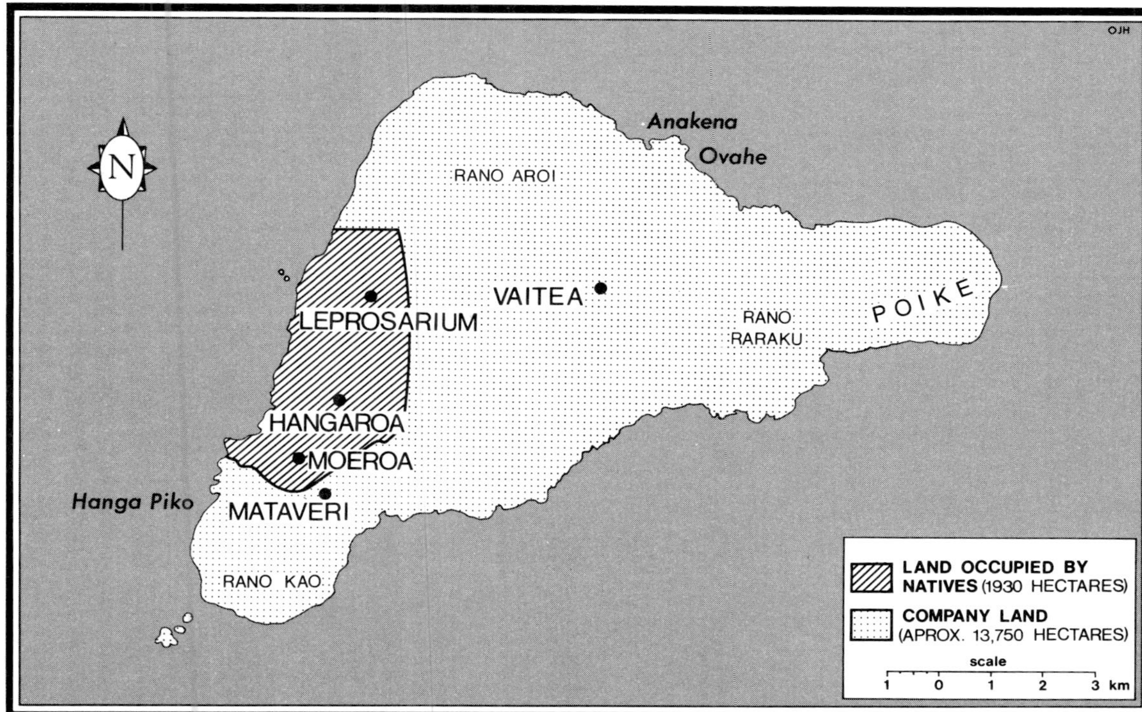

FIGURE 2,4 The division of the island between company and government in 1916 (redrawn from Vergara).

The Company's Treatment of the Indigenes

In early 1916 the anti-company campaign of concerned mainlanders found a leader in the shape of Rafael Edwards, Bishop of Dodona and Vicar Military of Chile. Military chaplains had been sent out on several naval expeditions. During their short stays on the island they performed the sacraments, including baptisms and marriages which may have been awaiting the official blessing for a year or more.[29] Bishop Edwards was shocked at the reports brought back by his chaplains.[30] The Rapanui were apparently living in appalling social conditions, bereft of outside help, and with their chapel in a severe state of decay.[31] In June 1916 the bishop left Valparaiso on the *General Baquedano* for an extended investigation of social conditions on Easter Island.

During his absence a growing concern about the forgotten inhabitants of the remote Chilean colony began to manifest itself in occasional newspaper articles of a speculative nature. It was known, for example, that leprosy was endemic in the island, and the demand of the *subdelegado* that a walled leprosarium be built to contain the twelve known lepers was met with enthusiasm by a society which regarded the disease with horror.[32] On his return, the bishop revealed that the lepers had been relegated to two huts north of Hangaroa where, lacking clothes, beds, cooking utensils, food, and medicines, they lived in an "unbreathable atmosphere which provokes nausea."[33] In his inimitable style the bishop continued:

> men and women, young and old, the lepers appear to be walking corpses, brutally mutilated . . . it is a spectacle whose horror sets the nerves on edge, paralizes the heart, and excites simultaneous feelings of pity and indignation within the breast.[34]

In late 1916 Bishop Edwards was made administrator of the leprosarium, and the University of Chile was asked to conduct a study of leprosy on the island.

Only a dozen or so lepers existed in 1916. The plight of the 250 other islanders also drew attention; as early as 1914 a newspaper article had asserted that the indigenes were totally naked and suffering from hunger and thirst.[35] So poor were their conditions of life that they were said to have petitioned the Chilean government to allow them to emigrate *en masse* to Tahiti.

> Poor islanders! Except for the Bishop of Dodona, who has concerned himself with them? Who has taken one

> second from the busy affairs of his daily life to consider the state of material and moral abandonment in which they live, whose fruits are nakedness, hunger, ignorance, and impiety? Who has raised his voice to implore pity for these unfortunate fellow countrymen? No one![36]

After the return of the bishop these paternalist diatribes were to be larded with abundant factual information.

To Bishop Edwards Easter Island appeared a rich and potentially productive land. The condition of the native inhabitants was therefore all the more starkly exhibited. His reports depict a broken race, almost entirely naked, eating only what the earth spontaneously produced, idle, shiftless, and unwilling to work.[37] This rather exaggerated description was fully in accord with contemporary opinion of the Polynesians who, having ceased to be "noble savages," had unfortunately not yet absorbed the Euramerican work ethic. There was clearly a gross lack of fit between Easter Island actualities and the bishop's model of man.

Responsibility for the plight of the islanders was laid squarely at the door of CEDIP.[38] Little thought seems to have been given to the almost total failure of successive Chilean governments to control company activities and ameliorate the living conditions of their island citizens. As is common in company state situations, the entrepreneur, whether guilty or not, becomes the most convenient whipping-boy when problems emerge.

In 1914 CEDIP had been accused of depriving the Rapanui of their land, of giving almost all of the scarce sweet water supply to the stock, and of driving the inhabitants from the coasts into the mountainous interior where the land was less fertile. Company permission was apparently required to leave Hangaroa, and should a hungry indigene be found stealing a sheep for his starving children, he was deported to mainland Chile on the next boat, there to die from the dual operation of unaccustomed climate and homesickness.[39]

Bishop Edwards added to these charges, stating that hunger among the Rapanui was in part due to company intransigence and the introduction of new wants. The former reliance on the abundant indigenous products had been reduced to "a few bananas, some sweet potatoes, other roots . . . raw or badly-cooked fish . . . a little sugar cane."[40] The growing preference was for imported foodstuffs, available only at the company store, where prices could be set at whim. In one instance, the bishop speaks of a sack of flour costing 100 pesos (the equivalent of one month's rent of the leased government lands).[41] Consequently, among the Rapanui "bread and flour are unknown; there is no maize, no potatoes, no rice, no coffee, no tea, no maté . . . nothing."[42]

To this rather culture-bound view Bishop Edwards added that although the island abounded in sheep, meat was rarely available to the inhabitants. When a meat ration was given to Rapanui workers during the shearing season, they were forbidden to take it home for their families.[43] All agricultural progress was hindered by the existence of only a single plough.

Working conditions were also said to be poor, and CEDIP was accused of instituting a regime of forced labour.[44] This had resulted in neglect of indigenous agriculture during those periods when the Rapanui were required to shear sheep, load and unload vessels, and other non-regular occupations. Where cash wages were given, they immediately returned to CEDIP via the company store. A letter was referred to in which Merlet had apparently asked the captain of the *Baquedano* to sanction forced labour. If the Rapanui proved unwilling to work, the company resorted to a lock-out, during which no work was offered, no goods were sold, and no native products were bought. This resulted in severe distress among the indigenes. In sum, Edwards suggested, the native inhabitants had become slaves of the company, which operated the island in a feudal manner reminiscent of the traditional *encomiendas* of the Spanish-American Empire.[45]

The immediate practical response to these reported outrages was a major drive to collect a wide variety of useful goods, from ploughs to needles, which could be sent to relieve the wants of the islanders. Of prime importance was the collection of clothes.[46] European clothing had been worn on Easter Island since the days of the explorers, from whom garments were stolen in quantity. This demand providentially coincided with mainland demands that the islanders be clothed, savage laxity in dress being perceived as an affront to bourgeois sensibilities.

Private charity produced a considerable array of goods, although it is not clear whether the 20 ploughs and sundry sewing machines requested by the bishop were forthcoming.[47] As an added attraction to those who wished to relieve the sufferings of "the poor indigenes of Easter Island . . . completely abandoned . . . without material or spiritual aid," all who contributed were guaranteed indulgences by the Church for 100 days.[48] In December 1916 a charity committee began work in Valparaiso, a city chosen not simply for its tenuous shipping links with the island, but because it was "the city from which the light of evangelism and civilization was carried to Easter Island."[49]

CEDIP did not remain quiescent under this hail of accusation. In a businesslike fashion Henry Williamson attempted to rebut the bishop's accusations point by point, although his letters to the press were hopelessly outnumbered, in terms of column inches, by those of the company detractors.

In dealing with the Rapanui treatment question Williamson perceptively observed that the issue depended wholly upon one's perceptions of and attitudes towards indigenous conditions of life. Any solution depended:

> upon the prism through which one looks. An evangelical missionary may consider that the company has been inhumane because it has not converted the indigenes from idolaters into catholics, from ne'er-do-wells into workers, from communists into respecters of private property, from immoral ways to chastity, from dirty to clean, from herbivores to carnivores. But a simple mortal might judge that the company, which is neither the government nor the church, has done quite enough in procuring houses for the natives, in inducing them to formalize their marriages, in preventing them from fighting and killing each other, in clothing the nearly naked females, in giving them land which they can cultivate if they so desire, and offering them ploughs and oxen, in providing cows for milk, in paying them a daily wage when they feel like working, and respecting their desires when they do not . . .[50]

Though it is now impossible to judge the truth of the matter, one feels drawn to the reasonableness of Williamson's point of view.

The literary output of Bishop Edwards and his chaplains during the period 1918-21 reveals a crusading spirit, amounting at times almost to hysterical zealotry. Father Bienvenido de Estella, in particular, made claims about the work of the church which were refuted by Vives Solar, a Chilean offical who had lived several years on Easter Island.[51] One detects more than a little paternalism in Bienvenido de Estella's choice of titles, such as "Six Months Among the Easter Island Kanakas."[52] Contemporary writers insisted that the islanders regarded the use of "kanaka" as opprobrious.

An altercation which took place between Bienvenido de Estella and a CEDIP official reveals the polarity of attitudes between church and company.[53] In the second decade of the twentieth century Rapanui funerals still involved a great deal of feasting, singing, and dancing. Regarding this as barbarous, the two priests instructed the islanders to behave in a more civilized manner. Company officials remonstrated, suggesting that the islanders should be permitted to retain their traditional ways. The reaction of the missionaries was to heap abuse upon the "Egotistical, monopolistic entrepreneurs" who refused to recognize the duty of all Westerners to bring the light of civilized morality to those still living in heathen fastnesses. On the other hand, one might question the company's altruism in that the selective support of native customs has been used by almost all colonialists as a means of entrenching their ultimate control.

It is almost axiomatic in any discussion of company towns or estates that the company is castigated for its treatment of its workers. Taking the middle ground between the protestations of CEDIP and the accusations of Bishop Edwards, one might well commend the company for its restrained interference with indigenous lifestyles and question the bishop's concern with imposing his standards by forcibly clothing, civilizing, and putting to work the entire population of a cultural group with a social ethos diametrically opposed to that espoused by this scion of a rich, entrepreneurial Welsh-Chilean dynasty.

Although the company treated the islanders paternalistically, and in leaving them largely to themselves was guilty of some inhumanity, it is unlikely that the tales of slavery, outright oppression, starvation, and brutality broadcast throughout the Chilean press can be taken at face value. Three pro-company accounts, no doubt solicited by CEDIP, were produced.[54] One derives from them a strong suspicion that the indigenes were quite capable of manipulating the opinions of temporary visitors. Bishop Edwards and his followers, ignorant of Polynesian folkways and sensitive to suffering and distress by virtue of their calling, may have been thoroughly humbugged.

One cannot ignore the possibility of self-seeking and a desire for publicity on the part of the anti-company campaigners. Unlike the social problems of Chilean cities, those of Easter Island stirred the public imagination. Yet, in

> Valparaiso alone, where there are thousands of poor girls who have no alternative but the streets to make a living . . . there are people . . . who are trying to make themselves famous by lecturing on the "Poor Kanakas" of Isla de Pascua, when they have so much under their noses to remedy first.[55]

The history of Britain and other Western nations amply illustrates the fact that missionary orders receive far more support if their work is directed at foreign or distant heathen than if they seek to ameliorate local or internal conditions, thus undermining the *status quo*.

Easter Island Again Viewed as an Agricultural Settlement

At the height of the Easter Island controversy one R.H. penned a lengthy series of articles in the Valparaiso press during the last four months of 1916. In these articles he rehearsed, in considerable detail, all the arguments used in the 1880s when the decision to annex was under discussion. A somewhat turgid correspondent, R.H. was also out of touch with reality.

At his best when defending Chile's sovereignty over the island, his protestations of its superb position as a naval base and a trans-Pacific coaling station had been superseded by events. By 1916, except in the minds of those who were incited by the war to revive fatuous geopolitical schemes, the locational advantages of Easter Island were recognized to be virtually nil. A far more viable proposition was concerned with the agricultural possibilities of the island, based on the official dedication of the island to agrarian colonization after the termination of Merlet's original lease. The indefatigable R.H. devoted many column inches to an analysis of the island's potential for agricultural improvement, and in doing so drew upon the knowledge of CEDIP employees as well as upon a report prepared by one Dr. Knoche for the government.[56]

On the basis of such prognostications two separate but not irreconcilable colonization schemes developed. The first was a revival of the Toro plan on a larger scale. His arguments based on the rich soil of the island, the possibility of cultivating almost its entire surface (clearly a perception of one who had never been there), the fame of the *chileno* as a farmer, the willingness of Chileans to emigrate, and the fact that the island had once fed several thousand indigenes, R.H. declared that "four thousand Chileans could live there."[57] Another body of opinion asserted that the island should indeed be an agrarian colony, but the colonists should be the islanders themselves.

> They are already settlers! They are no longer merely beasts of burden at the service of a narrow, uncharitable private interest.[58]

The chief obstacle to both schemes was the effective control of the entire land surface of the island by the Compañía Explotadora de la Isla de Pascua.

CONFLICT RESOLUTION

The anti-company campaign was monumentalized in two hurriedly-produced volumes. In *La Isla de Pascua* (1918) Rafael Edwards repeated his allegations of misery, want, and brutality, spoke of "the slaves whose chains have been broken," and asserted that the chief requirement of the indigenes was for reasonably-compensated work, possible only through the planned development of resources:

> But this will be useless unless there is maintained in Easter Island an authority independent of the economic interest which alone exists at this time.[59]

The company's rebuttal of all allegations was contained in a volume of the same title, which brought together in printed form a large number of the documents which Merlet had been collecting for some time.[60] The aim of this book was to:

> dissipate in the minds of the Government, the Magistracy, and Public Opinion, the anti-company feelings which have been engendered by several publications which, although no doubt well-intentioned, are rooted in lack of knowledge.[61]

CEDIP proposed that the government should take back its lands and work them itself, leaving the company free to develop its own territory.[62]

Newspaper vituperation, however, was more instrumental in sensitizing Chileans to the dispute. Anti-company writers asserted that CEDIP, with complete control of the island, had acted:

> as one might expect, exploiting its island as absolute lord and exercising, over the unfortunate (islanders) a medieval despotism.[63]

In contrast, R.H. and others referred to Bishop Edwards as a "worthy apostle" engaged in a "modern crusade" which was "as much patriotic as Christian."[64] The bishop himself attested that the campaign united the worthy causes of patriotism, religion and charity.

Newspapers eagerly published an exchange of letters between the bishop and Williamson.[65] Williamson was forced into the position of having to defend both the motives of his company and his own impugned loyalty to Chile. On the agricultural question, he denied any possibility of success for the proposed agrarian colony. Besides this attempt to reconcile public opinion to CEDIP's continued operation, Williamson was careful to reassure the Chilean president, the Minister for External Affairs, and other high functionaries of his loyalty to Chile.[66] Simultaneously, he challenged the veracity of Bishop Edwards and the resurgent Toro by rejecting trial by press campaign and demanding that an impartial investigatory committee be set up to review the evidence for CEDIP ownership of the bulk of Easter Island.[67]

Meanwhile, government officials had conducted hearings on the Easter Island question, taking special note of the report of the captain of the corvette *Baquedano*. On 7 November 1916 the Ministry of External Affairs, Colonization Section, decided that Merlet and CEDIP had not complied with the obligations set forth in the lease of 1895, and that the "prevailing regime on Easter Island has resulted in the misery of its inhabitants, is a hindrance to its progress, and will cause further evils if it is not immediately terminated."[68] Accordingly, the new lease agreement of early 1916 was revoked. The Inspector General of Colonization and Immigration was instructed to take immediate control of the government lands and to provisionally set aside portions of land for the use of the indigenes.

A commission was set up to investigate the judicial and administrative problems of the island with a view to safeguarding government interests and improving the living conditions of the inhabitants. Among the appointed commissioners were Bishop Edwards, the captain of the *Baquedano*, government officials from several departments, and a rehabilitated Policarpo Toro. As is usual in the modern history of Easter Island, mainland events supervened and a temporary solution, rapidly found, became the basis for future operations. The Merlet-government court case ground to an inconclusive halt, allegedly because of "instructions from above."[69] International incidents on the Peru-Chile border called Bishop Edwards from Santiago. Without his driving presence the commission collapsed.

During this atmosphere of tension CEDIP, with its exceptionally good contacts in influential circles, was able to convince the Ministry of External Affairs to grant a new lease of the government-owned lands. Known as the *Temperamento Provisorio*, the new lease treated the island as a single unit for the first time.[70] In this way the government asserted its claim to ownership of the entire land surface in a manner least offensive to the company, which remained in effective control.

The document enjoined CEDIP to regulate land use, conserve the stock, prevent any further loss of statues or other artifacts, provide land for a leprosarium, give help to the local fishery, provide the *subdelegado* with meat for Rapanui use, provide provisions for naval vessels, and support a

Chilean administrator and his family. Three thousand hectares (7,400 acres) in the Hangaroa area were parcelled out among the indigenes. The lot of the islanders was somewhat improved by these measures.[71] Unlike the Merlet lease, however, these duties were balanced by the omission of any obligations with regard to rent, maintenance of Chilean settlers, construction and maintenance of piers and coaling stations, provision of medical assistance to ships' crews, or maintenance of annual links with mainland Chile. A more realistic stance was clearly being taken by government circles, themselves unable or unwilling to devote the energies of the state to the development of their Pacific island.

FURTHER PROBLEMS

Despite its lack of a clear title and the temporary nature of its lease, CEDIP continued in quiet possession of Easter Island until President Ibañez, a reformist, reopened the question in 1927. The impetuous Ibañez decreed the 12-year old *Temperamento Provisorio* terminated on 19 April 1929, and the government made plans to register the whole island as state property.[72] Again the company mounted a stiff opposition. As Ibañez was forced out of office in 1931, with a consequent resurgence of political anarchy, CEDIP continued as effective administrator of Easter Island. With the restoration of political stability a second commission was authorized in July 1933, presided over once more by Rafael Edwards. This commission again recommended that the government should legally register the entire island as state property.[73] Accordingly, on 11 November 1933 the land surface of the island legally passed out of the hands of CEDIP.[74]

Proposals and counterproposals were interchanged between government, commission, and company with regard to the future economic use of the island.[75] In particular, CEDIP asked for a 30-year lease of the entire island in exchange for a final renunciation of all its land claims. By 1935 the company was willing to settle for a 20-year concession to "exploit all the land surface of the island, except the 2,000 hectares (5,000 acres) reserved for the natives."[76] Having little hope of alternative projects, the government felt compelled to let the island to a private entrepreneur for yet a fourth time; the lease was signed on 19 March 1936.

Despite its attainment of sovereignty in 1888 and legal ownership of the land surface in 1933, the Chilean state seemed loathe to reconsider its traditional stance, that of attempting to develop national territory by effectively ceding it to a private company. This attitude, in part the result of a chronic shortage of capital, was not unique to Easter Island, for the northern, southern, and eastern high-altitude extremities of Chile were developed in a similar manner.

However, as the island was officially under military jurisdiction, the naval authorities in Valparaiso made a determined attempt, for the first time, to regulate the routine operations of CEDIP. To this end the navy set up a third commission in April 1936, which drew up a *Reglamento de régimen interno de vida y trabajo en la Isla de Pascua*.[77] Of its 80 articles, no less than 23 dealt with working conditions, in an attempt to bring Easter Island into line with mainland labour codes. In their concern with details of salary, sickness benefits, death grants, and the like, these regulations placed the company firmly in the position of welfare agency as well as employer. The company state which had existed more or less untouched since the accession of Merlet was thus confirmed by government regulation.

Indeed, CEDIP was regulated into a position of even greater paternalism, for it was ordered to pay its workers not only a salary but also complete daily rations. In its control of the annual vessel, all employment, and the island's food supply, as well as the export economy, CEDIP remained the actual ruler of Easter Island. The small naval and civilian contingent was, under naval regulation, placed in the same position of company dependency, on a day-to-day basis, as the indigenes. In this atmosphere of effective company control, tempered by the naval presence and radio communication with Chile, Easter Island was prepared to continue its emphasis on profitable sheeprearing until after the middle of the twentieth century.

THE DEMISE OF THE COMPANY

According to Hunt, the official Williamson, Balfour historian, the parent company had attempted to sell CEDIP as early as the 1920s.[78] The interminable dispute over land titles had rendered any such sale impossible. Soon after World War II, however, Williamson, Balfour and its associated companies experienced a chronic dearth of liquid capital. Accordingly, Williamson, Balfour sold CEDIP, complete with government concession, to another Anglo-Chilean firm in 1946.[79] Always a farsighted enterprise, it seems the parent company withdrew from its Easter Island venture at a most opportune moment.[80]

The Chilean governments which followed World War II were radical in nature and concerned to effectively increase state control of the extremities of the nation's rather unwieldy territory. Government plans for a final takeover were begun in the late 1940s. The rationale behind these plans repeats, to some extent, the arguments of Chilean authorities at the time of the 1888 annexation and the anti-company campaign of 1916. Throughout this 60-year period Chilean perceptions of Easter Island had, in many ways, changed remarkedly little. This was in part due to the continuing remoteness of the island. In 1950, as in 1890, it was still visited only by company ships and naval vessels.

In the early 1950s the island was perceived as having several possibilities for development. Although echoes of its geopolitical advantages were heard, and a little thought was given to tourist possibilities, the dominant theme at this time was the evergreen agricultural possibilities of the island. Plans for the island's future were devised by the *Corporación de Fomento de Producción* (CORFO), the powerful government development agency.[81] Easter Island was again regarded as a possible agricultural supplier for mainland Chile. In particular, and despite the continuation of wool production, the island's economy was to be diversified by the production of maize, semi-tropical products, such as bananas and sugar, and fish, which would be processed in a modern plant. Government lines would provide an adequate shipping service which would effectively incorporate the island into the national economy for the first time.

The actors involved in bringing the Chilean government to the point of taking full control of Easter Island were many and varied. CORFO was active in the early 1950s, sending agronomists, civil engineers, and fisheries experts to the island.[82] Government shipping agencies expressed interest in serving the island, and the airforce began plans for an aerodrome. Initial flights by the Chilean Parragué and the Australian Taylor seemed to demonstrate that Easter Island would form an important stepping-stone on future scheduled flights between Australia and South America.[83] The Friends of Easter Island Society in Santiago was an active lobbyist for agricultural expansion and modernization in the form of an upgrading of medical, educational, and sanitary facilities, and the installation of such facilities as running water and electric power throughout Hangaroa village.[84] It is perhaps significant that González Videla, the president under whose aegis the takeover plans were made, was honorary president of this society.

Patriotic motives were well to the fore. González Videla told the society that "Easter Island is and will be eternally Chilean."[85] The naval authorities, already officially administrators of the island for many years, were not unwilling to take complete control. There was apparently no objection from the Rapanui who were reported to be "*impregnados de chilenidad*."[86] Accordingly, in November 1953 the company's lease was finally revoked and the naval authorities took upon themselves economic and social, as well as administrative control. Ibañez' decree states categorically why Chile officially decided to increase the effectiveness of military rule; "the island's position in the Pacific Ocean renders it of overwhelming geostrategic importance for national defence, and especially for defence of the continent."[87] It is likely, however, that continued naval rule was another of the temporary expedients by which Chile had succeeded in keeping Easter Island under an autocratic administration since 1888. The island continued under military rule until the mid-1960s. After a brief period of civilian government (see Chapter 8) it reverted to the military authorities after the Chilean coup of 1973.

PLATE 13 Man-modified landscape between Tongariki and Rano Raraku ▶

SECTION THREE

LANDSCAPE CHANGE

When any class of objects has habitually presented itself
to our perceptions in invariable conjunction with
particular relations, then, on the sudden appearance of
one object of the class divested of those accompaniments,
the essential difference of the relation is,
by an involuntary process, transferred to the object itself,
which thus offers itself to our perceptions with
all the strangeness of novelty.

Scythrop Glowry

Thomas Love Peacock, *Crochet Castle* (1831)

PLATE 14 Inner slope of Rano Kao crater ▶

5 THE PHYSICAL ENVIRONMENT

A monstrous pumice-stone, an enormous scoria, . . . a prodigious slagheap . . . that is the best definition of Easter Island.

Collage from Alfred Métraux and Robert Casey

During the long debates over Easter Island's potential for development, several diametrically opposed points of view emerged (Chapters 2-4). One body of opinion considered the island a superb haven for naval vessels; opponents stated that the island possessed no natural harbours. Agrarian colonizers announced that the whole island could be tilled, and would become Chile's tropical plantation base. Opponents argued that the island was arid. In the twentieth century, much was made of the possibilities of processing fish and animal meats for export to the mainland. Opponents claimed that the distances involved were too great.

Earlier chapters have explored these perceptions and demonstrated that it was on the basis of such perceptions, or misperceptions, that policy decisions were made from the 1880s to the 1950s. The present chapter seeks to resolve the debate by briefly describing the fundamental features of Easter Island's geology, relief, vegetation, climate, and soils. Such a description, referring as it does to the state of the island before the settlement of Western man in the nineteenth century, is also a necessary prelude to the discussion of landscape change which appears in the subsequent chapters.

ORIGINS AND GEOLOGY

In times geologically recent but beyond the memory of man, Easter Island rose, like Venus, from the waves. It rose between latitudes 27°03' and 27°12' South and longitudes 109°14' and 109°27' West. This is an extremely isolated position (Figure 2,0). The nearest island, S... Gomez, is 340 kilometres (210 miles away), a mere reef inhab... seabirds. To the east, no land is encountered until one re... coast, a distance of 3,550 to 3,700 kilometres (2... Westwards, lonely Pitcairn Island, the neares... imately 1,900 kilometres (1,200 miles) fro... population cluster is reached before Tahiti, ... (2,200 miles) distance. Easter Island's closes...

note are Valparaiso, Chile, and Papeete, Tahiti, over 3,200 kilometres (2,000 miles) away respectively to east and west.

This assertion of the emergent nature of the island remained long in doubt. Eighteenth century cosmographers, trained in the classical Greek notions of a symmetrical earth, postulated the existence of a huge southern continent, the existence of which was necessary to balance the major land masses of the northern hemisphere. *Terra Australis Incognita* was avidly sought, but even the three great exploratory cruises of James Cook failed to discover a land mass, though the chart of the Pacific was soon liberally sprinkled with island discoveries.

As the proposed continent was manifestly not to be found, it became necessary to invent its disappearance. Barclay, commander of H.M.S. *Topaze*, which visited Easter Island in 1868, propounded the theory of a lost continent which was once connected with South America.[1] As with the Old World's Atlantis, the sunken continent of Mu was visible only by virtue of its highest peaks appearing as the myriad islands of the Pacific Ocean. Part of the large continent of Lemuria, which formerly occupied both the Indian and the Pacific oceans, Mu sank beneath the waves two to four million years ago.

Such assertions are accompanied by an insistence that the statues of Easter Island were carved by Lemurians before submergence. Unfortunately for this argument, these artifacts occupy extreme coastal positions, suggesting little change in the shoreline since their erection. Coastal erosive action is of such magnitude that if the statues had been erected even several thousand years ago, many would have already been engulfed. Moreover, depths of 2,000 fathoms occur eastward and northward of Easter Island, reaching 4,000 fathoms as the coast of South America is approached. Even in the shallower area to the southeast, depths are of the order of 1,500-1,800 fathoms. Given that these oceanic depths occur in close proximity to the island, were the ocean floor to be uplifted to sea level the land area presently comprising Easter Island would be at an elevation of about 4,000 metres (13,000 feet) above sea level, possibly above the snowline, and hardly the most suitable location for the time-consuming carving of giant statues.

Despite the vigorous propagation of the Lemuria doctrine by Madame Blavatsky and other early twentieth century theosophists, the submergence theory has counted archaeologists among its adherents. Macmillan Brown, whose *Riddle of the Pacific* was a *cause célèbre* of the 1920s, rejected the subsidence of an entire continent.[2] He envisioned Easter Island as the centre of a vast Pacific archipelago, rather like Le Guin's *Earthsea*, which subsided after man took up residence thereon. This theory was built upon: the lack of recent volcanic activity on Easter Island; certain Polynesian legends of sunken land masses; seventeenth century buccaneer's reports of islands never seen thereafter though often sought; the undoubted unity of Polynesian language and culture in the great triangle between Easter Island, Hawaii and New Zealand; and on the supposed inability of the Easter Islanders to have built their island's monuments without outside aid. The latter supposition led, in the 1970s, to the far more absurd statements of Mazière and von Daniken.[3]

Unfortunately for this theory of yet another Lyonesse, Polynesian legends contain far more accounts of epic, culture-transmitting voyages from island to remote island than of major submergences of whole archipelagoes. Moreover, Easter Island could not have a central position within such an archipelago. While islands to the west are present in large numbers, there are virtually none to the east in the region of major deeps.

Modern geological evidence refutes the theories of a continental or archipelagic origin for Easter Island. Such an origin implies the existence of continental rocks, whether sedimentary or metamorphic, in the geological strata which make up the island. Indeed, Macmillan Brown stated that he had found slates, granites, and conglomerates on Easter Island, and that certain strata appeared to have been laid down in a shallow inland sea. Other visitors between 1880 and 1920 also made references to granites and slates. However, more detailed examinations by geologists, notably Chubb in 1925 and Bandy in 1933, failed to discover any trace of continental rocks.[4]

Chubb suggests that what was regarded by visitors untrained in geology as slate was, rather, a lava with platy jointing, while the supposed granite was a very coarse porphyritic basalt or dolerite. Similar errors have been made elsewhere in Polynesia, and microscopic petrographical analysis has further confirmed the absence of any mineral which might have been derived from a continental formation. Continental rocks may indeed exist two or three miles below the surface of the island, but any fragments carried up during volcanic activity must have been completely annihilated by the lava as it ascended to the surface.

Yet the catastrophic origins of Easter Island cannot be dismissed, for the island is wholly volcanic in origin. Easter Island legends contain definite references to cataclysmic events. Some legends suggest that the first immigrants left their country of Maori, on the continent of Hiva, because the latter was found to be slowly sinking below the ocean surface. According to this tradition even Sala-y-Gomez, 340 kilometres (210 miles) east of Easter Island, was part of Hiva. Mazière refers us to the legend that:

> Easter Island was a much larger country, but because of the sins of its people (the god) Uoko tipped it up and broke it with a crowbar . . .[5]

How far such legends are genuine accounts of ancient beliefs or modernized versions imbued with Christian and Western concepts remains debatable. What is clear is that Easter Island emerged without human witnesses.

Volcanic Origins

A distinction is generally made between continental and oceanic islands. The former stand upon the continental shelf; there is the strong possibility that, as with the Falkland Islands (Malvinas), they were once part of the adjacent continent. An oceanic island, on the other hand, lacks a continental basement of old granitic or sedimentary rocks and is surrounded on all sides by extensive deeps so that only a major emergence of several thousand feet would bring it into contact with a continent. Two types of oceanic islands may be distinguished; high, volcanic islands and low, coralline types are both abundant in the Pacific. Easter Island is clearly a high, volcanic mass rising from great depths, the result of eruptions which originated on the sea bed.

The sea bed in the east central Pacific is known as the Albatross Plateau, a vast area less than 2,000 fathoms in depth, but surrounded on all sides by profound deeps. On the margins of this plateau material bursting forth from submerged folds has resulted in submerged mountain chains such as the East Pacific Ridge. Such upwellings of the molten magma circulating beneath the earth's crust have occasionally resulted in peaks of sufficient altitude to reach above sea level and form volcanic islands or barely submerged seamounts on which coralline atolls form. Although there are no islands over the central area of the Albatross Plateau, its edges are marked by the Marquesas on the western and the Galápagos on the eastern margins. Near the southern edge are the islands of Juan Fernández, Pitcairn, Sala-y-Gomez, Easter Island, and the Gambier (Mangareva) archipelago (Figure 2,0). The geological history, structure, and petrographical details of these volcanic islands are similar, and the overall emergence of these cones has been linked with plate tectonics and the phenomenon of continental drift.

Easter Island legend relates the appearance of Easter Island from the waves:

> The volcanoes appeared in the days of the first race. First came Rano-Aroi; secondly came Rano Kao; thirdly came Rano-Raraku; but many years passed between their coming.[6]

Geological opinion also suggests that Easter Island's emergence was accomplished in three stages, although the order of appearance differs from that of the legend.[7] The headland of Poike, forming the easternmost promontory, was the first cone to emerge from the Pacific (Figure 1,5). It was followed by Maunga Terevaka, the major volcanic mass which dominates the northern and central parts of the island, encompasses the crater of Rano Aroi, and supports chains of subsidiary cones. Finally, symmetry was achieved by the emergence of the Rano Kao volcano to form what is now the southwestern promontory. But sea water still separated the cones of Rano Kao, Poike, and Rano Raraku, the latter a volcano of the Terevaka stage which emerged a little to the west of the Poike mass. Either a series of small seismic uplifts or an outflow of lava from the Terevaka cone caused a retreat of the ocean to its present limits and a consequent uniting of the three volcanic masses to form a single island.

Rock types

As rock types are of considerable importance in shaping man's use of island resources, a brief analysis is in order.[8] The mass of the island consists of grey vesicular basalt. Poike basalt is darker in colour; the Terevaka olivine basalt is more coarse-grained and covers about one third of the land surface. Rano Raraku, however, largely consists of a light porous tuff. The softer matrix of this formation is an extremely light pumice with a specific gravity as low as 1.7. Another fine-grained, purplish-grey, soft tuff deposit forms the three small cones of the Maunga Parehe area north of Poike.

The Rano Kao stage provided the most complex assortment of lava types. Typical grey basalt lava flows were, in this stage, accompanied by: a very dense, black, glassy andesite at Cerro Otu; an andesite with a platy structure around the Rano Kao crater rim; a yellowish rhyolitic tuff, west of Rano Kao, which is so light that it will float on water; a red, ropy pumice which forms the small cone of Punapau west of Otu; and finally the black and greenish-brown glass of the Cerro Orito obsidian deposits. Obsidian is rare in the Pacific islands, and this formation comprises only 0.02 per cent of the crystalline basalt. Nevertheless, for the native inhabitants the Orito obsidian, Rano Kao platy andesite, Punapau red pumice and Rano Raraku tuff had an economic and social importance out of all proportion to their size. While the tuff provided suitable material for cutting statues, the red pumice was required for statue hats or topknots. The platy andesite was a most suitable building material for stone dwellings, and obsidian was widely used for cutting tools and spear heads (Figure 1,6; Chapter 6).

LANDFORMS

The island that emerged from this series of volcanic upheavals has been much reduced in size by wave action. Some estimates suggest that it was originally almost twice its present size of approximately 166 square kilo-

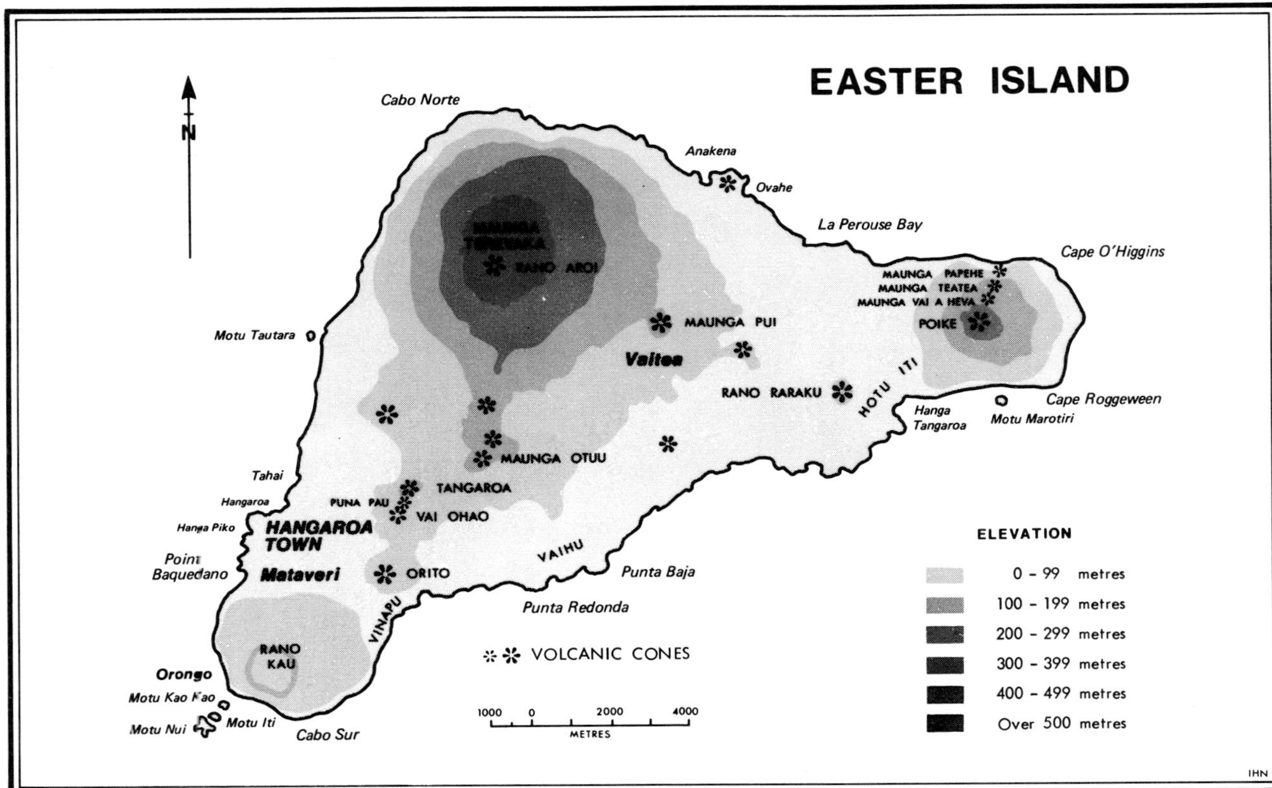

FIGURE 1,5 Physiography of Easter Island.

metres (64 square miles).[9] With a volcano forming each of three major promontories the island is roughly triangular in shape, like a tiny Sicily, although to the eighteenth century mind it resembled "a cocked hat". The three sides of the island are approximately 22, 18 and 16 kilometres (14, 11 and 10 miles) in length, giving a circumference of about 55 kilometres (35 miles) and a greatest width of about 11 kilometres (7 miles).

From the crater rim of Rano Kao the panorama includes the three peaks which form the apices of the island, separated by a rough hilly area below 90 metres (300 feet) above sea level which forms the central part of the island. Easter Island is wholly dominated by the three major volcanic masses. Maunga Terevaka, at 530 metres (1,767 feet) is the highest point, with Poike at 412 metres (1,350 feet) and Rano Kao rising to well over 300 metres (1,000 feet). All three are composed chiefly of volcanic ash, although Rano Kao includes interbedded lava flows. This composition has encouraged the formation of gentle slopes, now mainly grass-covered, which afford easy movement for travellers. The most remarkable feature, probably due to the lower porosity of the rock forming volcanic plugs, is the existence of freshwater lakes within the volcanic craters. These have the Polynesian designation *rano*.

Terevaka is distinguished by the considerable number of parasitic cones which radiate along lines of weakness from its summit. The most prominent chain comprises five cones running east-southeast. Rano Aroi, the highest and most westerly of these cones, lies near the summit of Terevaka and contains a small crater lake wholly overgrown by vegetation. Rano Raraku is the most easterly parasite; its crater contains a lake and its southern wall has been extensively reshaped by aboriginal quarrying. Its southeastern side has been steeply cliffed by wave action, although the present coastline is over one kilometre (one-half mile) away. Another chain of subsidiary craters extends southwards from Terevaka and includes Punapau's small deep crater of red scorified ash and the black obsidian cone of Orito. Both of these cones have been modified by indigenous quarrying.

Katiki, the main crater, dominates the Poike headland on the eastern coast. It is shallow (5-6 metres (20 feet) deep; 75-80 metres (250 feet) in diameter) and dry. The three subsidiary ash cones of the Maunga Parehe area lie in a chain to the northeast. When Poike was a separate island it was extensively cliffed by wave action. On its western, inland edge the cliffs now form a considerable rampart from the south coast bay of Hotu-iti to Mahatua on the north coast. Rising to 90 metres (300 feet), these inland cliffs cut Poike off from the main body of the island, and are accentuated where the lava flows from Terevaka have abutted against the cliff foot.

In the southwestern corner of the island, Terevaka lava has similarly overlapped the ash strata of Rano Kao. The latter has no parasites, but may itself be a massive parasite on Terevaka. Its crater is the most spec-

PLATE 15
The smooth slopes of Poike

PLATE 16
Rough grassland covers most of Easter Island

tacular on the island. A very deep caldera contains a large, almost perfectly circular freshwater lake about one kilometre (one-half mile) in diameter. The lake is almost wholly covered by floating vegetation. Attempts to make soundings have resulted in no agreement on its depth; needless to say, the Rapanui suggest that it is bottomless. The crater walls are precipitous, rising from the lake at about 120 metres (390 feet) above sea level to over 300 metres (1,000 feet) at the northern crater rim. The southern rim has been exposed to extensive wave erosion on the outer edge and subaerial erosion on the inner. Climbers of the inner scree slopes, where detritus ranges in size from minute scree to boulders as large as an automobile, eventually find themselves upon an extremely narrow knife-edged ridge which falls precipitously to the sea several hundred feet below.

Effectively dividing the three major cones, the low central area of Easter Island meets the coast between Rano Kao and Terevaka in the Hangaroa area, between Terevaka and Poike in the La Pérouse Bay region, and forms the most extensive coastal lowlands on the south coast between Poike and Rano Kao. This rough central lowland, abruptly broken in many places by subsidiary volcanic cones, does not deserve the designation of "plain". Formed from the lava flows emanating from the three major cones, the lowland is far more rugged and much more difficult to traverse than are the slopes of the three dominant volcanoes. In lava of the *aa* type, weathering results in a rough "plain" with hard rock outcrops, and wholly strewn with large and small lava blocks. In places these blocks are so thickly packed that walking proves difficult for horse or human being. Human activity, chiefly through constructing stone walls from the lava blocks, has extended their scatteration.

Individual lava flows may be discerned, their edges and snouts forming further obstacles to movement in the shape of terraces up to 6 metres (20 feet) high. The traveller in this region may observe basalt flows, tufas, and lavas composed largely of pumice or slag, in appearance and weight rather like coke. Black and dark brown are the overall colours of these rock types, but the occasional reds, yellows, and oranges provide relief from the general scenic monotony.

On Easter Island, normal subtropical erosion processes have not occurred; in Bandy's words: "Easter Island shows (the) effects of disintegration rather than erosion."[10] Except for the three crater lakes (*rano*), the island entirely lacks surface water. These three permanent water bodies are terminal lakes with no apparent outlets. Not a single perennial stream, much less a river, exists. Such is the porosity of the volcanic rocks, rainfall is almost immediately absorbed before runoff can occur. Beneath the land surface, a subterranean drainage system of unknown extent contains some known pools where sweet water may be obtained by excavation. This subterranean drainage system carries subsurface water to the coasts where springs emerge, rather unfortunately, just below sea level. This brackish water was much used by the indigenes until the late nineteenth century.

Lack of substantial subaerial erosion accounts for the manifest retention of the original forms of the volcanic cones, lava flows, and craters. The cones are drained radially during heavy rain, and their rims exhibit some water-cut grooves. When torrential rains occur, intermittent streams may carry surface runoff along gullies cut into the flanks of Terevaka.[11] After a few miles, however, even these channels sink beneath the porous mantle of ash. The intermittent stream running southwards from Rano Aroi formerly ran in an underground channel, the roof of which has collapsed to expose a narrow gorge crossed by a series of natural bridges.

Visitors familiar with the severely accidented relief of most Pacific high islands are astonished to find Easter Island almost wholly lacking in major ravines and valleys. Small ravines, gullies, and washes have been eroded in soft ashy formations, but these features are universally the result of floods during the rainy season. A small number of deeper, dry ravines etched into the north coast may be the fossil remnants of former permanent streams which have long since dried up.

THE COASTLINE

In contrast with the subdued nature of subaerial erosion, wave action is actively eroding the island, forming cliffs on almost all sides. Where the coast is composed of lava the cliffs range from about 8 metres (25 feet) to 30 metres (100 feet) in height. But where, as at all three corners of the island, the coast is of softer, ashy material, severe wave erosion has resulted in the formation of extremely precipitous cliffs. North and west of Maunga Terevaka and around the Poike peninsula these cliffs reach up to 180 metres (600 feet). North of Poike the Maunga Parehe volcanic cone has been so cut away by sea action that the central vent is exposed. The most spectacularly precipitous cliffs reach over 300 metres (1,000 feet) on the south side of Rano Kao. Wave and subaerial action have resulted in the lowering of the *arête* which forms the crater's southern rim. Eventually the rim will be breached and the impounded lake may pour into the Pacific.

Elsewhere in the Pacific Ocean the impact of wave action is severely reduced by the moderating effect of an encircling coral reef. Although small coral colonies occur sporadically, the ocean temperature in the vicinity of Easter Island is not sufficiently high in winter to promote the formation of a large, permanent reef. This lack of impediment to sea action was most recently apparent during the *tsunami* which followed the Chilean earthquake of 1960. Three successive waves broke over the southern and eastern coastlines of Easter Island, running up to 550 metres (600 yards) inland. In the bay of Hotu-iti 15 statues up to 10 metres (33 feet) long and weighing up to 30 tons were hurled from the coastal ceremonial platform of Tongariki and carried about 90 metres (100 yards) inland.

Rather earlier demonstrations of the severity of wave action are apparent in the shape of small islets and stacks. The Rano Kao headland must originally have been much larger, for the three islets of Motu-kaokao, Motu-iti, and Motu-nui were clearly part of the southern slope of the original volcano. Marotiri is the Poike equivalent. Only Motu-nui is fairly flat, offering a considerable area of level ground; the other islets are sharp basalt towers with precipitous cliffs. Two small, low, flattish islets of black basalt, Motu-tautara, are the remains of lava flows from the western slope of Maunga Terevaka. They also represent the wave-cut shelf which occasionally appears one or two metres above sea level at the foot of the harder basaltic cliffs. No such platform has been cut in the softer ash formations, which offer far less resistance to the onslaught of the waves.

One far-reaching consequence of the nature of Easter Island's geology and erosional regime is the complete absence of sheltered harbours. While the tall ash cliffs are smooth and sheer, the low lava cliffs are often extremely rugged and wave-torn. Coastal caves and long lava fingers extending out to sea do not provide protection except for the very smallest boats. There are very few sand beaches, the most extensive being at Anakena on the north coast, remote from Hangaroa. Shallow bays and coves elsewhere almost entirely lack sand, which is replaced by wave-worn basalt boulders. Sharp spikes of lava in shallow waters render the ingress of anything larger than a small launch impossible. Larger vessels must stand off one kilometre (one-half mile) or so from the coast.

Along the seaboard and inland, caves abound. Many were formed as volcanic gas tubes, or by the differential cooling of lava flows. Characteristically, the longer and deeper cave systems are entered via a narrow vertical shaft located in a lava field. Tunnels frequently widen into sizeable caverns, some of which have been measured at 10 metres (32 feet) by 20 metres (65 feet), with 6 metre (20 foot) ceilings. In 1886 Paymaster Thomson found such a cave:

> with a mouth so small that entrance was effected with difficulty. Once inside, however, it branched out into spacious chambers that could shelter thousands of people with comfort . . . Human remains were found in this cave.[12]

Other caves are located in sea-cliffs, especially in the south. Where lava has overflowed a mound of softer tuff, the latter has frequently been eroded to form caves, most of which are extremely difficult of access.

WEATHER AND CLIMATE

Easter Island lies only a little to the south of the Tropic of Capricorn, on the same latitude as central Queensland. Because of its exposed position, however, its basically subtropical climate is profoundly modified by oceanic influences, notably via winds and currents.

During the period September to May the Southeast Trades blow almost constantly from the east and southeast. Between May and September frontal storm activity becomes dominant, with winds from the north and northwest. Winds sweep across the island almost continuously, and although stormy days are not common, calms are very rare. In order of frequency, the dominant winds recognised by the indigenes are *anoraro* (wide expanse) from the southeast, *tongariki* (column of kings) from the northeast, *vaitara* (cut-water) from the west, and *motu-rauri* (dark-leaf rock) from the south.[13] *Tepu-hanga* (blows drift on shore) is the breeze which appears when the dominant winds are slack. From September to March the high summer temperatures are moderated by a branch of the Humboldt (Peruvian) Current which, averaging about 21°C (69.8°F) in temperature, effectively restricts the growth of coral.

Because of these oceanic influences the climate is generally mild and very equable. Climatological observations were begun in 1901 but discontinued in 1915, to be reinstituted by the Chilean Air Force in the 1950s. From these fragmentary data the mean annual temperature appears to be in the region of 20.5°C (69°F). Around this figure the seasonal range is small, with a mean for the warmest months (January and February) of 23.4°C (74°F) and for the coolest months (July and August) of 17.8°C (64°F). Absolute maxima and minima are recorded as 29.5°C (85°F) and 10.4°C (51°F). Temperatures at the volcanic crests are somewhat lower, the difference between Mataveri (30 metres (98 feet) above sea level) and the rim of Rano Kao (over 300 metres (984 feet)) being of the order of 1.7°C (3.5°F).

Oceanic influences render the air constantly moist; relative humidity rarely falls below 80 per cent. On over 200 days per year some rainfall is experienced. Mean annual precipitation is approximately 1,198.2 millimetres (47.2 inches), with the heaviest rainfall occurring in two peaks in March (autumn) and June (winter), and with a period of below average rainfall from August to October (spring). Seasonal incidence, however, varies somewhat from year to year. Skottsberg's records indicate high figures for March (228.8 millimetres (9 inches)) and June (241.8 millimetres (9.5 inches)), with a low of 28.1 millimetres (1.1 inches) in October, whereas Heyerdahl records highs in June and July and lows in September.[14]

Moreover, total precipitation varies greatly from year to year. A low degree of activity on the part of frontal storms in June and July may result in a very dry year. In 1903, for example, the island recorded only 711 millimetres (28 inches) of rainfall, whereas in 1905 2,134 millimetres (84 inches) were received.[15] Light showers are the most common form of precipitation, but heavy downpours of tropical force can occur at all seasons. In March 1912 there were five days when over 20 millimetres (0.8 inches) of rain fell within a 24-hour period; in June 1913 167.7 millimetres (6.6 inches) fell in a single day. Heavy dews commonly form overnight, but there are no records of frost or snow. Because of rock porosity and the high rate of evapotranspiration, which exceeds precipitation levels during about one-third of the year, any rainfall quickly disappears underground. After a heavy shower the ground is commonly perfectly dry within a matter of hours.

Cloudy days are very common, as are the accompanying drizzles and mist. The crest of Maunga Terevaka is frequently veiled by banks of cloud. Gusts of wind can quickly envelop the island in a thick mist, drastically reducing visibility. And when cold Antarctic winds lash the island with rain during winter, any feeling of being on a Polynesian island in the South Seas is utterly lost.

SOILS

Despite the humid atmosphere within which the island is constantly enveloped, the development of mature soils is uncommon and the distribution of good soils very uneven (Figure 2,5).[16] Parent materials are either lavas or volcanic ash; soils formed from marine sediments are insignificant. Depth of soil varies directly with parent material, as does soil colour which varies from deep brown to various shades of reds and yellows. On the lava plains soil is often wholly absent, or at best restricted to crevices and accumulations around large boulders. Where present, the soil is shallow and very stony. It is subject to removal and deposition by winds, which occasionally produce small dust storms.

Ash cones and tufa outcrops, however, are much more readily disintegrated to form a thicker, finer soil than appears above the lava beds. Talus and sandy silt accumulate within the volcanic craters and along the gentle external slopes of the cones. A loose volcanic sand occurs in places. The best areas of fairly deep loamy soil are found on the lowlying west coast around Hangaroa and Mataveri, between the ash cones of Terevaka, Rano Kao, and a ring of subsidiary cones. Other good-quality soils are found in extensive patches and sporadic locations across the lower, southern portion of the island, and on the Poike peninsula. Soil quality is highest where volcanic ash has been deposited over sands and gravels in undulating relief with shallow slopes.

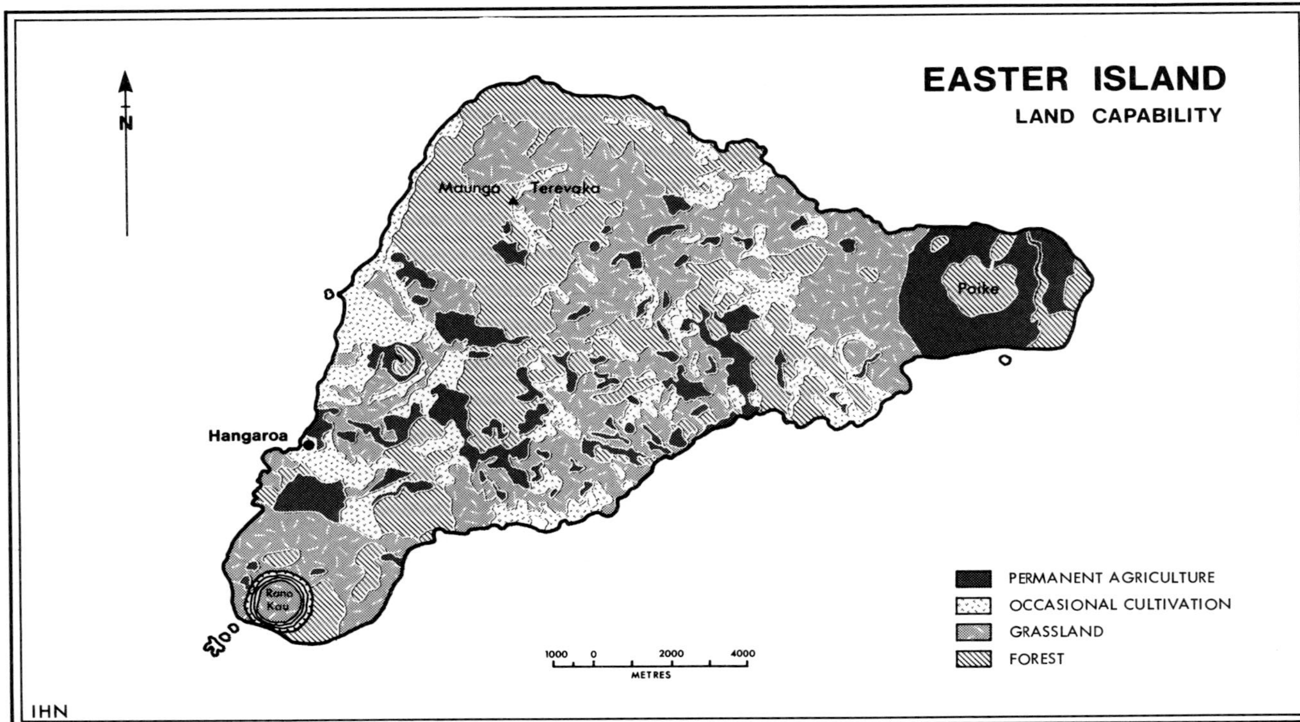

FIGURE 2,5 Land capability (redrawn from Odeplan, *Plan Sexenal*, 1973).

All soil types, however, lack a rich organic content. Even in the better areas the organic content is low, and everywhere rocky outcrops and stony patches impede the efficient working of the ground. Moreover, all soils on Easter Island are equally deficient in major elements such as nitrogen and phosphorus; trace-element deficiencies manifest themselves in crop abnormalities. Rapid water absorption in volcanic soils results in the formation of a hard surface crust, which further impedes cultivation and may hinder crop growth. Finally, the absence of streams and stream-channels encourages sheet erosion during downpours. During rainstorms the soil surface may be removed by broad sheets of fast-flowing water of inconsiderable depth. In the more rugged north gullying is apparent, and this is fast destroying the soil cover.

FLORA AND FAUNA

If one discounts the existence of Lemuria or Mu, one is left with the problem of attempting to trace the colonization of a newly-erupted, sterile island with plants and animals. The latter, in the case of Easter Island, had to cover distances of at least 3,000, and more often 5,000 kilometres (2,000 and 3,000 miles), before establishing themselves in the new environment. Ecologists disagree over the ability of plants and animals to migrate unaided over such distances. There is considerable agreement, however, that islands which are extremely isolated tend to have a characteristic biology.[17]

In particular, the flora and fauna of isolated islands are characterized by an extreme poverty of species, especially of the higher plant and animal orders. Algae, plankton, bacteria and other small organisms, spores, some airborne seeds and insects, and even certain bird species may arrive unaided across 3,000 kilometres (2,000 miles) of ocean. Larger species may equally likely have been introduced inadvertently or deliberately by man, particularly in Polynesia where voyages of several thousand miles were not unknown. On the other hand, as Darwin demonstrated in the Galápagos, isolated islands are frequently characterized by the existence of endemic species which appear nowhere else. These have developed, over long periods of time, specific adaptations to a particularly finite environment.

Easter Island conforms to all three characteristics. Whole families and genera of both plants and animals are completely absent. Some species appear to be peculiar to the island. Without introductions made by Europeans the island would be almost uninhabited by non-human vertebrates. And among the larger animals and plants found on Easter Island by the first European explorers, it is most probable that many first arrived in the canoes of hardy Polynesian migrants.

Vegetation

When Lloyd Praeger studied the botany of Achill Island, just off the west coast of Ireland, in 1904, he identified 416 species compared with about 1,700 species available in Britain as a whole. Skottsberg, in a 1917 survey of Easter Island, which is almost identical in size with Achill, was able to discover only 31 indigenous flowering plants, 14 ferns, 14 mosses, 23 lichens, and one fungus.[18] Although more recent botanical surveys have extended the species count to over 100, the extreme lack of species variety remains the dominant characteristic of the island's vegetation. Skottsberg remarks: "There is in the Pacific Ocean no island of the size, geology, and altitude of Easter Island with such an extremely poor flora."[19] Most obvious to the casual observer is the predominance of grassland associations and the almost complete absence of trees, except around Hangaroa village. The only trees of any size have been introduced within the last century.

Easter Island's vegetation history is in dispute. Lack of organic soil material, especially leaf mould, suggests a long term absence of tree cover. Legends attribute the introduction of plants to Hotu Matu'a, a folk hero and traditionally the first settler. He brought a variety of trees and shrubs, among them sandalwood, which have since completely disappeared. The names of these legendary plants suggest that most were of Malaysian, Australasian, or Polynesian provenance, although a few were allied to South American species. Although Macmillan Brown believed that the island had never been extensively wooded, the legend of Polynesian introductions is supported by several observations made by early European explorers such as Roggeveen.[20]

Later, more careful observers, however, indicate a lack of trees as early as the late eighteenth century. Cook remarked that "the country appeared quite barren and without wood."[21] Forster in 1777 noted: "there was not a tree upon the island which exceeded the height of ten feet."[22] Palmer in 1868 and Cooke in 1886 gave accounts of groups of small trees scattered in clumps upon hilly ground, and Eyraud in the 1860s confirmed the existence of shrubs and bushes in many places.[23]

From this evidence it is very probable that the pre-European vegetation cover, perhaps profoundly modified by indigenous fires, resembled a park-like savannah. As in East Africa, a predominantly grassland appearance was relieved by clumps of low shrubs and occasional small trees. Trees may have been reduced in number by fires, the extension of cultivation and, after Bornier's arrival, by grazing stock. Legends recount a former period of more luxuriant vegetation; sporadic archaeological excavations and some pollen analyses support this claim.[24]

Whatever the biohistory of Easter Island, the climax vegetation today is an oceanic meadow or grass heath, composed largely of tough bunch grass dominated by *Sporobolus Indicus (heri hoi)*. It may be compared with the dominant tussock grassland of New Zealand's South Island. With other species such as the endemic *Axonoptes paschalis* and *Stipa horridula*, the *Sporobolus* forms a grassland association which dominates the long slopes of the volcanic cones. It is also common on the stony, lower land along the southern coast, but the sporadic accumulations of boulders found throughout the lowlying areas provide water-retentive locales which are graced by bright green fern bunches. For similar reasons mosses are found in rock crevices and between grass tussocks. At higher altitudes, such as on the upper slopes of Maunga Terevaka, there is also a notable increase in moss and lichen cover.

Although the grassland association imparts to the island its characteristic, monotonous, heathland appearance, it gives way to other associations along the seaboard and in the crater lakes. Though the rocky shores are surf-beaten, the grassland has spread over the cliffs to form broken patches in nooks and crannies. Elsewhere the shoreline tends to support a characteristic, if sporadic, vegetation cover. This association is dominated by the grass *Paspalum Forsteranium* with other salt-tolerant forms such as *Asplenium*. Rocks are lichen-encrusted. Of the lichens *Physcia picta* is dominant, covering even vertical rock faces with its large, thin, white crusts.

Of the three major craters, grasses predominate only in the wide, open, sandy interior of Rano Raraku. The lake here is an expanse of open water ringed by a thick fringe of bulrushes and endemic varieties of *Scirpus riparius* which prevent easy access to the water. In contrast, the Rano Aroi lake is largely overgrown with reeds and peat moss. These associations are best developed in the crater of Rano Kao. Here the lake, which is 600-700 metres (1,950-2,300 feet) across, is almost wholly surfaced by a thick, floating peat bog. Composed largely of *Campylopus* mosses and low grasses, the bog appears flat. It is, in fact, most uneven, with treacherous wet places and drier raised areas. The latter may bear the weight of a man, and even cattle have been said to have picked their way across the bog. Encircling the peat bog is a belt of *totora* reeds and bulrushes, and between this and the shore is a narrow (5-7 metre (16-23 foot)) zone of open water wholly filled with a matted network of *Polygonum* rhizomes, across which one may carefully tread. The north side of the crater shelters a clump of stunted trees. The last dwarf specimen of *toromiro* was found here by Skottsberg in 1917, but has since died.

Toromiro was one of the economically useful plants and trees originally introduced by the indigenes. Others, such as the *hauhau* and *mahute*, have been considerably reduced in numbers. Today the main tree groves are of imported eucalypts and conifers, the role of which will be discussed in the following chapters.

PLATE 17
Surface and inner slopes, Rano Kao

PLATE 18
Dense vegetation at base of slope, Rano Kao

Animals

If isolation has resulted in floristic poverty, it is reflected also in corresponding limitations on the variety of animal life.[25] Although it is difficult to distinguish endemics from introduced species, it is likely that the former are very few in number, and comprise mainly insects, spiders, worms, and snails. A considerable proportion of the animal species is made up of late immigrants. Before the advent of man terrestrial vertebrates were entirely lacking; vertebrates were represented only by seabirds, fish, and seals. Moreover, the birds which visit the island, most notably terns, boobies, petrels, tropic birds, frigate birds, and gulls, feed wholly upon fish. That there were no terrestrial birds before the Europeans, especially of seed-eating species, is both a cause and a consequence of the lack of species variety in the vegetation cover. Easter Island has none of the indigenous forms which, like the Soay sheep and the St. Kilda wren, have rendered other islands remarkable.

Even the seabirds avoid the island proper, preferring to nest on small off-shore islets. Here the environment is certainly not of the best. Backstrom reported that the soil of Motu-nui was so hard that the *taiho*, a local sub-species of the petrel *Pterodroma heraldica*, was unable to dig its habitual burrows and was compelled to lay its eggs on the surface.[26] The fish population is subject to conflicting reports. Brown suggests that fish are not plentiful, owing to the lack of a coral reef and its fish-sustaining debris.[27] Métraux cites the thousands of seabirds on Motu-nui as evidence of plentiful fish.[28] It is notable that fish have played a very varied role in island diet, which also included eels, crayfish, cuttlefish, shellfish, and turtles.[29]

Eighteenth century visitors were amazed at the vast numbers of chickens which they found on the island. The Easter Island fowl has declined in numbers since that time, and has lost its peculiarities, which included the occasional production of blue eggs.[30] Before the introduction of the Norway or ship rat the island was inhabited by the edible Polynesian rat which, like the chicken, was brought by the original settlers. Animals greater in size than rat or chicken, though now abundant on the island, are wholly European introductions, and as such will be treated in the following chapters on landscape change.

PLATE 19 The "Hebridean" landscape of Easter Island ▶

6 THE CONTEXT OF CHANGE

> Your sheep that were wont to be so meek and tame and so small eaters, now as I hear say become so great devourers and so wild that they eat up and swallow the very men themselves. They consume, destroy, and devour whole fields, houses, and cities.
>
> Sir Thomas More

Two major groups of actors were instrumental in radically changing the landscape of Easter Island in the century which followed the first impact of the early 1860s. This landscape transformation was effected almost wholly through the imposition of an economic system previously alien to the island, the rearing of sheep for wool export. The initiation of this revolutionary economic system was the work of the Tahiti-based Brander-Bornier partnership and its co-heirs, during the period 1868-1888. From that date the sheepranching function of the island was systematized and further developed from Chile by Enrique Merlet and his successor, the Compañía Explotadora de la Isla de Pascua, during the period 1893-1953. The motive force behind each group was Scottish commercial enterprise, reaching Easter Island from two directions, by way of Australasia and southern South America. Before the effects of this enterprise can be assessed, however, some indication of pre-European landscape, economy, and society is required.

RAPANUI CULTURE AND LANDSCAPE

Although the question has exercised the minds of many writers on Easter Island themes, the origin of the Easter Island indigenes is of little importance in the present analysis. Despite the many books and articles, learned and otherwise, which have attempted to prove that the indigenous peoples of the island originated as Egyptians, Berbers, Greeks, Indians, native British Columbians, Andean Indians, Melanesians, and others, the overwhelming weight of evidence points to a Polynesian origin. Since the work of physical anthropologists in the 1930s there has been little basis for dispute concerning the physical characteristics of the present native inhabitants; in body type, blood group, and numerous other somatic traits those islanders with the least admixture of European blood are clearly of Polynesian type.[1]

Previous to European settlement, the Rapanui were also Polynesian in culture, although many modifications of basic Polynesian traits had occurred in order to cope with the island's peculiar physical environment. As developed in the island groups west of Easter Island, the archetypal Polynesian food economy involved a triad of roots, fruits, and flesh. Domesticated vegetable matter provided the greater part of the daily alimentation, the most important roots and fruits being banana, breadfruit, coconut, pandanus, sugar cane, sweet potato, taro, *terminalia*, and yam. Most of these originated in Asia, and were carried eastwards by the Polynesians across the Pacific as far as the South American coast.[2] Flesh food was derived largely from fish and other marine edibles; the Polynesians had independently domesticated only three animals, the dog, the pig, and the fowl. A large Polynesian variety of rat was also considered edible. Material culture was bound up with woodworking, tree products being used for food, clothing, housing, weapons, and sailing craft. Shell, bone, coral, and other nonvegetable matter served many purposes, and where stone was easily workable the Polynesians used it in the erection of ceremonial centres. In Tahiti such *marae* were common, involving ceremonial platforms, stone altars, and humanoid images.

The basic Polynesian language stock is the foundation of all major dialects in the vast oceanic triangle between New Zealand, Easter Island, and Hawaii. Both Polynesian legends and archaeological evidence suggest that a common culture was disseminated throughout the Polynesian triangle by successive waves of migration. In their large outrigger canoes, some capable of taking over one hundred persons and their equipment, and travelling in a fanlike formation to maximize the sighting of landfalls, the Polynesians were capable of moving from island to island over distances of several thousand miles. Modern computergraphic analyses suggest that the peopling of Polynesia from the west was more feasible than from the South American coast, despite the fact that travellers from the latter would have had winds and currents in their favour.[3]

As Polynesians spread across the Pacific, the peculiarities of new environments called forth new cultural adaptations or, at the very least, led to a change of emphasis in the element-complex of the basic cultural pattern. In New Zealand, for example, the heavy forests, marine life, and active vulcanicity were unlike anything the Tahitian immigrants had ever seen. The availability of large game in the form of the *moa*, and of a variety of tree types, permitted the horticulturalists to develop a characteristic architecture and hunting lifestyle. In contrast, migrants moving northwards and eastwards encountered islands of easily workable volcanic rock, and a Polynesian variant of megalithic architecture developed in Tahiti, the Marquesas, and Hawaii. Indicative of a food surplus and a strong central authority, this stone-based subcultural emphasis reached its zenith on Easter Island in the immediately pre-European period.

Polynesian migrants probably arrived in Easter Island from the Marquesas in the early part of the first millennium of the present era; it is possible that other in-migrations occurred during the succeeding thousand years.[4] Natural disasters or political disputes were frequently generators of migrations; the basic legend of Easter Island's first peopling is thus part of a common traditional stock.

The legend tells that all was not well in the land of Hiva. Hau Maka dreamed of a better place in which Hotu Matu'a, a chief of the Maori region, might live in peace and plenty. His spirit quartered the oceans, finally alighting at the remote island of Te Pito o Te Henua (Navel of the World, later Easter Island). When the spirit returned, Hau Maka sent several youthful explorers to reconnoitre the new land. But Hotu Matu'a did not wait for their report, and set out for Te Pito o Te Henua in two large canoes. In the several versions of this legend his reason for leaving Hiva varies from volcanic eruptions and marine transgression to family disputes of epic proportions. He arrived in the bay of Anakena before the exploring party had left the island. With him Hotu Matu'a brought builders and priests, fishermen and farmers, plants and animals. Hotu Matu'a gave to the barren island its flora, its fauna, and its human population.

It was possible to transfer the greater part of Polynesian non-material culture to Easter Island. Material culture, however, was profoundly modified by the scarcity of shell, coral, and wood, and the superabundance of stone. A stone-based culture rapidly developed, the various volcanic rock types being suitable for the creation of ceremonial centres, statues and images, petroglyphs, housing, fish-hooks, adzes, spearheads, and other implements. An obsidian deposit, rare in Oceania, eventually proved most valuable for weapon manufacture.

The traditional longhouse of Easter Island, a structure resembling an overturned canoe and found elsewhere in Polynesia, was based on stone foundation curbs. Anchored into sockets in the circumferential curbstone, the walls and roofs were of tree branches and *totora* reed thatch. At Ahu Tepeu, north of Hangaroa, are the remains of a single longhouse foundation approximately 45 metres (50 yards) in length. The platy volcanic rock of the Rano Kao rim proved to be admirably adapted to the construction of complete stone houses, a number of which comprised the ceremonial village of Orongo on the crater rim.

Because of the abundance of readily workable soft rocks, the Eastern Polynesian propensity for building ceremonial sanctuaries was carried to cyclopean heights on Easter Island. The island is characterized by the arrangement of ceremonial centres around its seaboard circumference (Figure 1,6). Although several types exist, the predominant artifact is the image *ahu*, an elevated stone stage or platform upon which large stone statues were erected. In a few cases, great care was taken to choose appropriate stone blocks and slabs to give a smooth fit and finished appearance to the *ahu*'s seaward wall. It is on this basis that commentators such as Heyerdahl have compared Easter Island megalithic building with

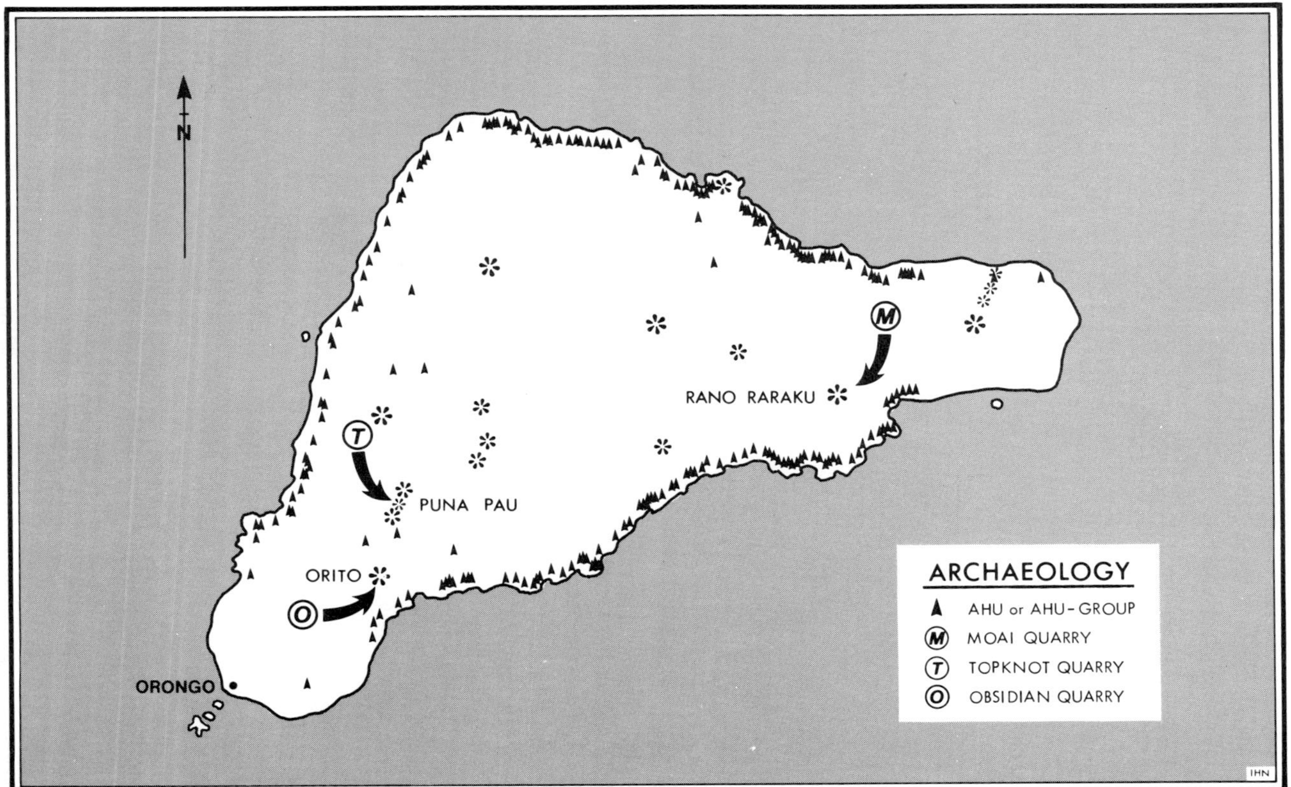

FIGURE 1,6 Major archaeological features of Easter Island.

that of the Incas. Almost every *ahu* faced inland, with an inclined plane forming a court on the landward side.

Unlike the typical *ahu* of Eastern Polynesia, which was usually topped by small coral, basalt, or wooden images, the Easter Island image *ahu* was surmounted by stone statues each of many tons weight and frequently seven to nine metres (20 to 30 feet) in height. These *moai* were carved from a prominent rock outcrop forming the outer rim of Rano Raraku. Here a statue-quarrying system operated, and many statues, up to 20 metres (70 feet) in length, remain in various degrees of completion. *Moai* mounted on *ahu* were generally provided with red scoria hats or topknots, all derived from the Punapau crater near Hangaroa. The largest moai ever mounted on an *ahu* weighs approximately 77,000 kilogrammes (170,000 pounds), and its topknot a further 11,000 kilogrammes (25,000 pounds).

If the possibilities for Polynesian stoneworking were enormously enhanced on Easter Island, the woodworking element of Polynesian culture was very poorly provided for. Humus-deficient soil, aridity, and exposure ensured a scarcity of large timber. The problem of wood resources was partially solved by making full use of the various types of hard and soft volcanic rock. It is probable, however, that the first settlers brought with them several trees of economic value. None of these trees reached much over three metres (ten feet) in height, and trunk diameters were generally small, yet it appears that such trees as the *makoi*, *toromiro*, and *hauhau* were available in sufficient quantity to furnish wood for paddles, small canoes, house frames, implement hafts, and small statues.

Specifically, *Sophora toromiro* was used in construction and for handles. *Triumfetta semitriloba (hauhau)* yielded fibres for string and rope. *Thespesia populnea (makoi)* and *Sapindus saponaia (marikuru)* provided fruits and other substances useful for ornamental purposes. The perfumed sandalwood (*naunau*) was also available. The *totora* reed, the feathers of fowls, and the long grasses were other sources of ornamental, constructional, or clothing materials. Clothing was also derived from *Broussonetia papyrifera (mahute)*, the paper mulberry.

Absence of a heavy vegetation cover exacerbated the effects of the island's cool winters and arid summers. Several staple Polynesian food plants were incapable of growth; the breadfruit succumbed, and the coconut fruited but poorly. It has been estimated that of the 53 plant species eaten in the 1960s, only 13, at the most, were available before 1800.[5] Similarly, of the 7 terrestrial bird species, only one was available before 1800; seabirds kept to the small islets off Rano Kao and rarely ventured over the main island. Thus the original settlers of Easter Island were compelled to adopt a very much more restricted diet than was available elsewhere in Polynesia. It was mainly a vegetable and root diet, with an emphasis on taro, yams, sweet potatoes, ti, sugar cane, and bananas. With the canoes came the domesticated fowl and the wild, though edible, rat.

These meagre meat supplies were supplemented by seabirds' eggs, by shoreline gathering, and by marine life, especially tuna (*kahi*), although the waters off the island are not heavily stocked with fish.

A relative paucity of sea life, lack of terrestrial fresh water, the prevalence of strong winds, and the aridity of the soil called for special constructional enterprises on the part of the early inhabitants.[6] A series of stone towers (*tupa*), usually found on the coastline, were probably watchtowers for turtle hunters. Along the coast small stone reservoirs were constructed to impound the fresh water of sealevel springs and prevent its contamination by seawater. As on arid coralline islands, plants liable to suffer from strong winds, salinity, or aridity were grown in natural depressions or small pits whose efficiency was enhanced by the erection of encircling stone walls.[7] A cyclopean example of this practice of planting in moist, humus-filled depressions was the use of the inner crater slopes of Rano Kao for the production of the most delicate trees, notably the paper mulberry and the banana.

Agriculture was well-organized. Practices which approximate to mulching, fertilizing, contour-ploughing, and terracing were evident.[8] Several eighteenth and nineteenth century explorers remarked upon the order and symmetry of the field layouts.[9] Except for the low stone walls around individual or clumped banana and *mahute* trees, however, there were no walls, fences, or hedges. The landscape would have given the impression of a *champaign* country of tall waving grasses, broken only here and there by stands of low trees and areas of cultivation. In the cultivation process the digging-stick was the most important tool, remaining in use into the twentieth century.

Agricultural land was largely confined to coastal areas; the slopes of Poike, though of excellent soil and largely free of stones, were probably under grass because of lack of water. According to archaeological remains and the accounts of visitors, settlements were found around almost the entire coast. Although usually located in conjunction with cultivable land and sealevel springs, some villages were perched on high cliffs. Only the precipitous east coast of Poike shows little sign of occupance. Both the mountains and the rough plains of the interior were sparsely populated. Village sites proliferated because of the division of the Easter Island population into ten patrilineal groups, or clans, each of which had its own territory (Figure 2,6). These ten groups coalesced into two exogamous moieties. The western and northwestern tribes, collectively known as the *Tu'u*, appear to have dominated the best fishing grounds. The eastern confederacy, the *Hotu-iti*, controlled the best growing areas and rock quarries.

This two-fold political division was to prove a major basis for rivalry and warfare as the island population grew. Estimates of the pre-European population have varied from 3,000 to 4,000. If this population stretched the food resources available from this rather unprolific Polynesian environ-

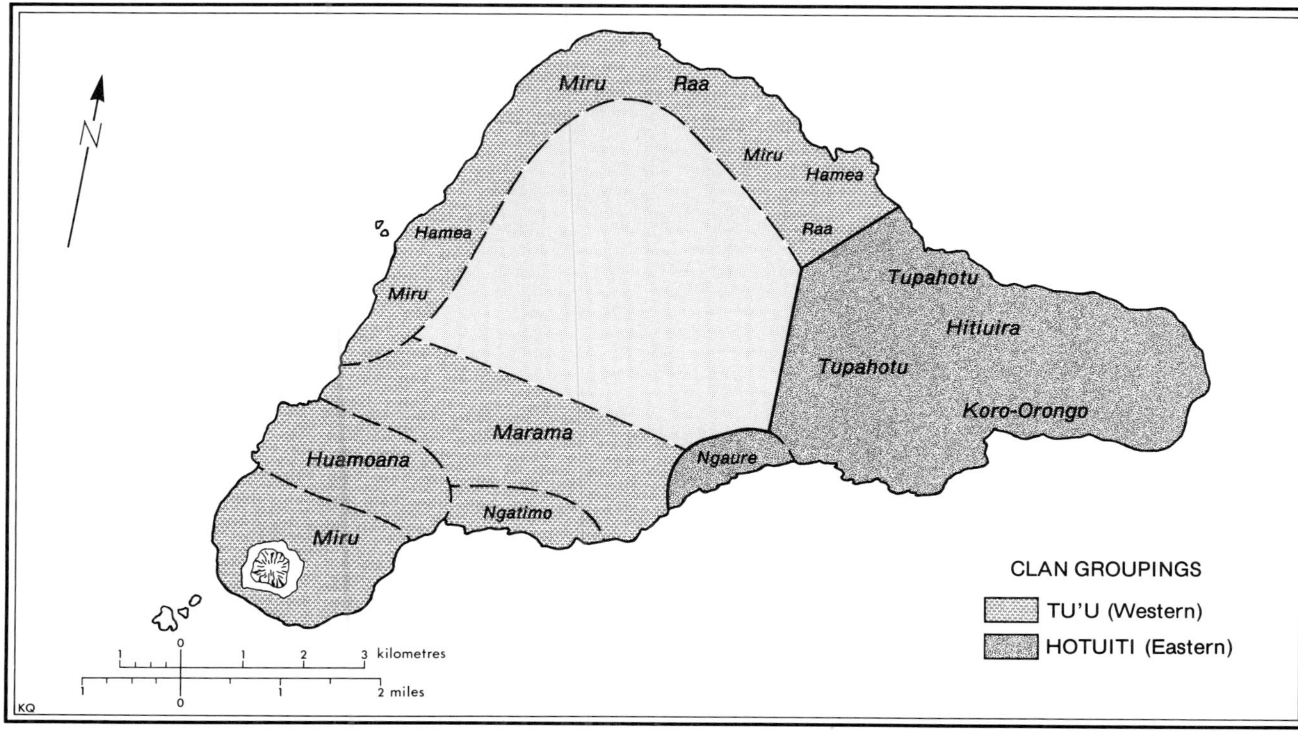

FIGURE 2,6 Prehistoric tribal divisions (sources: Routledge, Métraux, McCoy).

ment, it is not surprising that intertribal warfare became a way of life in the later prehistoric period. A peak of ferocity was apparently reached in the later seventeenth and early eighteenth centuries. Both ethnological evidence and the large numbers of obsidian spearheads (*mataa*) found in archaeological excavations point to fierce warfare at this time. The slaughter of the children and aged of a defeated tribe, as well as cannibalism, were natural population checks. The island's abundant caves were used as refuges, as were offshore islets. Insult or revenge was most readily perpetrated by toppling the statues from an opponent's *ahu*. Thus the period which is thought to have been the summit of achievement in terms of monumental construction in Easter Island is also the period during which the inhabitants began to destroy their own heritage. The earliest European explorers provide some testimony of the throes of internecine warfare, including details of newly-toppled statues and erect statues which were later overthrown.

As was described in Chapter 1, any population pressure was brutally relieved in the 1860s by the combined impacts of slaving, famine, disease, emigration, and cultural disintegration. By the 1870s the island was prostrate, its population shrunken to less than five percent of its former proportions, its fields abandoned, its monumental stonework overthrown or in decay. Into this vacuum penetrated Europeans, bringing with them varieties of animals and plants which were to completely transform the island's economy, society, and polity.

EARLY INTRODUCTIONS

Few of the early explorers made any attempt to introduce European animals and plants into Easter Island. The first known attempt to modify the meagre resource base came in 1786 when the La Pérouse expedition planted beets, cabbage, carrots, corn, cotton, gourds, lemons, and oranges in areas of appropriate soil around Hangaroa. Goats, sheep, and pigs were given to the islanders. Later visitors make no mention of these life forms; it is likely that the plants, their utility being beyond the experience of the indigenes, were allowed to die. The animals were, no doubt, a welcome but shortlived addition to the meagre meat supply. Other introductions were probably made by passing boats, but the arrival of new plants and animals on any scale had to await the establishment of the Catholic Mission shortly after the fatal impact of the early 1860s.

In their few years on Easter Island the missionaries managed to reintroduce many of the plants and animals originally brought by La Pérouse. Vegetable and fruit introductions were especially important in improving the local diet, and beans, corn, figs, peaches, pumpkins, and oranges were among those planted by the missionaries. Until the arrival of Europeans, the largest known mammal was the Polynesian rat. It is, therefore, not surprising that the sheep originally introduced by Brother Eyraud were immediately killed and eaten by the indigenes. As the mission developed, however, it proved possible to restrain the inhabitants from consuming the shipload of cattle, donkeys, horses, pigs, rabbits, and sheep which was delivered from Chile by Father Roussel. Cats were also introduced at this time. It is to the missionaries, in the half decade before 1870, that Easter Island owes its present variety of livestock.

Those livestock types which came to dominate the island were sheep and, to a lesser extent, cattle. Although introduced by the missionaries as food stock, these beasts were most suitable for commercial development, as carried on by the contemporaneous Brander-Bornier partnership, by the Salmon and Jaussen interests, by Merlet, and finally by CEDIP. As the whole island's economy, landscape, and social orientation were transformed by the process of commercial sheep ranching, a detailed discussion of sheep farming will follow.

It remains to note here the other important new animals and plants which were brought to the island after the missionaries but before the full development of company power in the twentieth century. Of the plants, the *miro-Tahiti* tree, the grape, many minor vegetables, and the *guayaba* are the most common. Coffee and cotton were also attempted, but never became of economic value. Toro's introduction of the breadfruit from Tahiti was a failure.[10]

Chilean settlers and Merlet were responsible for the introduction of terrestrial bird life in the late nineteenth century. Although the Chilean scavenger, the *loica*, could not be acclimatized, a small hawk (*manu toketoke*) was successfully introduced from the mainland in an attempt to reduce the depredations of the common rat, which had by this time superseded the Polynesian variety. The hawks, however, proved to be more interested in partridges, which took readily to the tussocky grasslands. Partridge eggs became as important to the indigenes of the early twentieth century as seabird eggs had been to their prehistoric ancestors. Cats, dogs, and several species of small birds, including the ubiquitous sparrow, also found suitable niches.

Certain birds were brought in to reduce insect numbers.[11] Formerly free of major insect pests, though always infested by flies, Easter Island is now plagued by cockroaches, flies, crickets and other small life forms. Like the small Polynesian lizard, most of these came ashore inadvertently from vessels calling at the island. Bryan states that mosquitos were introduced from Tahiti and bedbugs from Chile.[12] Cockroaches are now found in such numbers that predators cannot cope with them. Several species of flies abound in the pasture lands and after the 1870s receive dishonourable mention in almost every journal. Thomson exclaimed in 1886: "Myriads of flies infest every part of the island."[13] A quarter of a century later Mrs.

Routledge stated: "It was often necessary to wear headgear and dine in gloves."[14] The author has frequently found sleep impossible because of the attentions of ants, flying ants, mosquitos and cockroaches.

LATE NINETEENTH CENTURY SETTLEMENT PATTERNS

As noted earlier, the native inhabitants originally lived in small hamlets in coastal locations. Early explorers, although preferring the bay at Hangaroa (known as Cook's Bay) as a landfall, did not find a large village there. The La Pérouse expedition of 1786 saw several huts, some large stone-built houses, and an *ahu*. A similar small village existed at Vaihu.[15] In 1866, shortly after the first impact, many of the remaining native inhabitants had gathered in the Anakena and La Pérouse Bay areas of the north coast.

The European newcomers of the 1860s chose the Hangaroa-Mataveri area for its two sheltered small inlets, its wide expanses of level fertile land, and its proximity to the Rano Kao crater for water and as a garden site. Except for the fertile but waterless slopes of Poike at the island's eastern extremity, the region lying between the slopes of Rano Kao and Maunga Terevaka possessed the widest expanse of land suitable for cultivation (Figure 2,5).

Dutrou-Bornier's initial estate of 706 hectares (1,744 acres), purchased for 100 piastres in 1868, comprised half the Rano Kao crater and its gentle outer slopes in the Mataveri area (Figure 2,3). On fairly level land, close to a ravine at the foot of the Rano Kao slope, Dutrou-Bornier erected a wooden farmhouse. Mataveri had been an important gathering point for intertribal festivities connected with the annual cult ceremonies at the sacred village of Orongo on the Rano Kao crater edge (Figure 1,6). This cult appears to have died out in the period 1866-78. Missionary influence was in part responsible for this, but Routledge suggests that the Mataveri-Orongo ceremonies were

> finally crushed by the secular exploiters of the island, whose house of Mataveri . . . rests on the foundation-stones of the cannibal habitation.[16]

Like the early Christian fathers who deliberately erected churches on pagan religious sites and absorbed heathen rites into sacred liturgy, Dutrou-Bornier showed remarkable insight in placing his farmhouse atop the stone blocks of Easter Island's only island-wide ceremonial site. By substituting the farmhouse for cult buildings and the annual shearing festivities for the Orongo ceremony he effectively replaced a sacred religion with the trappings of a commercial counterpart.

Mataveri was blessed with a cove navigable for small boats at Hanga Piko, a freshwater spring at the base of the cliffs nearby, and access to Rano Kao. Beaten earth tracks were made from this focus of power towards Hangaroa to the north, east to Vinapu and Vaihu, and south, up the slopes of Rano Kao, to the crater. From the crater rim a steep winding path, still in use, led down the crater's inner wall to a warm, moist, sheltered zone at the junction of crater wall and lake. Here Bornier developed a small "jardin potager" for the supply of kitchen vegetables. When a well was sunk near the house, Mataveri became a valuable property with ample agricultural land on the rolling plain around the house and several hundred acres of pasture land on the Rano Kao slopes.

By including both Mataveri and Orongo in his first land purchase, and by siting his house on former ceremonial buildings, Bornier effectively proclaimed himself lord of Easter Island. Equally significantly, the missionaries established their somewhat smaller initial estate further north in the partially deserted native village of Hangaroa (Figure 1,3). Here a second power focus emerged. Unlike Bornier, who was content to erect a house and farm buildings, the missionaries constructed a small church and school, complete with flagpole. Beaten earth tracks joined those of the Mataveri estate.

The village of Hangaroa, known in the 1860s and 70s as Sainte Marie de Rapanui, became the major population centre of the island; indigenes began to gather around the missionary settlement. Not all the remaining inhabitants were willing to move to the twin poles of civilization represented by sacred Hangaroa and secular Mataveri. In order to reach the eastern indigenes the missionaries were compelled to erect a second church at Vaihu, serving the south coast of the island (Figure 3,2).

Mataveri, Hangaroa and vicinity presently house the whole population of Easter Island. The process by which the post-impact indigenes were removed to Hangaroa is uncertain. In the early 1860s the native population was distributed throughout the island, with definite clusters at Hangaroa, Anakena, and Rano Raraku (Hotu-iti).[17] Thomson suggests that the missionaries first attempted to resettle the indigenes of Anakena, La Pérouse Bay, and the east generally, around the two chapels of Hangaroa and Vaihu. Some probably remained outside the pale of conversion during the missionaries' stay, however, for some of Bornier's post-missionary land deeds were witnessed by an Anakena chief. Father Roussel coerced the Rapanui to move towards Hangaroa, but the wholesale clearance of the inhabitants from their ancestral lands was probably completed by the Brander-Bornier partnership. Anxious to allow their sheep unrestricted freedom to range the island, fearful of the depredations likely to be made on the animals by the hungry, and wishing to have the small population under control and within easy reach when employment needs arose, the sheepmasters rounded up the remaining hold-outs on the northern and eastern coasts, compelling them to live in Hangaroa.

The date of this final corralling of Easter Island's human stock is not known. Newspaper reports of the late 1880s still speak of a settlement at Vaihu.[18] A letter from John Brander junior, however, dated 13 February 1897, suggests that the clearance and resettlement took place a considerable number of years earlier:

> the Rapanui were and have been forbidden to disturb the stock and . . . they were compelled to live in the village of Hangaroa and for convenience sake allowed to live in a certain part of Mataveri.[19]

As Brander and Salmon were both on the island for about four years during the late 1870s and early 1880s, it is likely that the final resettlement of the indigenous population was accomplished during that time. Clearly, it was most convenient for the sheepmasters that the island be neatly compartmentalized into two sections, a small, fertile, government-owned area as a reserve for the natives, with the remaining bulk of the island, including most of the native and mission lands noted on Bornier's map of 1871 (Figure 3,2) as a sheepwalk.

From contemporary maps (Figures 3,6 and 4,6), the descriptions of visitors, and the court records of the litigation between the Brander and Bornier co-heirs, it is possible to construct a picture of the landscape of Easter Island at about 1880, a decade after the expulsion of the missionaries and a decade before the arrival of the ill-fated *colonos* and, later, Merlet. Most of the island lay derelict, its ceremonial centres and villages abandoned and in ruins. Former garden plots, even in Hangaroa, were giving way to grass and shrubs. Only two major settlement nodes were apparent.

Hangaroa was by far the larger, but was inhabited wholly by indigenes dwelling in scattered huts each in its own garden grounds. Gana's map of 1870 depicts thirteen houses in Hangaroa, with five at Mataveri. Other maps show a similar distribution. At this time a score or so of houses would be sufficient for the entire population. The European raison d'etre of the village, however, had gone after 1871. A missionary inventory of that year, when the mission left the island, includes merely two chapels (one at Vaihu), a stone house, and a wooden house. Other than raw land and animals, other improvements were restricted to three canoes, two water cisterns, and four small fields surrounded by drystone walls.[20] By the early 1880s the chapels and school were falling into disrepair, and the crude stone quay in Cook's Bay was disintegrating under the attack of waves.

The smaller node of Mataveri was clearly the power centre of the island after 1871. Sited on the lower slopes of Rano Kao, and guarding several

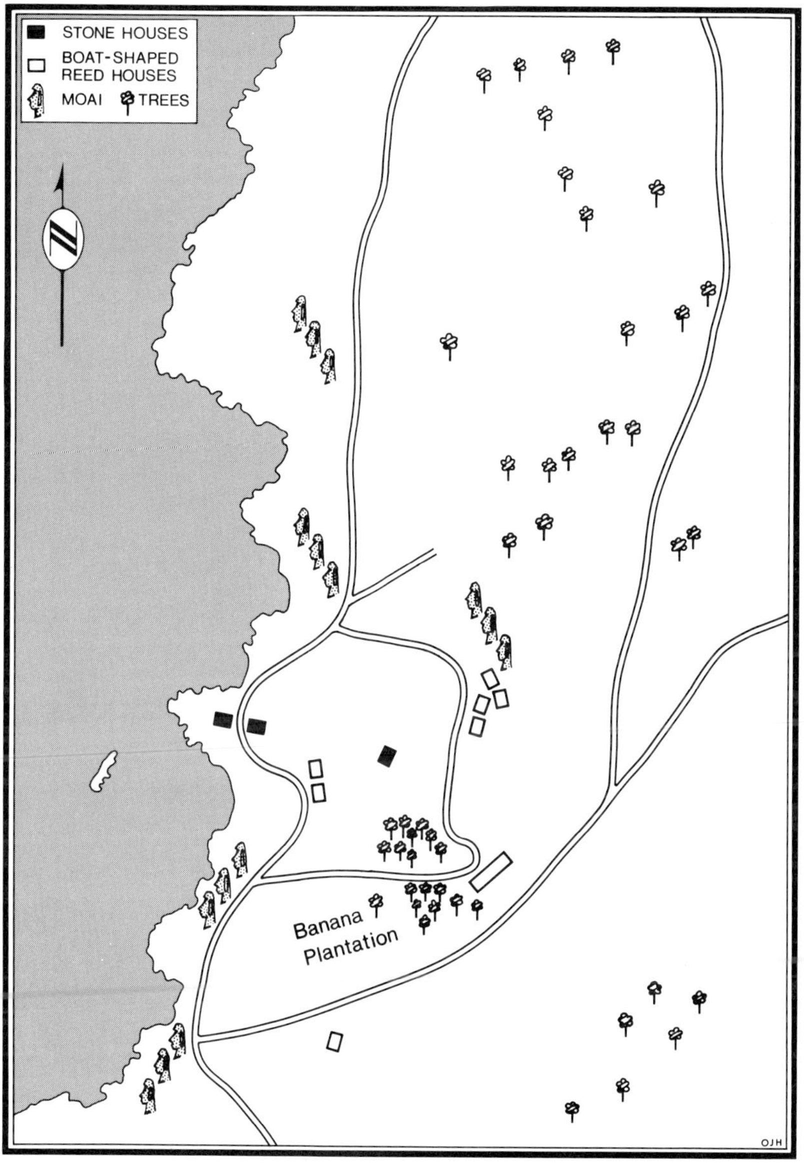

FIGURE 3,6 Settlement in the Hangaroa area, 1786 (redrawn from La Pérouse's *Atlas*, Plate 10).

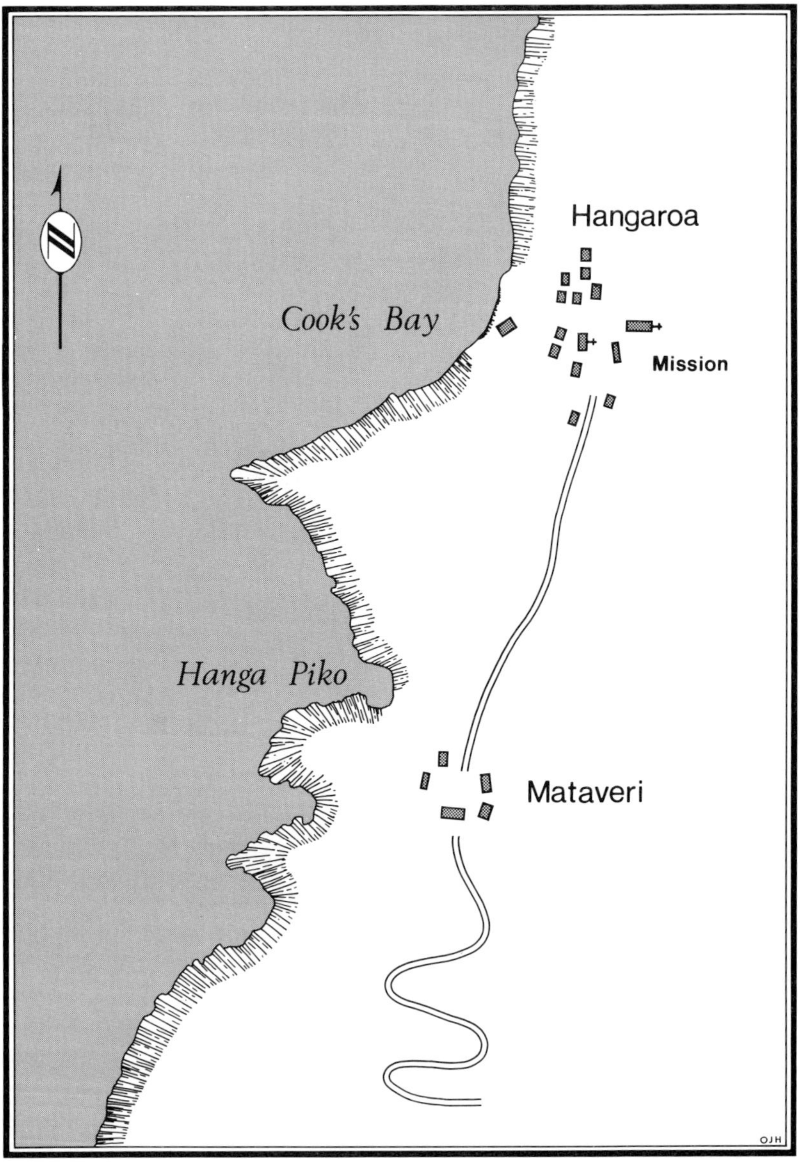

FIGURE 4,6 Settlement in the Hangaroa area, 1870 (redrawn from Gana).

sources of sweet water supply, it effectively dominated Hangaroa (Figure 5,6). The court records and lease agreements of the period give some indication of improvements made at Mataveri between 1868 and 1880.[21] Living quarters at the Mataveri home farm consisted of a large six-roomed house of wood with a galvanized zinc roof, the whole raised from the ground on foundation stones from native houses and sporting a large veranda (Figure 6,6). This largest building measured 12 metres (40 feet) x 10 metres (33 feet) x 7.5 metres (25 feet) in height. A small four-roomed wooden house, a three-roomed wooden house, two small huts serving as kitchen and coach-house, and an unfinished house frame were disposed around the farmhouse. A wooden stable roofed with thatch served as a workshop for carpentering and blacksmithing. Two small paddocks, with walls over 1.5 metres (5 feet) in height, lay in front of the main house. Hanga Piko cove, by 1880 the only important embarkation point, was regarded by Brander as "one of the best in the island."[22] Here were located a thatched cart-house, a plank-roofed wooden warehouse for wool storage, and a boat-shed. The inventories also list an assortment of furniture and implements, including five tables, "two ploughs in good condition," and "an iron key in bad condition."

Major boundary fences of lumber had been set up from Hanga Piko to Mataveri, and again from Mataveri to Vinapu, thus "enclosing the hill and crater of Rano Kao."[23] Within this boundary fence were two large, lumber-fenced stockpens and five small pens bounded by drystone walling. A vine arbour at the farmhouse was matched by fig, mulberry, and other fruit trees, and similar trees planted by the missionaries continued to flourish in Hangaroa.

In 1880 a third settlement node still remained at Vaihu, inhabited by A. Salmon, owner of former mission lands and Easter Island factor for the Branders. Vaihu consisted merely of a chapel, a stone building, and a dwelling-house of two rooms. It was not a permanent settlement, however. After the departure of the missionaries in 1871 it had lain deserted until the arrival of Salmon in the late 1870s.[24] While Brander occupied Mataveri, Salmon remained domiciled at Vaihu until replaced in 1888 by Toro's settlers.[25] With the departure of the settlers and arrival of Merlet in the 1890s, this third settlement node was abandoned, except for shepherds.[26] All the Rapanui were confined to the Hangaroa area except when on company business. This left the sheepmasters of the twentieth century free to develop the bulk of the island as a sheepwalk, a process involving considerable landscape transformation.

THE IDEOLOGY OF IMPROVEMENT

To fully appreciate the transformation of Easter Island's landscape and society after the arrival of the entrepreneurs, it is necessary to trace the cultural origins of entrepreneurial operators and their island managers.

FIGURE 5,6 Mataveri and Hangaroa in 1916 (redrawn from Routledge).

FIGURE 6,6 The CEDIP manager's house at Mataveri, 1916 (redrawn from Routledge).

Almost invariably, these were of Scottish origin. The Branders, the Darsies, and the CEDIP partners were all from eastern or southern Scotland. Though lowlanders, they cannot have been unacquainted with the profitability of sheepraising in Scotland, Australia, and elsewhere. Indeed, some of the earliest trading links developed by Williamson, Balfour in Chile involved the exportation of wool to Britain.

The impact of a newly-established commercial wool economy on traditional subsistence societies has been well-documented in Britain. In England, during the medieval and Tudor periods, increased demand for wool and mutton led to the highly unpopular enclosing of much arable land for sheep pasture. Many of the deserted villages whose remains abound in the English landscape date from these periods. Villages were evacuated wholesale, their former inhabitants being compelled to find urban employment or to swell the growing numbers of "sturdy beggars" on the English roads.

Similar change came to Scotland only after 1745, but was sufficiently violent to aid in the destruction of a complete culture, that of the semi-tribal Gael. It is instructive to follow the course of late eighteenth century sheep farming in Highland Scotland in some detail, for the cultural genocide it helped bring about in Scotland was to be repeated in Easter Island a century later, and by the same Lowlander entrepreneurs.

Until the mid-eighteenth century the Highlands and Islands of Scotland were a Celtic fringe of clan societies, united by a common culture, economy, and language, but divided by bitter intertribal feuds. Agriculture was poor, oats being a staple product. More reliance was placed on the raising of sheep and black cattle for local consumption. The basis of land tenure was not the land itself, nor its products, but the number of fighting men in could sustain.[27] The clans enjoyed an essentially subsistence economy in a harsh, isolated environment, but their attachment to the land was strong.

After the utter defeat of the Scots in 1715 and 1745, the English conquerors, abetted by Lowlander sympathizers, began a deliberate policy of cultural suppression through pacification, road building, the introduction of a money economy, and the proscription of Highland weapons and dress. The tribal system collapsed as the chiefs became anglicized, lost their Gaelic, and became absentee landlords. Their demands for hard cash to support Lowland lifestyles could not be met from the traditional subsistence farming. Consequently, the new lairds were eager to lease their lands to Lowland sheep farmers, or to "improve" their acres for pasture on their own account. In either event, the change from a subsistence mixed crop and animal husbandry to a pastoral monoculture meant that, as earlier in England, large numbers of former tenants were now landless and redundant.

Wars and population growth, increasing the demand for meat, wool, and timber, brought the Highlands and Islands into the English metropolitan hinterland for the first time. Hillsides were stripped of woodland. Black cattle exports made both lairds and Lowlanders rich, but were increasingly replaced by sheep after the 1760s. By 1800 the sheepmasters were established in almost all of the former clan districts south of the Great Glen.[28] Expansion continued northwards and pastoral "improvements" continued into the second half of the nineteenth century, contemporaneously with the introduction of sheep and cattle into Easter Island. Assured southern markets, lack of overseas competition before the era of refrigeration, and the rich pastures afforded by former arable land were major attractions. As the availability of winter fodder was a vital constraint, it was important for success that the better arable land be fenced off for fodder crops.

The former tenants were turned off the land they had farmed for centuries. During the brutal period known as the Highland Clearances, clansmen were forced from their houses, which were burnt before their eyes. There was no alternative employment, for a sheepmaster could "live and make rich in a desart, with his sheep and a very few servants."[29] Harassed by their former chiefs or by southern aliens whose language they could not speak, by missionaries and by the Society for the Propagation of Christian Knowledge, and having lost most of their possessions, the former clansmen were either resettled in bleak fishing villages on stormy coasts, or were compelled to emigrate to the unknown regions of Lowland Britain, Australia, or North America.

It was the Age of Reason. Industrial enterprise, commerce, agriculture, town planning, and landscape gardening were all involved in a vast transformation process. In the agricultural sphere the radical reorganization of farmlands on scientific principles, and on a commercial basis, was generally referred to as "Improvement".[30] Although improvement in Lowland Britain usually involved new crops and cropping systems, in the Scottish Highlands, by now a bare "wet desert," profitable improvement came only with the introduction of the hardy Cheviot sheep. As sheepranching appeared to be the "highest and best use of the ground," the sheepmasters generally saw little amiss in their "reducing the population in order to introduce valuable improvements . . . the necessity of removing the former inhabitants to make way for shepherds."[31]

Only a few landlords inveighed against this wholesale transformation of Highland life and landscape.

> Nothing can be more detrimental . . . The first thing is to drive away all the present inhabitants. The next is to introduce a shepherd and a few dogs; and then to cover the mountains with flocks of wild, coarse-woolled and savage animals which seldom see their shepherd or are benefited by his care.[32]

The above quotation succinctly describes the initiation of sheepranching in medieval England, eighteenth century Scotland, and nineteenth century Easter Island. For its maintenance, the new sheep economy demanded little beyond a few shepherds' homes, some fencing or walling, and the creation of paddocks for the control of fodder, breeding, treatment, and shearing.

Few former inhabitants were able to take part in any of these sheepraising enterprises. Sheepranching is capital-intensive rather than labour-intensive, and benefits greatly from economies of scale. A single fully-employed shepherd, aided by dogs and some few well-distributed fences or walls, may control a flock of over one thousand sheep. An extensive land base is required for such a flock, with different grazing types at varying altitudes and with varying aspect, so as to suit animals of all ages at all seasons and in all weather conditions. Moreover, major initial capitalization is required to cover risk of loss in the new environment, transportation to markets, basic landscape improvements, and credit costs. No small family enterprise could hope to be competitive.[33]

Sheepfarming on Easter Island, introduced by Brander and continued by other Scottish entrepreneurs, had an effect remarkably similar to that which followed its introduction into Western Scotland. The initial concept of sheeprearing on small Pacific islands was not without precedent; among other cases, in 1863 a Scottish family purchased Niihau, an island in the Hawaiian archipelago, and ran it as a cattle and sheep ranch. This island and its population remained under total family control into the second half of the twentieth century.[34]

In the case of Easter Island sheepranching emerged at the ultimate point of contact of two diffusion streams both emanating originally from the same British source. The earlier connection was the more tenuous. Australia, by the second half of the nineteenth century, was proving its value as sheep country. Australian sheep were taken into the Pacific, and it was from this source that Dutrou-Bornier brought the first commercial rams and ewes to Easter Island. The second diffusion reached Easter Island via the Falklands, Patagonia, and Tierra del Feugo, all of which were utilized for sheeprearing by a series of Scottish enterprises during the late nineteenth century.

Meeting at Easter Island in the shape of the Branders and CEDIP, these two Scots-based sheeprearing diffusion paths were the initiators of the radical changes in settlement patterns, economy, employment, and landscape features which took place there after 1870. The processes begun by the Brander-Bornier partnership in the period 1868-88 were continued by the Merlet-CEDIP regime in the following century.

PLATE 20 Outbuildings at Mataveri, erected during the "improvements" of the 1920s ▶

7 IMPROVING LANDLORDS

> Today, despite flagpoles in front of the administration house, and gold frogs on the breast of a prefect of police, government, authority, and retribution are symbolized in the native mind by that deity of the new culture: The Company. Men have come and gone . . . But always The Company has persisted, its power unshaken by criticism or revolt, its hold upon the land seemingly more eternal than that of the old stone gods.
>
> Robert Casey, 1932

Freed from the annoyance of Rapanui settlements outside the Hangaroa-Mataveri axis, the sheepmasters of the late 1890s were able to develop the bulk of the land surface of Easter island without let or hindrance. Their knowledge of sheeprearing was originally derived from Scottish experience modified by cultural transfer through Australasia and southern South America. With its rolling cone-shaped hills, its abundance of stone, its grassy uplands, and its lack of treecover, Easter Island resembled a Hebridean landscape. Several natural materials, similar to those used in Scotland, were available for landscape transformation in the interests of sheep-rearing. Other necessary materials were imported from Pacific Rim countries. Once the surviving population had been penned into the Hangaroa area, the turning of Easter Island over to the commercial production of wool and animal byproducts demanded or resulted in radical changes in the animal population, vegetation, and the built environment.

ANIMALS

At the time of Bornier's accession to the lordship of Easter Island only a few animals, brought by the missionaries, were in evidence. When these were transferred to his dubious safekeeping after the missionary evacuation in 1871, Bornier reported that the mission stock consisted of 250 sheep, 14 cattle, 7 fat pigs, 4 horses, 3 ponies, and 2 donkeys.[1] Bishop Jaussen's court claims of the early 1880s to ownership of two-fifths of the sheep, seven-twelfths of the cattle, two-thirds of the horses, and all the donkeys on the island suggests that in 1871, when the Brander-Bornier partnership was officially inaugurated, Easter Island contained about 700 sheep, 25 cattle, and 10 horses. These figures are approximately confirmed by the partnership agreement, which states that Bornier had installed 500 sheep, 30 cattle, and 10 horses on the island (Table 1,7).[2]

During the 1870s the Brander-Bornier partnership made great efforts to increase the stock. By 1879, according to the official inventory, there were 9,600 sheep, 200 cattle, 43 horses, and 5 donkeys, although the pigs had become wild.[3] Over 400 head of Merino sheep stock had been brought from Australia by Bornier in 1872. Bornier's "simultaneously commercial and civilizing work" had managed to raise the animal stock of the island from less than 1,000 in 1871 to over 10,000 within the decade.[4]

After Bornier's murder the stock was in the hands of the Branders and Salmons for over a decade. By 1884, although no fixed number could be ascertained on account of continued sales, losses, and breeding, it was believed that the island contained 14,000 sheep, 350 cattle, 60 horses, and 5 donkeys.[5] Three years later, when Brander and Toro were negotiating the sale of the island to Chile, the animal numbers were restated as 14,000, 720, and 150, the donkeys being ignored (Table 2,7). The Salmon figure for sheep was used thereafter in contracts between the Chilean government and Merlet.[6] Between 1887 and 1889 the mission's pigs and donkeys were reclassified as Brander property.[7]

None of these figures can be considered accurate. As with the unavailability of exact lot boundaries, which was the source of disputes between company and government for forty years (Chapter 4), so Brander's lease agreements with Toro carefully stated that an exact head count was impossible.[8] By 1889 the majority of the cattle had run wild, ranging freely across the island; only an estimate of their numbers could be obtained from field observations. The sheep counts were more accurate but referred only to adult beasts, "it having been impossible to count the lambs."

With the recession of the Tahiti interest and the growth of the Anglo-Chilean connection after 1895, sheep numbers were again increased and the island became little more than a vast sheepranch. By 1911 Knoche was speaking of "thousands of sheep",[9] and as many as 2,000 cattle.[10] A more accurate survey by Bryan in 1920 revealed 1,400 horses (1916 estimate of 800), 4,000 cattle (2,000), and 24,000 sheep (18,000), a total of almost 30,000 animals.[11] Although accurate time series figures for later years are unavailable, estimates suggest that at the height of CEDIP's exploitation of Easter Island the 1920s figures had been more than doubled, to about 70,000 head. The National Economic Census of 1943, however, found that CEDIP had only 41,412 sheep, 775 pigs, 387 cattle, and 98 horses. In contrast, the native population owned 922 cattle, 329 horses, 1,222 pigs, but no sheep.[12] The vast increase in stock numbers in the first

TABLE 1,7 Animal Population 1871

	Brander-Bornier	Mission (according to Bornier)	Mission (according to Jaussen)	Approximate Totals
Sheep	500	250	200	700-750
Cattle	30	14	14	44
Horses	10	7	6	16-17
Donkeys	—	2	2	2
Pigs	—	7	15	7-15

TABLE 2,7 Animal Population 1887-9

	Brander (1887)	Salmon (formerly the mission; 1887)	Brander (1889)	Total (1887)
Sheep	8,400	5,600	7,440	14,000
Cattle	300	420	350	720
Horses	50	100	78	150
Donkeys	—	—	2	—
Pigs	—	—	7	—

four decades of the twentieth century was due not merely to natural increase but also to a concerted effort to "improve" the island on the part of CEDIP.

THE DECISION TO IMPROVE

The original intention of the Brander-Bornier partnership of 1871 had been to exploit Easter Island in every possible manner, though concentrating on the rearing of "sheep and other animals, commerce in wool and all island products suitable for export," mainly to the Society Islands and Tahiti.[13] Sheep were therefore the initial focus of commercial attention; horses and donkeys were brought in simply as necessary adjuncts to the sheepraising operation. Cattle were introduced as a secondary commercial enterprise, but were probably less profitable than sheep. Although horsehair, hides, and other cattle products, including dried meat, were exported, this trade never became as important as wool. Beef exports were never a viable proposition; isolation and the small stock precluded export of fresh meat even after the inauguration of refrigerator vessels. Like the horses and the seven fat pigs before them, many cattle led a semi-wild, feral existence.[14]

John Brander junior remarked in 1887 that much improvement of this situation was required, for:

> Easter Island has been so far a grazing country, the stock being allowed to roam over the whole island, only driven into the pens when required. Half of the cattle are still wild, require taming. Grass grows over the whole island, there are very few trees, stones, a large quantity, and water is to be found in the three craters, in numerous waterholes and crevices of the rocks.[15]

Brander's "plan of improving the island" involved killing off all the bulls, old cows, large bullocks, and most of the horses, and selling or killing most of the sheep, which produced an inferior wool in quantities of only about sixteen tons per year. The profit from meat, hides, tallow, and bones would cover the cost of this operation, as well as that of a new bull, a new stallion, and new rams "of first class wool" to supplement the existing merinos.

An outlay of eight thousand dollars in machinery, pumps, well-boring apparatus, water pipes, fencing, and the construction of new buildings and waggons would, prophesied Brander, result in an efficient sheep farm:

PLATE 21
Cattle round-up
c. 1917

PLATE 22
Cattle, stone walls,
and wire c. 1917

> Pay a great deal of attention to the sheep and I believe that the island could produce from sixty to one hundred tons wool per annum in time.[16]

Brander's prediction was accurate. The improvements effected by CEDIP resulted in a wool clip which, during the 1920s and 30s, fluctuated around 70 tons per year.

At the time of Brander's suggestion, in the late 1880s, the land was largely unfenced, thus rendering controlled grazing impossible, water remained a scarce commodity, and for transportation reliance had to be placed upon a few old ox-waggons, donkeys, and horses. Moreover, Brander stressed to Toro in 1889 that the animal stock was in no way in perfect condition.[17] Many of the wilder cattle were very thin, and many of the sheep were attacked by a sickness known as *arestín*.

During the Toro and Merlet periods, 1888-1903, improvements were haphazard but not unimportant, involving the introduction of new garden vegetables and fruits, shade trees, and walls. Enrique Merlet brought in partridges and attempted unsuccessfully to foster ducks on the Rao Kao crater lake.[18] During the decade 1911-20, however, the violent dispute between CEDIP and the Chilean government (Chapter 4) provoked the preparation of at least three reports on possible agrarian improvements.

Dr. Walter Knoche, Director of the Central Meteorological and Geophysical Institute of Chile, was dispatched to Easter Island on the *Baquedano* in April 1911 as leader of a commission whose tasks were to establish a meteorological station and make a general scientific survey. In a lengthy report outlining the work accomplished during the commission's 12-day stay on the island, Knoche reported that he had installed both a weather station and seismic apparatus, complete with a Chilean attendant, although it was hoped that the latter would eventually be replaced by Percy Edmunds, the CEDIP manager on the island.[19] There was no trace of the rabbits introduced in the 1860s. The pigs had disappeared, and there were few dogs and cats, although several of the latter lived wild. After botanical, zoological, demographic, and ethnological comments, Knoche suggested that the island had no strategic importance, being far from major shipping lanes.

It was, however, the only semitropical region in Chile. Merely the latest of a series of agrarian visionaries who envisioned Easter Island as a tropical plantation (Chapters 2, 4), Knoche suggested that the island should be "converted into a magnificent garden of the Republic" which would supply Chile with sugar, bananas, pineapples, and other tropical produce. The island, he asserted, would also make a far better penal colony than the existing one on the Juan Fernández islands. This was the only recommendation of Dr. Knoche that was ever implemented by a Chilean government.

A second report was prepared only three years later by one Pedro Adams of Osorno, who accompanied Enrique Merlet on the company ship in 1914.[20] Directed at the company, this report eschewed any suggestion of plantation agriculture, and concentrated on the possibilities of pastoral improvement. Adams found the 2,000 cattle to be in fairly good condition, especially the work oxen which were large and well-developed. One suspects that he did not closely examine many of the feral cattle; those he saw he reported to be fat, healthy, and amenable to control. The sheep, however, were in poor condition, and increasing only slowly. Many lambs died off at the age of 4-5 months, when the small, skinny, degenerate ewes could or would no longer suckle them. Of the sheep brought from Australia, many had died.

Adams blamed almost all of the pastoral problems of Easter island on the quality of the pasturage. The indigenous grasses were tough and contained little nourishment; young lambs no longer able to suckle could not digest such hard grasses. Because of the poor grass cover cows yielded little milk and of poor quality, so any cheesemaking enterprise was clearly impossible. For similar reasons the many horses were universally small and weak. The dominant grasses encouraged sheep pests, were resistant to invertebrate grass predators, and readily killed off other grasses through the ecological processes of invasion and succession.

Adams recommended the continuation of the rejuvenation of cattle quality, already begun by CEDIP with bulls imported from a Señor Scott's mainland *hacienda*. A similar effort for the sheep was urgently required. No further stallions should be imported, as the last import had been unable to adapt to the pasturage and had been killed by the feral stallions. Pigs would be useless in Easter Island; with a soil of very low humus content there was little for them to forage, and few possibilities existed for providing suitable specialized feeds or scrap food for them.

Infrastructural recommendations included the need for more fields to be created by wall building, the continuation of excavations for wells by means of explosives, the importation of more shade trees, and the establishment of weeping willows to protect water supplies. New ploughs should be heavy and strong in order to resist the blows caused by the numerous stones in the soil. Industrially, the most suitable development would be a factory for the production of *charqui* (jerked or dried meat). Because of the lack of suitable port facilities, live cattle could not easily be embarked on vessels, and would more readily be disposed of in the form of barrels of lard and tins of meat.

The third report of the second decade of the new century came from the pen of William Alanson Bryan, "Professor Zoology and Geology, biological engineer," of Hawaii. As Hawaii lay north of the equator "under almost the same conditions of temperature and climate that Pascua occupies in South latitude," and at about the same distance from mainland markets, it appeared to CEDIP that Bryan's suggestions for improvement would be more apposite than any emanating from persons domiciled in central or southern Chile.[21] Based on a visit to Easter Island in 1920, Bryan's lengthy report was made directly to CEDIP. In Bryan's opinion the local manager, Edmunds, was doing his best in the face of isolation, lack of suitable tools and facilities, and the inefficient and unreliable labour of the indigenes:

> The available labour supply which consists of about forty adult natives is exasperatingly unsatisfactory and utterly unreliable. Its efficiency is about on a par with that of an equal number of twelve year old city boys in the country on a holiday. The lack of efficient, dependable labour is the greatest present difficulty in the proper management of the existing ranch.[22]

Given suitable improvements, Bryan suggested that even if the land under crops was increased to 4,000 hectares (10,000 acres) by a possible Chilean settler colony, the remaining land would readily be able to carry 10,000 head of cattle and 20,000 sheep without being overstocked. In 1920 the 29,400 animals enjoyed a little less than 0.6 hectares (1.4 acres) each, on which basis Easter Island was "far from being overstocked." The most necessary improvements were extensive fencing to conserve pasturage and water supplies, improved water supply, and heavy ploughs because "all volcanic soils are heavy and hard to plow." Although there were good soils in the Mataveri area, and on Poike, "about three-fifths of the total area must be classed as rocky land, fit only for cattle and sheep pasture."[23]

Bryan's chief concern was to improve water supply on the arid island, without which it would be impossible to increase stock numbers to any degree. From the number of undersea springs, the abundance of brackish water along the coast, the prevailing rock types and the prevalence of lava tubes and subterranean caverns, Bryan predicted ample supplies of underground water. Some of this water, possibly existing under artesian conditions, would readily be tapped by deep wells. Water was subsequently found in two of the three locations indicated by Bryan. Alternative sources were crater lakes; "up to the present absolutely nothing has been done to conserve, develop, or make available this splendid natural and well-distributed supply of surface water, which anywhere else would be capitalized at many thousands of dollars."[24] Rano Kao lake, the largest body of water on the island, could become a major water source for the adjacent ranch, harbour, village, agricultural lands, and stock if a pump and pipeline were installed. With suitable storage tanks about 15 square kilometres (6 square miles) of the best land on the island could be irrigated, and the 300 metre (1,000 foot) fall could be used to develop hydroelectric power. A third water supply alternative was to blast shallow wells at seepage sites and equip them with small windmills.

After "an adequate, well-distributed water supply, . . . the very cornerstone of successful development," Bryan opined that CEDIP required better harbour facilities, tools and equipment, roads, fences, afforestation, grass quality, and animal quality.[25] Harbour facilities, hardly improved since Bornier, would be rendered more useful by blasting a wider channel, better quayage, rearrangement of shedding, new handling equipment, and a floating buoy for moorage. The use of flat-bottomed lighters would more than double the work possible in one day. Such improvements might even render Easter Island a more frequent port of call for passing vessels.

Bryan also found that the buildings, fences, tools, stock, and methods in use on the island in 1920 were all up to forty or fifty years old.[26] Percy Edmunds, the ranch manager, still occupied the farmhouse raised by Bornier in Mataveri in the 1860s, and was able to point out the freebooter's grave.[27] Bryan felt that the manager required at least two literate assistants, one with training in vetinary science or agronomy. The other should be in charge of plant, and one of his first tasks should be the repair of old fences and the construction of new walls "dividing the land so as to control breeding, feeding, water etc."[28] In particular, water holes required fencing; Bryan found dozens of dead animals polluting the waters of the crater lakes. Improved access to these lakes was necessary, as, in Rano Raraku especially, many animals became mired and died in their attempts to traverse the thick reeds around the lake edge.

Roads, still covered with loose stones, required improvement so that waggons could readily penetrate to every part of the island. The use of a motor vehicle, it was suggested, would improve the manager's efficiency by 200 percent. Wood supplies could be increased by planting fast-growing eucalypts and other trees. Existing trees had been planted almost exclusively around Mataveri; this was a waste of good agricultural land and did nothing to provide shade and shelter to the range stock. Bryan found the stock in poor condition, the horses "without value and excessive." Like

PLATE 23
Mataveri outbuildings

PLATE 24
Old stables
at Mataveri

Adams before him he urged "an infusion of new blood. Breeding animals of good quality should be immediately introduced."[29] *Charqui* production would be the best mode of using cattle.

Much, however, depended upon grass quality, as Adams had suggested earlier. Of nineteen graminaceous species Bryan found that thirteen were natural or of early introduction from other tropical regions. But of the six "grasslike plants of more recent introduction" two were cultivated cereals, and two more obviously garden foodplants. "No considerable effort has been made to supplement the native list of rather inferior forage grasses with the valuable feed and fattening species."[30] Like Adams, Bryan noted that the coarse *mauku* grass, probably from Tahiti, was rapidly crowding out more useful species.

Finally, Bryan suggested a long list of plant species which he felt might be introduced to CEDIP's profit. These included better varieties of banana, sugar cane, grapes, sweet potatoes, yams, pineapples, and citrus fruits as well as new or little-tried crops such as cotton and sisal. Although he believed that an agricultural colony could be established, he was adamant that the rational development of Easter Island required that the whole island be under one management.[31] Given fifty years of undisputed possession and the expenditure of less than one hundred thousand dollars, Bryan assured the CEDIP proprietors that the island could become a major exporter of wool, meat products, sugar, sisal, pineapple, other citrus fruits, and many minor products.

He did not omit aesthetics. Noting that most known ornamental shrubs would thrive on Easter Island, he added:

> The possibilities of developing the Island as a veritable Garden of Eden only necessitate the introduction of a large assortment of well-known and even rare ornamental plants (which) if introduced would soon transform the colorless and almost flowerless island into a mass of bloom.[32]

IMPROVEMENTS IN THE 1920s AND 1930s

From Bryan's account it would seem that those Chileans who believed, as early as the 1880s, that Easter Island could become a tropical plantation, were justified in their support of Toro's settlement schemes. What was lacking then, and continued to be lacking for the next generation, was the capital and the will to develop the island. Little change had occurred in the period 1880-1920, for both Merlet and CEDIP had continued to work with the old Brander-Bornier equipment, buildings, and stock. In the face of recurring disputes between government and company, the latter had wisely decided to severely limit the costs of the Easter Island operation. By 1920, however, more secure in their new lease arrangements, and urged equally by Adams and Bryan to improve vegetation, stock, infrastructure, and fencing, CEDIP decided on a programme of investment.

Williamson, Balfour were, in fact, compelled to take a more direct interest in the island after the death of Merlet in 1918. Moreover, they were unable to sell the island because of their lack of an officially registered title to the land surface. In these conditions a risk venture made under a favourable lease arrangement was not excessively daring. "We are aiming at spending three or four thousand pounds per annum on the island and hope to get back five or six thousand pounds," wrote a prominent Williamson, Balfour partner.[33] Shortly after Bryan's report had been digested, improvements were inaugurated in the areas of livestock and pasture quality, wall- and fence-building, and water supply and other infrastructural improvements.

Vegetation Changes

Despite the pleas of Bryan and Adams, little effort was made to import new grass species of greater nutritional value. Regrassing the island would have required a long-term effort hardly possible in view of the company's tenuous legal title; the improvement of stock, which could readily be removed or sold, was a better commercial proposition. Considerable effort was made, however, to rid the pasturage of the coarsest grasses such as the *mauku*. This was accomplished by a programme of selective burning.[34] As practised in Scotland, Patagonia, and other pastoral areas, a selective burning programme can be productive of a remarkable regeneration of pastoral value. It permits the eradication or reduction of unwanted species, provides fertilizing ash, and supports the growth of a high quality aftercrop of sweet young shoots.

In general, however, the vegetational aspect of Easter Island's landscape was not radically changed from its appearance in 1870. Compared with Patagonia and Tierra del Fuego, Easter Island's grass cover was rich. In those southern regions several acres were required to support a single sheep; on Easter Island a stock ratio of up to two sheep per acre was possible. The dominant grass species formed what Knoche regarded as a "natural savannah," often reaching a metre (3.3 feet) in height and usually bleached yellow in the hot summer sun, thus forming a natural hay. Several of these grass species are of European, American, or Australian origin, but the times and means of arrival are not known. An elucidation of the development of Easter Island's grassland requires the attention of an historical biogeographer.

The growth in sheep numbers, however, had a considerable impact on certain vegetation types. Sheep are delicate, selective feeders. In the Scottish Highlands the influx of large sheep flocks resulted in the efflorescence of the less-heavily grazed grasses such as *Nardus* and *Molinia*. These, together with bracken, spread over the hills in the wake of the sheep, reduced pasture quality, and could be kept down only by rigorous burning. Regular burning and the poverty of grassland species prevented this occurrence on any scale in Easter Island, but the analogy with the Scottish experience holds true with regard to the effect of sheep on arboreal vegetation. Sheep readily consume the young shoots of tree species; they may strip trees of bark on the lower trunk. If allowed to roam freely, sheep will effectively prevent the natural regeneration of trees in a partially-deforested area.

Before the advent of the European it is probable that the park-like savannah, which comprised Easter Island's total non-cultivated vegetation picture, contained a fair number of trees. Polynesian legends, archaeological investigations, and pollen analyses support the case for a somewhat more arboreal vegetation type than is found on Easter Island today.[35] Imported trees grow fairly well.

The recency of the demise of the native woodlands is recorded in the journals of visitors. The earliest explorers were strongly divided as to the extent and nature of Easter Island woodlands. Although Forster in 1777 noted "there was not a tree upon the island, which exceeded the height of ten feet," we are given no indication of the extent of small trees and shrubs; shrub vegetation, however, seems to have been quite common as late as the 1860s (Chapter 5).[36] Much of this woody vegetation was destroyed by indigenous practices before the first settlement by Europeans. In 1868 Palmer found the boles of large trees, such as the *toromiro*, coconut, and hibiscus, decaying in several locations.[37]

Eighteen years later, however, Cooke wrote of the existence of *toromiro* in "considerable numbers," but:

> all, or nearly all, dead and decaying by reason of their being stripped of their bark by the flocks of sheep which roam at will all over the island.[38]

Like much of eighteenth-century Scotland, Easter Island was finally denuded of its meagre tree cover by the depredations of the sheepmasters and their flocks. In the face of persistent grazing and gnawing, only tough grasses, lichens, and mosses survive.

Contemporary evidence suggests that the sheep introduced in the 1860s quickly reduced the endemic shrubby *toromiro* which was once common on the northern side of the island and which, with trunks of up to 50 centimetres (20 inches) in diameter, had been a major prop of the native economy.[39] In 1870 Gana saw clumps of dead *toromiro*, which he attributed to the ravages of sheep and cattle. The last *toromiro* on Easter Island, its trunk 10 centimetres (four inches) thick in the 1930s, survived into the second half of the twentieth century only through its location in the Rano Kao crater, protected from sheep by its rocky inaccessibility.[40]

As if in response to the destruction of indigenous trees by their flocks, the early sheepmasters played their improving landlord role by introducing a variety of alien trees. By the first decade of the twentieth century the ranch at Mataveri had become the scene of experimental plantings of *algarrobo*, various types of acacias, several species of eucalyptus, pines, araucarias, cypresses, and coconut palms.[41] Fruiting trees such as oranges, figs, mulberries, peaches, and vines were also tried, some of these introductions dating from the 1860s. Several tree species were spread throughout Hangaroa from Mataveri and from the initial stock brought by the Catholic mission.[42]

In the protected Rano Kao crater the initial gardening efforts of Dutrou-Bornier were succeeded by deliberate plantings of acacias, ti, bananas, figs, vines, and other tree crops. Many of these were still assiduously cultivated into the 1950s, but although fruit is still available in the 1980s, the crater gardens are now wild and overgrown, interspersed by the occasional small conifer and a single bright patch of bougainvillea. After Bryan's visit the guayaba, a low bushy tree with edible fruit, was introduced. This rapidly spread in the vicinity of Hangaroa and by the 1970s had covered large areas of formerly cultivated ground.

Of all the introduced tree types the most prominent, and most significant in the process of landscape transformation, is the eucalypt. Several species of eucalyptus were brought from Australia in the late nineteenth century; Bryan felt that these were not the most suitable species for the Easter Island environment.[43] Nevertheless, the eucalypt had several advantages for the sheepmasters. It was excellently adapted for use as timber; the eucalypt is very fast-growing, sometimes reaching a diameter of 20 centimetres (eight inches) in five years. As it shed its bark, rather than its leaves, it provided continuous shade for animals, a factor of major importance during the arid summer. Leafy and thick-trunked, it could also be used as a windbreak, again a major value for an island so exposed. Eucalypts are less susceptible to damage from sheep than other trees, as a permanent bark cover is not necessary for survival. Furthermore, the tree would also be safe from the indigenes, who had not hesitated to chop down new species in their quest for suitable material for the carving of wooden images, a major trade item with calling vessels. CEDIP's attempts to plant trees beyond Mataveri were increasingly restricted to eucalypts, the wood of which is essentially uncarvable.

The chief disadvantage of the eucalypt is that its bark does not readily disintegrate, but forms a tinder-dry litter below the tree. Eucalypts are also notorious in Easter Island for drying out an already arid earth. Nevertheless, eucalypt groves were planted in several locations throughout the island to provide the flocks with shelter from sun and wind (Figure 1,7). Outside Hangaroa and Mataveri, a region which soon became wholly surrounded by tree growth, the majority of the eucalypt clumps were planted on the slopes of Rano Kao, along the south coast, and in the central area of the island around the ranch substation in Vaitea. More isolated clumps were placed on Poike and Maunga Terevaka. In contrast, modern conifer plantations have been almost wholly restricted to Rano Kao, with some experimental plantings elsewhere.

The improving sheepmasters, therefore, were responsible for the final demise of the meagre indigenous woodland, and for the dotting of the landscape with clumps of new species. The clumping of trees, and their arrangement in lines as windbreak screens, especially around Mataveri and Vaitea, is reminiscent of the emparked estates created by eighteenth-century gardenists in Britain. Indeed, to CEDIP the island was wholly its personal estate, with its great house and a village beyond its gates (Figure 5,6), a landscape to be made over in its own image.

Walls and Enclosures

Sheeprearing demanded not only different types and patterns of trees, but also an almost wholly new landscape feature, the fence. Easter Island fences are almost wholly drystone walls. Stone walls were not unknown to the indigenes, but had been used only in house construction and for the protection of individual fruit trees from wind damage. It has also been suggested that the ruinous remains of small enclosures scattered throughout the island were originally built by the native agriculturalists to protect their crops from voracious sheep and other domestic beasts.[44] Like Scottish crofters whose crops were devoured by sheep, and still suffer from the depredations of deer, the islanders were compelled to raise walls around

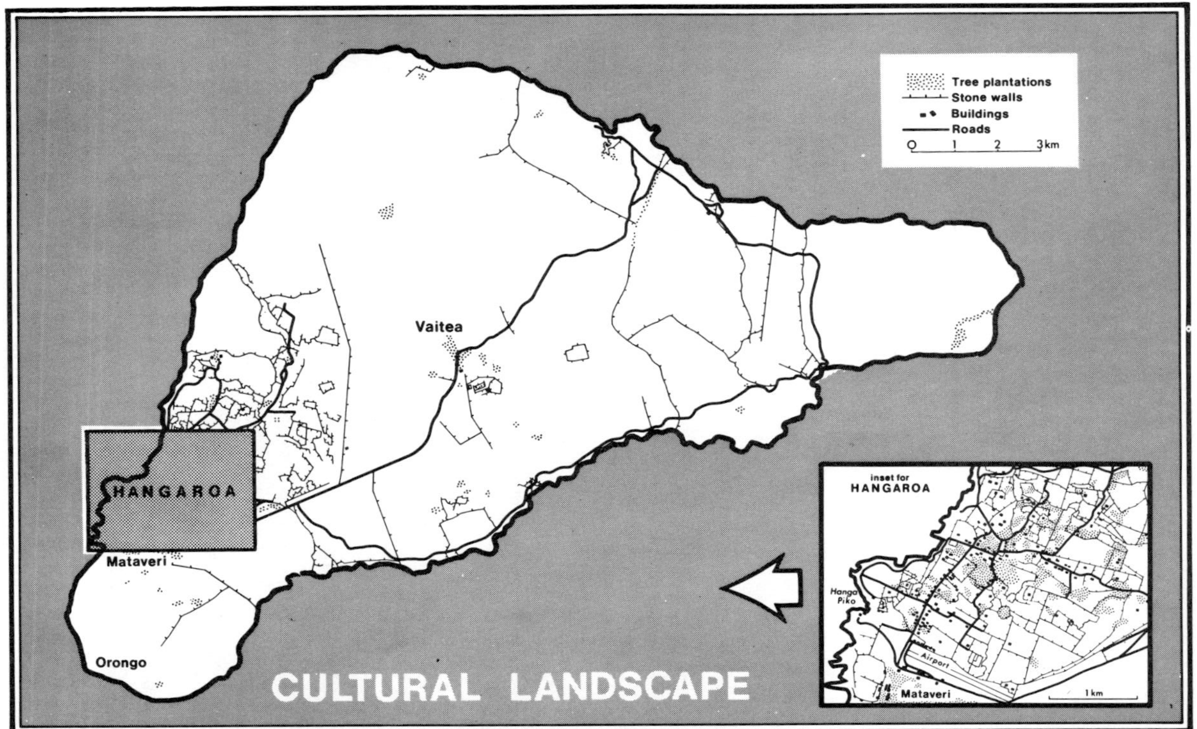

FIGURE 1,7 European landscape features, mid-twentieth century (source: FACh maps).

PLATE 25
Below Rano Raraku, an "improved" landscape of roads, walls, shelter-belts, paddocks, and a shepherd's cabin

PLATE 26
Eucalypt clumps and walls, Rano Kao in background

their garden plots. Many of the irregular walled areas in Hangaroa were enclosed by the indigenes after the coming of the sheep (Figure 1,7).

In general, however, the indigenes did not erect walls or fences. Even when compelled to do so after the 1860s, their own enclosures were irregular and tended towards curvilinearity. In sharp contrast, the walling of Easter Island, accomplished almost wholly under European guidance, involved laying out lengthy straight stone walls, product of the European's linear, carpentered world.[45]

Bornier, with a fairly plentiful supply of timber from the few remaining trees, from shipwrecks, and from importation, was able to fence his original Mataveri estate in wood (Figure 2,3). Such extravagance, in an island bereft of timber, could not be continued after the 1870s, for imported wood was prohibitively expensive, flotsam appeared irregularly and in small quantities, and shipwrecks could not be relied on. The solution was to make every possible use of the abundant stone of Easter Island.

Wall-building began on a small scale with Bornier and Salmon and continued well into the twentieth century. Its purpose was to divide the island into manageable sectors so as to improve pasturage quality, control breeding, and facilitate animal treatment. Bryan lamented the lack of fences as late as 1920:

> The existing fences, mostly of stone, built by several managers with different ideas, are very sadly out of repair. Aside from the fencing about the settlement, the Island is practically one immense cattle range. New fence lines should be laid out and constructed . . .[46]

After Bryan's report a concerted effort was made by CEDIP to improve the walling on a rational plan (Figure 2,7).

Easter Island's stone walls, known by the Chilean term *pirca*, resemble the drystone walls of the Andes, New England, Greece, Northern Britain, and other stony environments. Cementing is not used; irregularly shaped stones, many of them cleared from adjacent forage paddocks, are held together by mutual tension to produce walls of about 1.5 metres (5 feet) in height and 0.6-1.0 metres (2-3 feet) thick. Nowhere do the *pircas* match the skilled indigenous stonework as found in several major *ahus*. Only rarely do they approach the quality of traditional drystone walling in Highland Britain. Many show signs of hasty erection, with ill-fitting stones and a lack of accurate keying. Some walls are so irregularly built that large gaps appear between the component stones, giving the whole wall a lacy, perforated appearance.

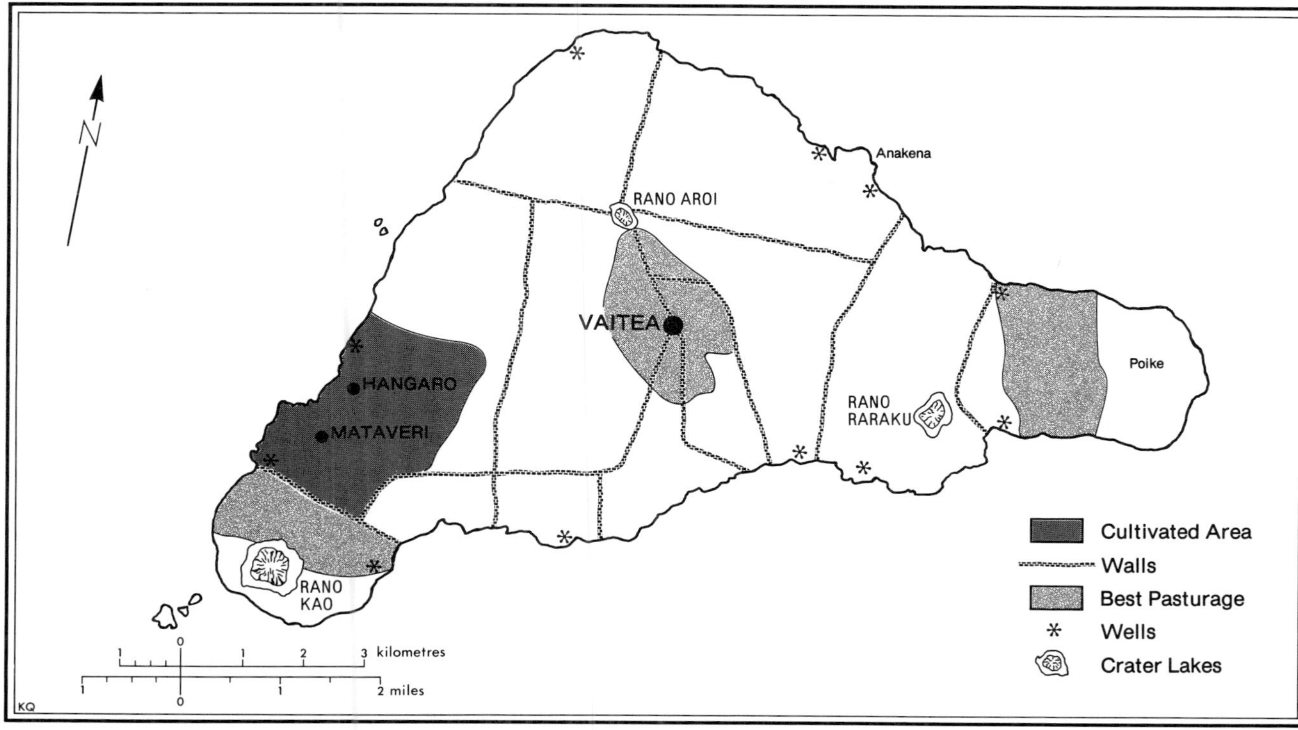

FIGURE 2,7 The planning of a sheep-ranch. Not all the walls indicated were actually built; compare Figure 1,7 (redrawn from Cruz-Coke).

Although loose stones are found scattered throughout the island, there was little reluctance to use the already-shaped stones of ancient monuments; indeed, these were found by Métraux in native-built anti-sheep enclosures.[47] On the coasts, as at Tongariki, *ahus* became integral sections of the wall pattern. In several *pircas* one may still distinguish stones taken from *ahus*, from the traditional native boatshaped houses, and from other structures. The curb stones of the traditional houses were especially useful. Métraux, writing of a former village north of Hangaroa, states: "There are the remains of several houses, though some have been pulled down by Williamson-Balfour Company agents for stones to build their walls."[48]

The walls were built by native labour under company direction; it is unlikely that the post-impact population protested the final despoliation of the artifacts whose destruction they had themselves begun. The wanton destruction of archaeological sites, however, cannot be condoned in the case of Orongo, the unique ceremonial village on the seaward crest of Rano Kao. The stone houses of Orongo were systematically pillaged by island residents who carried the plate-like stone slabs down to Mataveri and Hangaroa by the cartload. Such a useful building material could not be ignored; as in contemporary bombsites and house demolitions, the abandoned material was regarded as valueless unless recycled by someone with special needs. The remains of Orongo's ceremonial dwellings could until recently be seen in scattered locations in and about Hangaroa.[49]

The distribution of *pircas* (Figure 1,7) indicates that two separate walling processes were at work during the sheepmaster period. In the Hangaroa area, where the native population was concentrated and where all cultivation was carried on, a bewildering mosaic of walls has resulted in a patchwork of irregular enclosures. This pattern is evidence of a multitude of uncoordinated decisions concerning the fencing of individual plots. Walls parallel each other, creating seemingly inefficient field shapes, encircle each other, or fail to enclose entirely the intended land parcel. In many places trees and shrubs act as supplements or substitutes, themselves often supplanted by modern posts and wire.

Beyond Hangaroa the irregularity of the Polynesian walled landscape is replaced by the linear order of the walled sheepwalks. The disposition of the company's walls suggests at least a basic subdivision plan begun by the first Europeans and continued by Toro, Merlet, and CEDIP (Figure 2,7). A major objective was to divide off the populated area of Hangaroa from the sheep pastures beyond. This was accomplished by the Bornier fence which cut off Rano Kao and by a further, parallel fence between Mataveri and Hangaroa (Figure 5,6). The remaining section, although incomplete, begins on the south coast near Vinapu and continues in a series of long straight sections towards the northwest coast between Hangaroa and Maunga Terevaka. One writer has castigated the company for constructing this boundary fence, citing its major purpose as the encirclement of the Rapanui who were not allowed to venture beyond the wall without company permission.[50] The removal of all the islanders to one location and their enclosure by a boundary wall certainly gives the impression of a segregated native reservation.

From the company's point of view, however, this was perhaps the most essential wall on the island. It clearly demarcated the several thousand acres which were finally deemed government-owned land for Rapanui use (Chapter 4) from what CEDIP regarded as its own property. Supplemented by guards, gates, and wire, it posed some deterrent to the rustling of sheep and cattle, which has been endemic since the arrival of these beasts. Indeed, the chief reason given for the enforced resettlement in Hangaroa was "to secure the safety of the livestock."[51] The results of Rapanui resentment of such treatment are dealt with in the following chapter. The walling-in of the indigenous population drew no strong objections from the Chilean authorities, as they were engaged in the same process with the Mapuche of southern Chile after the 1880s. Moreover, during the first two decades of the twentieth century, when much of the walling-in of Hangaroa was completed, Chile was officially represented on Easter Island by a *subdelegado* who was also the CEDIP manager. The analogy with Scottish crofting, however, suggests a supplementary reason for the wall, which was apparently important to Toro and his settlers. From the agricultural point of view the wall may have been as much to keep foraging animals out of the Hangaroa garden plots as to keep human beings within the pale.

The remainder of the wall network was devised for the effective control of the stock. Although many walls are incomplete, it is clear from their general trends that the goal was to partition the island into a series of large enclosures, probably in the region of one dozen or more in number.[52] Before overgrazing set in, animals could be transferred from a depleted paddock to one of higher grass yield, the depleted paddock then being burned over to discourage unwanted growths and promote grass regeneration.

Policarpo Toro apparently began the wall which runs from Tongariki to La Pérouse Bay, thus isolating Poike. West of this, five lengthy sections of wall running mainly north-south combine with the aforementioned wall to form five large enclosures. These walls were begun by one Cooper, a CEDIP employee who acted as *subdelegado marítimo* at the turn of the century, and were continued by his CEDIP successors. Between this walled eastern third of the island and the Hangaroa walls, however, no major attempt was made to create walls running across the island's greatest width, although many small sections of wall exist.

These small sections are associated with subsidiary sheep stations, themselves made possible by the creation of several wells and windmills as part of a successful water supply improvement programme. The proper control of the sheep flocks required a few employees to live temporarily in small isolated huts outside the Hangaroa reserve. Small dwellings with adjacent paddocks and corrals were located at strategic coastal points, notably at Vaihu, where the original walling had been begun by the missionaries and Salmon, at Anakena, at Tongariki below Rano Raraku (although this may originally have been the 1914 Routledge expedition's "country house"), and at Vaitea in the centre of the island.[53] Of these, Vaitea was of the greatest importance, as it became a semi-permanent settlement and the site of the annual shearing from the 1920s onwards.

Occasionally, wall-building was abandoned and lines of trees, generally quick-growing eucalyptus, were planted. One such living fence, as recommended by Bryan, forms almost one-third of the major north-south fence begun by Cooper on the eastern side of the island. Although clumps of trees are common in Hangaroa and the leprosarium to the north of the town, one major line of trees, lying immediately south of the present airport, was planted in the 1920s as a shelter-belt for Mataveri. From the 1920s onwards wire fences were used extensively to complete gaps in *pircas* and to form new paddocks.

Fences of living trees, wire, and drystone walls, the latter increasingly ruinous, divide the present landscape of Easter Island into ten major enclosed areas (Figure 1,7). At the eastern extremity of the island are the five enclosures already described, plus the Poike peninsula. In the west, three major enclosed areas are occupied by Mataveri (now the airport and armed forces zone), the Rano Kao grazing and afforestation area, and the Hangaroa agricultural and urban zone. Between these two extremities the tenth unit, occupying approximately half the island and stretching from the north coast of Maunga Terevaka to the south coast at Vaihu, comprises a single incompletely fenced region centring upon the sheep station of Vaitea.

Infrastructure

Improvements in animal and vegetation quality, and the erection of walls, were accompanied by an upgrading of the island's commercial infrastructure. The reports of Knoche, Adams, and especially Bryan were instrumental in impelling CEDIP to improve its island facilities. The serendipitous foundering of the company vessel *Falcon* permitted not only the rebuilding of the Mataveri ranch house but also the construction of more adequate houses for the Hangaroa population. A number of new machine sheds, stables, warehouses, and subsidiary buildings were erected at Mataveri and Hangaroa. One of these bears the date 1929.

During the 1920s also, a ranch substation was developed at Vaitea, with a farmhouse and a range of accompanying outbuildings. Paddocks suitable for shearing and dipping arrangements were laid out, and some fodder crops were experimented with in enclosures of trees, wire, and walls. At this period also the two major roadways striking east from Hangaroa and Mataveri along the south coast and through the central plains were improved, although no surfacing material has yet been applied to any Easter Island roads or streets.

The most important innovation concerned embarkation procedures. Hanga Piko cove, largely unimproved, was used for all imports and the exports of wool, hides, and other products. As no large vessels could enter, launches and small boats were used to lighter goods between ship and shore. This dangerous and inefficient practice was compounded by the lack of quayage at Hanga Piko. CEDIP improvements in this area were instrumental in making Easter Island a viable sheeprearing proposition.

Bryan noted that:

> Work is almost invariably interrupted and delayed — sometimes for days — during the taking in and discharging of cargo owing to wind and swells . . . This deplorable condition has resulted in the loss of valuable cargo and ships, not to mention needless destruction of small boats.[54]

At Bryan's suggestion several flat-bottomed lighters were built to facilitate cargo transfer. Of unique construction, this type of lighter was in use into the 1970s, when military-style metal landing craft were substituted. Each lighter comprised a rectangular cage of wooden poles, within which a mass of upright oil drums provided both buoyancy and stability for the upper cargo-carrying platform of wooden planks.

To facilitate the manoeuvring of the lighters in poor weather conditions, the entrance channel to Hanga Piko was retrained by blasting to provide a fairly sheltered harbour arm. Part of the rough seawall which this effort required was composed of a ruinous *ahu* with accompanying fallen statues.

PLATE 27
Hangaroa cove, open only to small boats

PLATE 28
Hanga Piko quay with rafts

One side of the harbour was provided with several feet of stone and concrete quayage with metal bollards and other deck furniture. Inland from this was a sloping embarkation ramp and warehouses for wool storage and machinery housing.

THE ECONOMIC CYCLE

With improved roads, port facilities, water supplies, walls, and animals, Easter Island became an efficient and profitable commercial sheep station after 1920. Efforts to improve the stock, begun before the 1920s but continued energetically during that decade, began to show results in the form of enhanced profits. Despite such setbacks as the wreck of the *Falcon* in 1924, which damaged the whole year's wool clip, the investment made by Williamson, Balfour in the 1920s came to full fruition in the following decade. Between 1903 and 1931 CEDIP paid only two dividends. After 1932 the declaration of a handsome dividend became an annual event until Williamson, Balfour sold CEDIP in 1946.[55] From the end of World War I to the outbreak of World War II the sheep population had approximately tripled and the wool clip, now ranging between 70 and 100 tons per year, was of a vastly improved quality.

Throughout the interwar period a dual but semi-interdependent economic system prevailed on Easter Island. Within the boundary wall the Polynesian population continued to cultivate its land parcels in the government sector, growing a greater range of edibles than had previously been available. Dry taro, which thrives in loose, rocky soils, declined in importance, as many good taro sites now lay without the boundary wall. The *kumara* (sweet potato), however, remained the dietary staple. The varieties grown on Easter Island are almost wholly of original native introduction and, thriving well in loose ash soils, yielded remarkable crops in and around Hangaroa.

A few islanders grew maize, which was sold to CEDIP as fodder, although managers complained regularly that they would buy more if the Rapanui would grow it. None of the cash crops recommended by Bryan were grown on a commercial basis, although sugar cane, pineapples, figs, grapes, bananas, melons, and other fruits were items of local consumption. Nor did the recommended *charqui-* or fish-processing factories emerge, although a little dried meat was made and exported infrequently.

Although fish were caught off Hangaroa, the Rapanui meat supply remained irregular. Meat rations were provided for the few company workers, and for the majority of men and girls at shearing time. Only lepers and a few permanent employees of CEDIP received a regular meat supply, usually in the form of mutton. Most of the Rapanui, however, appear to have had access to meat through poaching expeditions carried on across the boundary wall by night. Despite wall, barbed wire, and watchmen, the loss of animals to poaching was significant throughout the fifty years of company rule and beyond. It was estimated by the CEDIP manager, for example, that between two and three thousand sheep were rustled in 1934 alone.[56]

As a Rapanui family was able to live on the produce of from one to two hectares (two to five acres) of land, but were each awarded five hectares (12 acres) by the Chilean government, much of the Hangaroa agricultural reserve remained unused (under CEDIP rule the Polynesian population remained well under one thousand). Knoche was unimpressed by indigenous cultivation techniques, which he regarded as "The most primitive form of agriculture," with fields "covered with weeds."[57] Nearly twenty years later, however, Métraux found that most plots were well cared for, quality of cultivation varying greatly with the owner.[58] Dietary supplements, such as coffee, rice, flour, sugar, and tinned goods, were obtained from the company store. The purchase of these, of course, required hard cash, which could only be obtained by working for the company. Cash could occasionally be obtained from visiting vessels in exchange for wooden artifacts, and the CEDIP manager sometimes purchased garden produce, hides, and wool from the Rapanui. The latter, however, were forbidden to own sheep. The resolution of this apparent paradox is explained by the company manager:

> They do a little trading in hides and wool . . . It is an economic process whose simplicity would arouse the envy of an international banker. They steal the sheep from us and sell us the hides. You will see that in such an arrangement waste is almost entirely eliminated.[59]

CEDIP representatives on the island were unable to prevent these poaching excursions. Indeed, during much of the second decade of the twentieth century the manager was the sole European on Easter Island except for a French carpenter and an Italian who lived Polynesian lifestyles in Hangaroa (Figure 3,7). In such circumstances retribution was impossible, as company police recruited from among the indigenes proved to be unreliable. Indeed, as early as 1915 one Bautista Cousin, a European CEDIP foreman, was murdered by the Rapanui.[60] Revolts against company authority occurred in each decade, and continued into the 1960s during the period of naval rule (see Chapter 8).

FIGURE 3,7 Hangaroa village in 1916 (redrawn from Routledge).

Beyond the Hangaroa boundary wall no Rapanui could pass, at least officially, without leave from the company. Sheepraising, the chief business of the island, was organized from Mataveri. The creation of walled enclosures permitted the inauguration of a "camp rotation," whereby flocks were moved regularly from paddock to paddock. As lambing was no great problem in the mild climate of Easter Island, the demand for labour in the CEDIP era was excessively discontinuous. A few shepherds and cultivators at Mataveri and Vaitea, and a maintenance gang for fence repairs, supplying water to animals, and policing the boundary wall and gates, involved only a handful of the Rapanui population as permanent employees. In 1904, for example, the company employed only eight indigenes.[61] By 1943 this figure had risen only to 14.[62]

The situation of an island devoted to animal raising, with a peripheral indigenous population engaged in semi-subsistence agriculture, though occasionally working for the alien entrepreneur, is analagous to the crofter-factor (laird's manager) relationship in the earlier sheepwalks and later deer forests of the Hebrides. The names of the managers and foremen who, generally in pairs from the 1920s, dominated island affairs from Mataveri, add to the pronounced Scottish Lowlander flavour of Easter Island life. Most prominent among these were Edmunds, Harris, Clark, Sanders, Munro, Morrison, McKinnon, and Murdoch Smith.

These factors made calls for labour during dipping and gelding, but most concertedly during shearing and embarkation. Some indication of the annual economic cycle and its demand for temporary labour is afforded by an analysis made by Bienvenido de Estella in 1920 (Table 3,7).[63] Until the 1920s shearing was generally carried out at Mataveri; it was considered most convenient to herd the flocks to the embarkation point. With the growth of the sheep population, the improvement of transportation, and the development of the camp rotation system, the ranch substation at Vaitea became the venue for the annual two weeks' shearing session. The central location of Vaitea reduced herding time and did not tire the sheep. The wool clip was then carried to the Hanga Piko storage sheds by waggon.

This rather irregular demand for labour seemed well suited to the Polynesian temperament. Native Hawaiians, for example, had taken readily to cattle ranching, but rejected the sustained daily monotony of plantation labour.[64] The Rapanui, alienated from their land by colonial domination, had lost any regard for sustained daily labour. According to Bryan, who was clearly an exponent of the work ethic:

> Of the inhabitants of the several Polynesian groups with which the writer is acquainted the Rapa Nui colony

PLATE 29
Sheep to the shearing, c. 1917

PLATE 30
Round-up of horses, c. 1917

TABLE 3,7 Employment of Easter Islanders by CEDIP, 1920

Occupation	Employees	Duration of Employment
Mechanic	1 male	permanent
Watchman	1 male	permanent
Shepherd	2 males	permanent
Gelding bullocks	20 males	annually (1 week)
Rounding up horses, counting, gelding, cutting hair	8 males	annually (3 weeks)
Dipping sheep	20 males	every 4 months (1 week each)
Rounding up sheep for shearing	6 males	annually (15 days)
Shearing	Variable	annually (15 days)
Gleaning loose wool	9 females	annually (15 days)
Shearing helpers	3 children	annually (15 days)
Baling wool	Variable	annually (variable)
Embarking wool	20 males	annually (2 weeks)

SOURCE: R.P. Bienvenido de Estella, *Los Misterios de la Isla de Pascua* (1920), pp. 185-6.

> seems the least disposed to regard labor of a consistent kind as a part of life. The tendency to work furiously for a while, followed by long periods of rest, eating, song, and sleeping, graphically describes their day. They are therefore best adapted to piecework, or as extra hands when rush work is to be done as loading cargo, wool shearing, etc.[65]

Had commercial plantation agriculture been introduced on any scale it is possible, as in Hawaii, that the importation of labour would have been necessary.

Shearing time, *la esquila*, was the only opportunity for the bulk of the population to cross the boundary wall. It had an atmosphere of festival, for it came to replace the traditional Mataveri and Orongo ceremonials as the major social event of the year. Its popularity was further enhanced by the availability of hard cash and fresh meat in quantity, and the inevitable sequel of embarkation, where wooden artifacts could be traded for soap, cigarettes, clothing, and other goods with the visiting vessel's crew. Until the twentieth century, however, the money economy did not wholly take root in Easter Island. Company payments continued to be partly in kind, and among the Polynesians mutual gift-giving and barter were universal. Blue jeans remain an acceptable barter item.

POPULATION RECOVERY

After the overwhelming population crash of the 1860s from an estimated total of about 4,000 to a minimum of 110 in 1877, the population of Easter Island made an increasingly rapid recovery (Table 4,7; Figure 3,1). An increase to about 200 by the turn of the century was partially due to the presence of temporary Chilean settlers (12 in 1888) and a number of foreigners.[66]

From the 1890s the number of Chilean mainlanders and foreigners fell drastically; until the 1960s non-Rapanui rarely accounted for more than ten percent of the resident population. For long periods there was no Chilean on the island, and the company manager was occasionally the sole European. By the turn of the century, however, immigrants were present. The *Baquedano's* census of 1904 revealed three Tahitians and three Europeans.[67] A Frenchman, Vincent Pont, arrived from Tahiti, took up residence in Hangaroa, and, as a carpenter, became a permanent CEDIP employee. Cardinali, an Italian, played a similar role. Hills, an Englishman, was the CEDIP farm manager. By 1911 a half-dozen Chileans (probably a single settler family which was still there in 1918) and a German were in evidence, although all told the aliens accounted for only about five percent of the total population.[68] Many of these aliens interbred freely with Rapanui women; Hill, Pont, and Cardinali are extant surnames in the 1980s. Subsequent CEDIP managers and their assistants, the Chilean naval contingent, and many visitors made major contributions to the island's gene pool. By 1934 Drapkin found only 159 of the 456 islanders to be probably of exclusive Rapanui ancestry. The remainder had considerable admixtures of American, British, Chilean, Chinese, French, German, Italian, Tahitian, and Tuamotuan blood.[69]

TABLE 4,7 Population Trends since the 1877 minimum

Date	Total Population (Métraux, 1940; Census)	Total Population (McCall, 1977)	Non-Rapanui Population (Métraux, McCall)
1877	111	110	
1882	150		
1886	155	168	11
1888	178		12
1892	201		
1900	213	227	14
1911	228		
1916	273		
1917	301	295	29
1922	298	311	8
1934	469		
1936		494	20
1940	563	546	18
1950		753	29
1952	807		
1960	1,134	1,155	125
1970	1,666	1,599	491
1972		1,866	511

Aided by these infusions, the island population recovered rapidly after the 1890s. In the period 1877-1911 the population doubled in a little over 30 years. When the loss of the Chilean settlers and a reduction in the European contingent in the latter part of the period is taken into account, a healthy natural increase rate of about two percent per annum is indicated. In both of the subsequent, and roughly equal, periods of 1911-34 and 1934-60, however, Easter Island's population doubled in approximately 25 years, despite the insignificant in-migration of mainland Chileans before the 1950s.

An abrupt 50 percent increase was recorded in the single decade 1960-70, and by 1980 the island population had risen to about 2,000. A doubling of population in the 20-year period 1950-70 indicates either an extremely rapid rate of natural increase, considerable immigration, or both. The in-migration of mainland Chileans since 1960 has been a major element in the current phase of population growth, and is inextricably bound up with the processes of modernization described in the following chapters.

PLATE 31 Ancient and modern in Hangaroa ▶

SECTION FOUR

MODERN TIMES

Discontent increases with the increase
of information. That is all.

Mr MacQuedy

Thomas Love Peacock, *Crochet Castle* (1831)

PLATE 32 Officials greet LAN-Chile arrival at Mataveri airport ▶

LAN-CHILE

8 MODERNIZATION SINCE 1965

> This is the essential *credo*: the dynamic forces are external; the patterns of modernization are imposed from above; tradition must inevitably give way to modernity; the problem is to overcome 'stubborn resistance'; the people to be encouraged are the 'achievement-oriented' elites.
>
> Harold Brookfield

The changes associated with the modernization of traditional societies may be swift, impacting, and revolutionary, brought about by a brief encounter, or slow, remorseless alterations impressed by decades of alien control. Easter Island's modern historical development is a compound of both processes. The near-fatal impact sustained in the 1860s was followed by a century of autocratic control by aliens. During this century of commercial exploitation changes took place gradually in both landscape and people. As the former was reshaped to serve the purposes of the sheep-ranch (Chapter 7), the latter slowly became aware of the fundamental features of the world that lay beyond the confines of their island.

Their awareness was radically increased, and their coping mechanisms strained to the utmost, during the latter half of the 1960s decade, when a second period of drastic and rapid change began. Until this time Easter Island had remained an anachronism, a semi-subsistence society where barter and payment in kind remained prominent exchange mechanisms, and where information regarding the outside world filtered through irregularly by radio or via the annual boat. In sharp contrast, the later 1960s witnessed the arrival of a large-scale Canadian medical expedition, an American military-scientific contingent, in-migration from Chile, and a scheduled air service to both Santiago and Papeete, Tahiti. In half a decade the inhabitants of Easter Island, long accustomed to being controlled by the company state run by CEDIP and its naval successor, were thrust willy-nilly into the commercial, wage-earning, entrepreneurial ethos of the mid-twentieth century.

ANTECEDENTS OF CHANGE

Change originates from both without and within. A considerable impulse for change was generated by the publicity accorded to a series of scientific expeditions which visited Easter Island between 1914 and 1964. The same period witnessed a number of indigenous uprisings against authoritarian control, culminating in the "revolution" of 1964-5.

Expeditions

Visiting scientific expeditions influenced the islanders by demonstrating the existence of previously-unknown luxuries in the shape of food, clothing, shelter, transportation, and domestic apparatus. Discontent with a company-controlled way of life was therefore aroused, and the seeds of relative deprivation were sown. Almost every expedition also produced a popular book on the island, even if scientific works failed to emerge. These popular works, some of which achieved wide circulation in several languages, were influential in altering external perceptions of Easter Island. The publicity given to the island in the period 1955-65 was probably of great importance in the Chilean decision to modernize.

Besides CEDIP management and a few Chilean naval personnel, Easter Islanders enjoyed external contacts only when vessels called at the island. Radio communication with the mainland, established in the 1930s, was controlled by the authorities. Visiting vessels were few, the island being far from major shipping lanes. The only scheduled call was made by the company boat which arrived once a year to reprovision the island and take off the wool clip. Naval vessels did not call annually or on a regular basis, for changes in government personnel were effected via the company boat which, by the terms of the lease agreement, carried administrative and service personnel free of charge. Occasionally a foreign warship or cruise vessel would call, but such visits were irregular and infrequent. Accordingly, indigenous perceptions of the outside world received a heavy screening via the twin deities of company and navy.

The only major external disturbance to the even tenor of island life came with the incursion of scientific expeditions. Such expeditions had called at the island in the nineteenth century, but usually only for a few days. Almost all the twentieth-century expeditions, in contrast, came prepared for a stay of several months. Often strongly archaeological in orientation, these expeditions demanded local labour for digs, transportation, and personal services, and thus became important temporary sources of money, food, and goods.

Only the more important expeditions whose sole or major objective was Easter Island are considered here. The first major expedition was mounted by Mrs. Routledge in 1914, with official British scientific support. Although scientific data were lost, the expeditionaries witnessed a native uprising against CEDIP, saw the sinking of the French vessel *Jean* by a German naval squadron, and were overwhelmed by the marooning on the island of the crews of French and British vessels sunk by the Germans. Mrs. Routledge produced a popular account of their experiences, inevitably entitled *The Mystery of Easter Island*.

Twenty years later Lavachery and Métraux led the Franco-Belgian expedition to Easter Island (1934-5). Métraux's *Ethnology of Easter Island* (1940) remains a standard work, but the author also produced the popular *Easter Island: A Stone Age Civilization of the Pacific*. After a further gap of twenty years, the Norwegian Archaeological Expedition to Easter Island and the East Pacific arrived in 1955. This group, which made the most profound impact on Rapanui life, was led by Heyerdahl, who had achieved wide publicity in 1947 as the leader of the Kon-Tiki exploit. Whereas Métraux and Lavachery had been concerned largely with ethnological data, including both material artifacts and legends, Heyerdahl's expedition concentrated upon archaeological work, and was responsible for the first carbon dating of Easter Island materials. Several members of this expedition have repeatedly returned to the island, a number of popular and scientific works have appeared, and the major results are gathered together in *The Archaeology of Easter Island* and *The Art of Easter Island*. Heyerdahl, moreover, effectively revived the myth of Easter Island by his best-selling *Aku-Aku: The Secret of Easter Island*.

After 1955 visitors began to multiply. Whereas CEDIP had always restricted the availability of passage on its vessels, after 1952 the annual Chilean naval supply ship frequently carried newspaper reporters and the curious. From these emerged, during the 1960s, a number of popular paper-covered travel books in Spanish; these fanned the growing Chilean interest in Easter Island affairs. Foreigners were also carried, and similar volumes appeared in French and were later translated into Spanish. The French reading public was also served by Mazière's *Mysteries of Easter Island*, product of the French Easter Island Expedition of 1963. Hard on the heels of the French came the Canadian Medical Expedition to Easter Island (METEI, 1964-5) which began to publish its microbiological work in the mid-1970s. A number of METEI participants have written travel books and popular accounts of the island in British and North American journals.

One unforeseen result of this series of visitors was a growing feeling in Chile that Easter Island had been neglected and that social conditions required amelioration. The work of Métraux, for example, was partially responsible for a surge of interest which led the Chilean authorities to establish the first resident doctor, the first permanent school, and the first resident priest since 1871. These initial attempts at modernization did not have immediate results. A healthier and better-educated population, however, was being prepared for the struggles which took place a generation later.

Rapanui Uprisings

Chilean authorities were also made aware of their colonial responsibilities by the actions of the islanders themselves. Throughout the period of alien domination indigenous rebellions have periodically taken place, beginning, perhaps, with the murder of Dutrou-Bornier in 1877 and continuing with the anti-Toro unrest of 1892 (Chapter 3). The murder of the last Rapanui king in 1899, possibly by Merlet, and Merlet's firing of Rapanui crops, also provoked anti-company demonstrations in 1900. Twentieth century uprisings have captured headlines in Chilean newspapers and even abroad, severely agitating both alien residents and mainland officialdom.

The Routledge expedition found itself embroiled in a major revolt during 1914, an outcome of the further abuse of power by Merlet (Chapter 4). At this time Percy Edmunds, the harassed CEDIP manager, and also *subdelegado marítimo*, was the sole representative of both company and government. Antagonism towards CEDIP had been growing for some years, especially because of Merlet's desire to use the Rapanui as cheap or unpaid labour on the sheepranch. In June 1914 Angata, an old woman, was led by a dream sent by God to declare that Merlet had died, that the island belonged to the Polynesians, and that a symbolic feast of company beef and mutton should be celebrated without delay.

1914 was the apogee of empire. Mrs. Routledge rather scornfully compared the rising to "a Gilbertian opera."[1] The Rapanui claims, however, as presented to Mr. Edmunds, were no more unreasonable than the rash of expropriations of alien enterprise which has swept the Third World since independence. In this premature expropriation attempt the Rapanui declared (as translated for Routledge by Edmunds):

> We desire to take all the animals in the camp . . . for you know that all the animals and farm in the camp belong to us, our Bishop Tepano (Jaussen) gave us originally . . . There is another business . . . who gave the animals to Merlet also who gave the earth to Merlet because it is a big robbery. They took this possession of ours, and they give nothing for the earth, money or goods or anything else . . .[2]

As the white party, including six expedition members, totalled only five men, one woman, and a boy, nothing could be done to prevent the islanders from slaughtering and eating cattle and sheep, from breaking into the wool warehouse and other property, and from ranging over the whole island, previously out of bounds to them. In view of their former strong links with Tahiti, it is perhaps significant that the rebels flew a home-made tricolor.

The siege of Mataveri was relieved only by the arrival of the Chilean warship *Baquedano*, whose captain, though restoring order at once, was clearly unsympathetic towards CEDIP and the British Scientific Expedition. He was unable to guarantee the safety of the latter, and considered the Rapanui had "behaved very well not to murder Mr. Edmunds."[3] With the ensuing death of Angata and the exile of several young islanders to Chile, the rebellion came to an end.

After the troubles of 1914, and the consequent lengthy controversy between Chile and CEDIP (Chapter 4), the single company manager was supplemented by an assistant, and a Chilean naval official was usually in residence. This did not prevent the murder of a white company overseer before the end of the decade. Métraux observed that disturbances had continued in the 1920s, and that "the natives are constantly incited against the company."[4] The tone of several contemporary visitors is distinctly pro-CEDIP.[5] Casey, however, was able to see the indigenous point of view.[6] Life for CEDIP overseers apparently remained precarious into the 1930s. According to a manager of the early 1930s: "There's no law out here. This place is like the American frontier in 'forty-nine."[7] Agitation, unrest, discontent, and labour troubles continued into the 1940s[8] and 1950s.[9]

NAVAL RULE AND POLITICAL CHANGE 1953-73

The history of Easter Island is one of autocracy. In the century since 1865 missionaries, commercial freebooters, multinational corporations, and military forces have sought to impose their will on the island. Accordingly, the political situation has always been ambiguous, with two or more foci of power, though usually of grossly unequal strength.

The Naval Presence

During the company state era, Chile maintained a presence in the shape of a prefect of police and some navy personnel, usually a radio operator and a *practicante* (nurse orderly) after the 1930s. Justice arrived irregularly in the form of the captain of a naval vessel. As Casey demonstrated in the early 1930s, however, it was CEDIP, not the Chilean representative, which "impressed its will on the land and exercised a godlike power over life and death."[10] For the company, through its ownership of the stock, precariously guarded by a Rapanui-manned company police force, as well as of the annual supply vessel, controlled the island's nonvegetable food supply. Feeble attempts at unionization among the Rapanui workers could be quelled by withholding cash, sugar, flour, and other items in great demand.[11]

Attempts by the resident Chilean authorities to interfere with company policies could be met with similar withdrawal of privileges or even by threats of violence.[12] As Ferdon remarks:

> You cannot successfully put a government representative on the island to watch a company when he is completely at their mercy for food, supplies, and even radio communication. There was no middle ground . . . he was either fighting the company outright and living off the islanders' good will or he was completely on the side of the company where good food and housing awaited him.[13]

It is not surprising that many officials took the latter course.

Nevertheless, the occasional visits of Chilean warships firmly established the Chilean Navy as a further, although impermanent, power focus.[14] Over the years, naval interest increased and by the time Williamson, Balfour sold out after World War II, CEDIP had become a "hot political potato."[15] The revocation of the company lease in 1952 (Chapter 4) and the subsequent installation of the Navy as controller of the island was intended as an administrative basis for social improvement. The Navy, however, began by administering the island as if it were a ship, "with a commander as governor, a second-in-command, a navy doctor, paymaster, three petty officers, four sargeants, three corporals, four marines, one seaman medical helper, and a naval carpenter."[16]

Military control of this type is generally not a strong preference of the citizen. The administration of noncitizens in the Pacific, however, has frequently taken this form.[17] Being chiefly concerned with the naval station at Pago Pago, the United States government placed the administration of Eastern Samoa after 1899 in the hands of the Navy Department. Similarly, a naval officer ruled Guam from the same date. In both instances the naval authorities ruled absolutely and paternalistically. Their commercial incompetence was emphasized by poor local resources and isolation from markets. Their introduction of a money economy was inconsistent with extreme paternalism, and in any case helped only those few who obtained work at naval installations. The discipline of previous regimes was reinforced; any signs of "mutiny" against the "commander" of the "ship" were summarily quashed. The same syndrome took place on Easter Island.

In the 1930s Métraux had stated: "The Williamson and Balfour Company is the only real link the natives have with western civilization."[18] The Navy took on this role. From 1952 the annual company vessel was replaced by the yearly naval supply ship. Imported goods were available from a naval commissary, rather than a company store. From 1868 to 1952 the sheepmasters had ruled the island from Mataveri. In the latter year the Mataveri ranch house was designated as the residence of the island's military governor.[19] From this ancient seat of power the Navy controlled the *fundo* (sheepranch), although when civilian help was called in the *fundo* was increasingly run from Vaitea; it was at Vaitea that several strikes for better wages occurred. Sheepraising remained the island's economic raison d'etre, and the naval authorities were enjoined to make wool production a profitable concern. Inheriting the attitudes of CEDIP, as well as its stock, the Navy forbade the Rapanui to leave Hangaroa without permission. Unlike the company, the Navy had sufficient personnel, discipline, and firearms to enforce this statute.

The Chilean literature, not surprisingly, contains many allusions to the beneficent nature of naval rule.[20] Despite the islanders' continuing lack of citizen's rights, which it had campaigned for, the mainland Friends of Easter Island Society made no complaints against the naval presence, which it had been instrumental in bringing about.[21] According to Campbell, the "*paternalista y generoso*" rule of the Navy was "the happiest moment in two centuries of Easter Island history."[22] From the point of view of the Rapanui, however, a typical Latin American coup had occurred, for only the ruler had changed. The basic social, economic, and political system developed in the company state era continued largely as before.

There is even some evidence that a certain number of the Easter Islanders would have preferred the old regime to continue, with a forceful naval presence as a counter-balance against company control.[23] Father Sebastian Englert, a Capuchin who had been the island's priest since 1935, was fervently opposed to naval rule, to the mainland campaign which had brought it about, and to its likely consequences:

> It is a profound error. To bring mainlanders to the island will disturb the islanders; those natives who have gone to the mainland have been corrupted. A perfidious cam-

> paign of lies has totally misrepresented the reality of the island . . .[24]

As paternalist as the company and the Navy, Englert ignored the growing demands for change which were burgeoning among those few Rapanui who had travelled to Chile or elsewhere.

The "Revolution" of 1964-5

A considerable wave of unrest swept the Pacific islands during the 1950s. French autocracy in Tahiti, for example, led to the emergence of a popular leader, strikes, anti-French violence, and a short-lived independence movement.[25] With relatives in Tahiti, Easter Islanders could not be unmoved by these actions. Moreover, in the early 1960s a French expedition spent several months on the island. Mazière and his Tahitian wife took a strong anti-Navy line, finding the military authorities officious and overbearing.[26] Mazière suggests that the distribution of meat and milk to the Rapanui was extremely restricted, although by this time many of the islanders had acquired their own beasts.[27] Moreover, Rapanui wishing to cross the boundary wall were compelled to seek written permission in the form of a pass.[28] The wall was supplemented by barbed wire, and its two gates were apparently locked at 6 p.m. Within the reserve were "1,000 Easter Islanders living in the most unbelievable wretchedness and lack of freedom."[29]

Mazière was especially concerned that Rapanui who wished to leave were prevented from doing so by the Navy. A strong desire to leave the island had been prevalent as early as the 1870s.[30] Some few had left in small open boats, mainly for Tahiti, as late as the 1950s. An investigation of this desire to leave was one of the few specifically sociological goals of METEI.[31] Reid suggests that in the mid-1960s up to 70 requests were made per year to sail to Chile with the annual ship.[32] Of these only about a score received permission, reasons for refusals including lack of space, lack of jobs or relatives in Chile, and fear of transmitting leprosy to the mainland. Restricted in their ability to travel to the country of which they were theoretically citizens, and confined to a minute section of their homeland, "because it *belongs* to the Chileans," the islanders' lives in 1965 were more spatially restricted than in 1865.[33] Further, priests and school staff who regarded the Rapanui essentially as children were effectively prolonging the infantilization process which is common in company states and had been in operation in Easter Island since the 1860s.[34]

By 1964, however, a generation of schooling, religious instruction, and medical attention had enlarged indigenous horizons. During Navy rule the number of islanders visiting the mainland was certainly greater than in the company era, in the early years of which deportation from the island had been used as a punishment. Selected school children spent entire years away from their families. Military service on the mainland made many male islanders aware of alternative lifestyles and economic opportunities. Moreover, the Rapanui had become aware that the citizens of Chile enjoyed universal suffrage. Although officially citizens of Valparaiso province, Easter Islanders in 1964 still had no vote at any level. Males, it is true, could vote for a native council, but membership of this advisory body was subject to the approval of the military governor.[35] In effect, the Easter Islanders of 1964 were as much a colonized people as they had been when annexed in 1888.

Revolution was probably inevitable. An islander who had returned from the mainland as a school teacher became the leader of the discontented. In October 1964 Eduardo Frei, a reformist, was elected president of Chile; Frei's presidency was characterized by public works programmes, agrarian reform, and a partial nationalization of the American-owned copper industry.[36] An open letter to Frei was sent from Easter Island, complaining of Navy rule. Complaints were made about unpaid labour, travel restrictions, confinement to Hangaroa, suppression of the Rapanui language, ineligibility to vote, and arbitrary naval decisions which could not be appealed.[37] Suggestions for economic diversification were made; it was hoped that "colonialism will end."[38]

As an initial act of defiance the school teacher was voted in as mayor-elect. The military governor declared the election illegal. Sabotage and interrogations followed. Rumours circulated that the revolutionary leader had been influenced by Mazière's support of a Polynesian Union based in Tahiti.[39] Perhaps coincidentally, a French warship appeared off Hangaroa in early January 1965. This was followed by a Chilean warship bearing an investigative commissioner and forty marines, between the Rapanui and whom several confrontations occurred. Colonial attitudes towards Easter Island are clearly exemplified in a marine's statement that the force had come to protect "Chilean people".[40] Revolutionary fervour was defused by the official proclamation of a new election, in which suffrage was extended to women, but excluded illiterates and non-speakers of Rapanui. Despite the lack of such normal electoral features as a secret ballot, the revolutionary leader was elected mayor on 12 January 1965.

The commission promised to seek a new constitution for the island. In fact, this was already under debate in an embarrassed Chile, and Easter

Island was rapidly granted the status of a civil department within the province of Valparaiso.[41] Officials were authorized to inaugurate a municipal system of government in Hangaroa. The first meeting of an official *junta de vecinos* (neighbourhood council) took place on 16 March 1966, and the municipal constitution came into effect only on 21 May 1967.[42]

The minutes (*actas*) of this municipality's meetings are unremarkable, and deal with such normal civil functions as the regulation of vehicles, building permits, liquor outlets, sanitation, markets, fish and fruit prices, and the like. Having no power to tax, the municipal authorities were supported by government grants and a percentage of the profits of the Viña del Mar casino.[43] By 1973 the municipality had made some progress as the official voice of the islanders. *Acta* 136, 28 August 1973, records a debate on how to celebrate the forthcoming Chilean national day, September 18th. The military coup of 11 September supervening, the previously-inscribed title, "*Acta* 137," remains without a text. As throughout Chile, civilian rule was immediately terminated.

MODERNIZATION: EXTERNAL IMPACTS

Two events of profound importance enhanced the changes begun by the islanders' assertion of their right to control local affairs. For the first time, a people whose only link with the outside world had been an annual vessel from Valparaiso were presented with a weekly air service to Santiago and, later, Tahiti. Moreover, shortly after the inauguration of the air link a large contingent of Americans settled on the island for several years. For the Rapanui it was their first long-term contact with a sizeable group of foreigners of non-Chilean provenance.

The American Presence

In the mid-1960s an agreement with Chile enabled the United States to set up a tracking station on Easter Island ostensibly for the surveillance of artificial earth satellites. By January 1967 about 80 Americans, largely military, were constructing the facility on Rano Kao, together with a base camp at Mataveri.[44] Scientific equipment, machinery, generators, fuel, housing, vehicles, and food supplies were imported. Communications were enhanced by weekly flights from Panama; being unable to land on Easter Island, the planes dropped mail, medicines, and other goods by parachute. As such materials previously reached the island only on the annual boat, it proved convenient to send them from Santiago to Hangaroa via Panama.[45]

The American presence appears to have been received favourably by the islanders.[46] *El Mercurio*, the conservative Santiago newspaper, reported that the Americans behaved respectfully, duly regarded island customs, and "drank only beer, of Chilean manufacture."[47] Some attempt was made to reap spillover benefits by the opening of bars and *discos* in Hangaroa.[48] One of the chief effects of the American presence, however, was to provide islanders with new behavior and aspirational models somewhat at variance with Chilean lifestyles.

On leaving the island in 1971 the American military contingent left a significant quantity of *materiel* on the island. Scientific equipment was left for the use of FACh (the Chilean Air Force) in its investigation of Pacific meteorology. FACh, which had been in nominal control throughout, also took over the American camp as an air base. An electricity generator, various types of vehicles and machinery, aluminum trailers, housing, and hangars were left for use by a variety of public agencies. Although the station was partially re-activated in 1975, only two American servicemen were brought in to man it.

Scheduled Air Services

The creation of an airfield at Mataveri was by far the most effective of the many agents of change which operated in Easter Island after 1965. The profound impact of rapid air communication with the outside world might best be appreciated by a consideration of previous linkages.

Until 1967 Easter Island laboured under the grave disadvantage of extreme isolation. For 70 years, since the time of Merlet, the island had relied upon a single boat per year from Valparaiso for food supplies, the exchange of government, religious, military and CEDIP personnel, and the export of the wool clip. Years in which several boats called were balanced by occasional years during which no boat appeared from Chile. Cancellation of the official annual vessel, which occurred in 1965 during the stay of the METEI expedition, caused considerable hardship. On this occasion island residents were left without soap, coffee, and sugar for four months, and without antibiotics for six. The government store ran out of food and clothing and closed for several months.[49] In the early 1960s, then, Easter Island was probably more isolated than it had been a hundred years before, when boat connections with both Tahiti and Chile occurred several times per year.[50] Little wonder that, as in most isolated islands, visiting vessels received a tumultuous welcome. The call of a ship remained a major social event into the 1960s, and is still the occasion for a gathering at the landing point.[51]

Trans-Pacific air routes became inevitable after Kingsford-Smith's epochal flight from California to Australia in 1928, which stimulated a scramble between Britain and the United States to occupy tenantless but strategic coral isles such as Canton Island.[52] The possibility of an air service to Easter Island was not seriously considered until 1951 when one Roberto Parragué flew an amphibious Catalina to Mataveri from the Chilean mainland in 19 hours.[53] A second Catalina arrived soon afterwards from Australia. Parragué made further flights, including one from Easter Island to Tahiti in 1965. Up to this time the provisional airstrip at Mataveri consisted of grass and wire matting, serviced by six Chilean FACh personnel.[54]

A scheduled transPacific air route from Europe via South America to Australia had been under consideration since the 1940s. Interest revived in the 1950s when France upgraded the Faaa airport on Tahiti in connection with tourist promotion and the French Pacific nuclear testing programme.[55] Because of the short range of civil aircraft at this time, Easter Island was considered a vital stepping stone on the Tahiti to southern South America leg.[56] Thus the island was able to help fill a major gap in the global air network before direct overflights between Santiago, Lima, and Tahiti began in the early 1970s (Figure 1,8).

Work began on the Mataveri airport in 1965. The fairly level stretch of land between Hanga Piko and Vinapu was chosen after a larger airport site at Anakena was rejected on the grounds of high cost.[57] In early 1967 FACh tested the new 2,000-metre (6,560-foot) runway with C-118 and Douglas DC-6 equipment.[58] The first commercial flight, using a LAN (Chilean Air Lines) DC-6B, took place on 3 April 1967, when the flight time from Santiago to Mataveri was almost nine hours.[59] In February 1968 the route was extended to Tahiti, and in 1970 the substitution of Boeing 707 jets cut flight time in half, and permitted an extension to Fiji by 1974. These improvements were followed by impressive increases in passenger traffic (Table 1,8). After 1971 a twice-weekly schedule was inaugurated. The Boeing equipment, moreover, enabled LAN to operate a weekly direct flight between Santiago and Tahiti, in competition with Air France's Lima-Tahiti route.

Full realisation of Easter Island's potential for the generation of air traffic was initially prevented by infrastructural inadequacies. Although Santiago-Mataveri flights often operated at 90 percent capacity, the single Mataveri runway was too short to permit the carrying of more than 85 passengers, in a 150-seat plane, on the Mataveri-Faaa leg. Until lengthening took place in

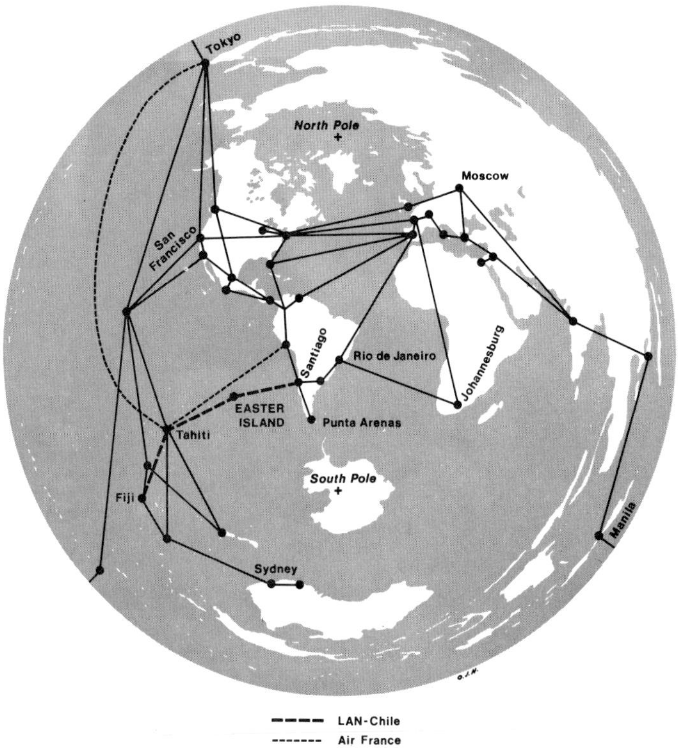

FIGURE 1,8 Transpacific air routes, 1975. Unusual projection from LAN-Chile promotional material.

the mid-1970s, every flight to Tahiti suffered a potential loss of 40 percent of its payload.[60] Figures for the first five years of the service suggest that overall operating costs were only just matched by income.[61] In January 1977 Air France terminated its competitive Lima-Tahiti route because of heavy losses.

MODERNIZATION: INFRASTRUCTURE

During the late 1960s the mainland government was concerned to expunge the island's former "colonial" status, to upgrade the conditions of life of a people who were both locationally and socio-economically marginal to Chile, and to achieve "the incorporation of the islander into the mainstream

TABLE 1,8 Air Traffic Santiago—Easter Island—Tahiti 1967-71

Year	Number of Passengers	Annual Increase (per cent)	Frequency	Aircraft
1967	444	—	monthly	DC-6B
1968	1,575	254.7	fortnightly	DC-6B
1969	1,851	17.7	fortnightly	DC-6B
1970	8,192	342.6	weekly	Boeing 707
1971	11,403	39.2	weekly	Boeing 707

SOURCE: adapted from ODEPLAN: *Plan de Desarrollo del Departamento de Isla de Pascua* (1972), p. 50.

of national life."[62] Accordingly, an elaborate plan for the improvement of utilities, social services, communications, transport, and housing was announced, with the deliberate intention of effecting rapid "transformation and modernization."[63] Infrastructural improvements were motivated on the one hand by the need to provide basic standards for a nascent tourist industry, and on the other by feelings of guilt regarding Chile's neglect of the island during the previous 80 years.[64]

Utilities

In 1774 Captain Cook found the water on Easter Island not only scarce but "so bad as not to be worth carrying on board."[65] Until the 1960s the majority of the population relied largely upon rooftop tanks for rainwater catchment; wells of sweet water at Mataveri and Vaitea were reserved for alien administrators. From the 1920s wells and windmills, and piped water from the interior crater lakes were used to water stock (Chapter 7). In 1914 the Routledge expedition was severely discommoded when the Mataveri roof tank ran dry; the METEI expedition of 1964 brought its own solar still.[66] As late as the 1950s, during exceptionally dry seasons, recourse had to be made to the crater lakes.[67]

After 1964 CORFO (the Chilean Development Corporation) made extensive test bores, finding major aquifers at Mataveri and behind Hangaroa. From 1967 houses and establishments in Mataveri and the central area of Hangaroa were provided with a piped water supply, though peripheral areas remained unconnected. Although Mataveri water is sweet, the water supplied to the town is slightly brackish, and many users retain supplementary roof tanks. Extension of the service is held back by the high capital cost of servicing scattered houses, many on 5-hectare (12-acre) lots.

Electricity supply was begun by the Navy and, based on a deisel generator, most of Hangaroa was given a basic service, including street lighting. Use of the donated American generator permitted an amplification of the system. By the early 1970s houses in Mataveri and central Hangaroa were fully electrified, and usage had grown to such an extent that a tariff was instituted in 1973.

Garbage disposal became a problem after 1965 when changing lifestyles and the growing importation of commercial goods increased its generation. The high cost of returning empty bottles and oil drums to the mainland renders necessary their disposal locally. The oil drums, however, have several uses, and are employed in house, fence, and raft building, for storage, and for water troughs.

Social Services

Although education in Easter Island remained disorganized throughout the CEDIP period, a small bilingual Rapanui-Spanish text entitled *Te Poki Rapanui* (The Easter Island Child) was published as early as 1923 by Vives Solar, a former *subdelegado*.[68] It included short homilies which vainly exhorted the Rapanui to imitate the Tahitians and Pitcairn Islanders in the planting of commercial crops, so that they too might "have good houses and live elegantly." In 1934, when the first regular public school appeared, almost 54 percent of the population was illiterate.[69] A female religious order ran the school until the late 1960s when, coincidentally with the growth of the Chilean expatriate population, a new building was erected and secular instructors appointed. Beyond primary level, however, education was available only on the mainland until 1978. By the mid-1970s several Easter Islanders were attending universities in Chile and the United States.

Medical facilities were also upgraded in the 1960s. Except for the leprosarium, staffed by nuns and visited annually by a naval doctor, no permanent medical facilities existed until the establishment of a naval doctor in the early 1950s. Although a naval nursing orderly was generally present, occasional medical missions had to be supported by private groups such as the Friends of Easter Island Society.[70] By 1965 leprosy had been reduced to only about a score of cases, only six of which required isolation. Other, more contagious, diseases, such as tuberculosis, were a greater problem.[71] As the island was so infrequently visited, a catarrhal fever, *kokongo*, swept through the island upon the arrival of any vessel.[72] Although of long standing, *kokongo* diminished within a few years of the inauguration of regular air connection with Chile.

METEI found Easter Island's makeshift hospital lacking modern diagnostic or operating equipment, with poor drug supplies and no immunization programme for most common communicable diseases. Moreover, islanders could be exploited by the single doctor, one of whom, in a total of 190 operations, performed 76 gall bladder removals.[73] Facilities were radically improved in 1965 when METEI donated its prefabricated 20-bed hospital complete with generators, laboratory, X-ray equipment, and ambulance. Ten years later this Canadian hospital was superseded by a new structure. Because of staffing problems, however, eye problems and most serious cases require travel to Santiago.

Transport and Communications

Improved radiotelephone, telegraph, and postal services followed the influx of mainlanders after 1965. Since 1972 over one hundred telephones have been installed. FACh set up a small radio station and by 1975 a television transmitter was broadcasting videotapes. The single naval supply ship was replaced by EMPREMAR, a state-owned shipping agency which established twice-yearly sailings between Hanga Piko and Valparaiso. Little improvement was made to the facilities at Hanga Piko and Hangaroa Bay, although the lighters constructed of oil drums were replaced in the mid-1970s by landing craft, and an alternative quay was begun on the north coast. Sea traffic, however, remained light. During the four years 1967-70 approximately 1,650 tons of goods were imported annually, the return cargo consisting of a wool clip varying between 60 and 75 tons per year.[75]

With Navy rule the number of motor vehicles on Easter Island radically increased. To accommodate these, roads were graded and Hangaroa's streets widened. As no surfacing was done, the streets of Hangaroa are clogged with red mud after a heavy rainfall. The widening and straightening of the streets to create broad avenues in the Latin American style was destructive of many trees, particularly a fine avenue of figs planted, appropriately enough, by the early missionaries.

PLATE 33
The road to
Hangaroa

PLATE 34
Fishermen at work
beside road to
Hangaroa

MODERNIZATION: URBAN HANGAROA

The deliberate modernization of Easter Island involved the transformation of Hangaroa from a straggling village, focussed upon the church, into a subtropical town linked to the Mataveri military base by broad, straight avenues (Figures 4,6, 3,7, 2,8).

Housing

In the 1870s the most common dwelling remained the indigenous, reed-thatched, boat-shaped house (Chapter 6).[76] At the turn of the century these traditional shelters had largely been replaced by timber, thatch, and galvanized metal cabins, built in the European style, and deriving their materials from shipwrecks.[77] In 1918 34 of the 46 houses were of wood, 11 of stone, and one of stone and cement.[78] Wood, still very much a scarce material, was the preferred medium. The CEDIP houses at Mataveri and Vaihu were of wood, as were the dwellings of permanent company workers located in Moeroa, the Hangaroa subdistrict closest to Mataveri. In contrast, about one third of Hangaroa's 36 houses were of stone, although the houses of the *subdelegado marítimo*, the Frenchman Pont, and of CEDIP's indigenous supporters were of wooden construction. The poorest inhabited dwellings were made from stray loose planks, cloth, and flattened metal.[79] Some of these cabins were as small as 3 x 5 metres (10 x 16 feet), and most were overcrowded and unhygenic. By the early 1930s Hangaroa had become "a cluster of clapboard and sheet iron huts."[80]

A general lack of furniture was remarked upon by visitors from Loti in 1872 to the expeditions of the early 1960s.[81] As late as 1965 it was estimated that 46 percent of the population lacked an individual bed.[82] Immediately prior to the naval takeover the indigenous inhabitants of Hangaroa occupied 109 houses, mostly of only two to three rooms each, and averaging three or four persons per room.[83] Many had a separate kitchen building, which is not uncommon in the 1980s, but only 20 had any form of sanitary facility. However, 25 cement houses were under construction, but remained incomplete because of delays in the transport of material from Chile.

For those who secured jobs with government agencies during the Navy period, housing conditions improved with better access to local stone, imported wood, and cement. As the supply of imported materials remained dependent upon boat deliveries, however, the Hangaroa townscape since the 1950s has been characterized by a score or more of unfinished dwellings. These are now complemented by complete but vacant houses left by families which have migrated to the mainland.

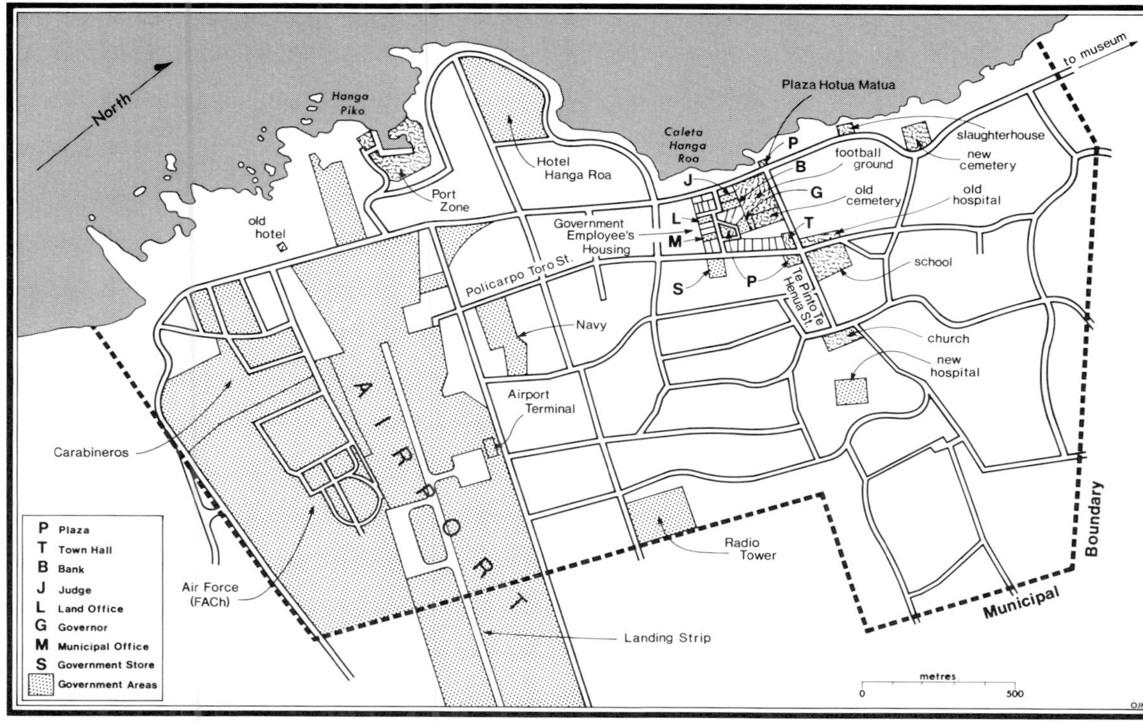

FIGURE 2,8 The urban plan of Hangaroa, 1975.

During the late 1960s several new housing types emerged to challenge the predominant one-storey hand-built wooden cabin. Trailers left by both Canadians and Americans were used as dwellings. Prefabricated housing units were brought from Chile to house Navy, FACh, *carabinero*, and civil government personnel.[84] Except for a few rather incongruous A-frames, the wholly single-storey housing is not destructive of visual landscape amenity, especially in the heavily treed areas of Hangaroa.

The Urban Plan

Since the 1860s the single major settlement zone has been characterized by two major foci (Chapter 6).[85] In Hangaroa proper the church formed the nodal point for the indigenous population. At Mataveri alien administrators occupied a distinct sector based on the farmhouse. This bipolarity is still apparent more than a century later, and is reflected in the characteristic layout of each area (Figure 2,8).

Street planning in the Mataveri military zone, occupied chiefly by FACh, the Navy, and the *carabineros*, reflects the occupants' predominant ethos of order and regularity. The compact gridded layout is relieved only by a few curved residential streets. In each of the three separate military compounds houses are arranged close together in rows. LAN, CORFO, and other agency housing is located close by.

In complete contrast, the bulk of Hangaroa resembles a sprawling subtropical agricultural town. Here the straight streets and regular parcellation of the military zone are replaced by a mosaic of irregularly-shaped land parcels connected not only by winding streets but also by an intricate system of pathways which cross fields, scale stone walls, and penetrate shrubberies. Most houses are set well back from the street in lots ranging in size up to 5 hectares (12 acres). Many lots are used for vegetable and fruit production, especially bananas, so that the townscape has a heavily-treed, plantation-like appearance. Houses are well separated from each other. On the periphery of the town cultivated land begins at the back door, although much formerly cultivated land is now covered in guayaba shrubbery, adding to the generally overgrown appearance.

The chief axis of Hangaroa remains the original main street, named Te Pito Te Henua, running downhill from the church to Hangaroa (Cook's) Bay. On or near this axis lie the church, the school, and old and new hospitals, the old cemetery, the football ground, two small plazas with erect *moai*, the tiny beach of Pea, and the small fishing community who inhabit makeshift hand-built homes in the squatter style.

PLATE 35
Chilean housing and bank, Hangaroa

PLATE 36
Cemetery on the urban fringe

Original
Missionary
Land Purchase
Church
H A N G A R O A
Site of
Chilean Housing
and Government
Caleta
Hangaroa
Cemetery

Site of
Airport
To
Rano Kao
Crater
Site of
Air Force
Base
MATAVERI
Former
Company
Ranch-house
Hanga Piko
Site of
Hotel

Polynesian Hangaroa and military Mataveri represent extreme differences in cultural world views. In the late 1960s an attempt was made to connect the two by interposing civil government facilities along the widened avenue, Policarpo Toro, running from the Hangaroa axis to the airport. A third focus was created around a small flagpoled plaza, about which were arranged the governor's office, land office, bank, fire station, municipal office, magistracy, and telegraph office. Housing for associated personnel was interspersed. Nearby, on Policarpo Toro avenue, were located the ECA store and the open market. This connecting street has become the modest commercial axis of the town, with several small stores and bottle outlets, a private tourist agency, the post office, and several houses selling carved artifacts. As distances between houses and facilities are great, and no public transportation exists, the superabundance of horses on Easter Island proves useful by providing an important means of intraurban transportation.

◀ **PLATE 37** Aerial photograph showing settlement structure of the immediately premodernization period

PLATE 38 Fish (Kon-Tiki Museet artifact 2182) ▶

PLATE 39 Tourists at Rano Raraku ▶

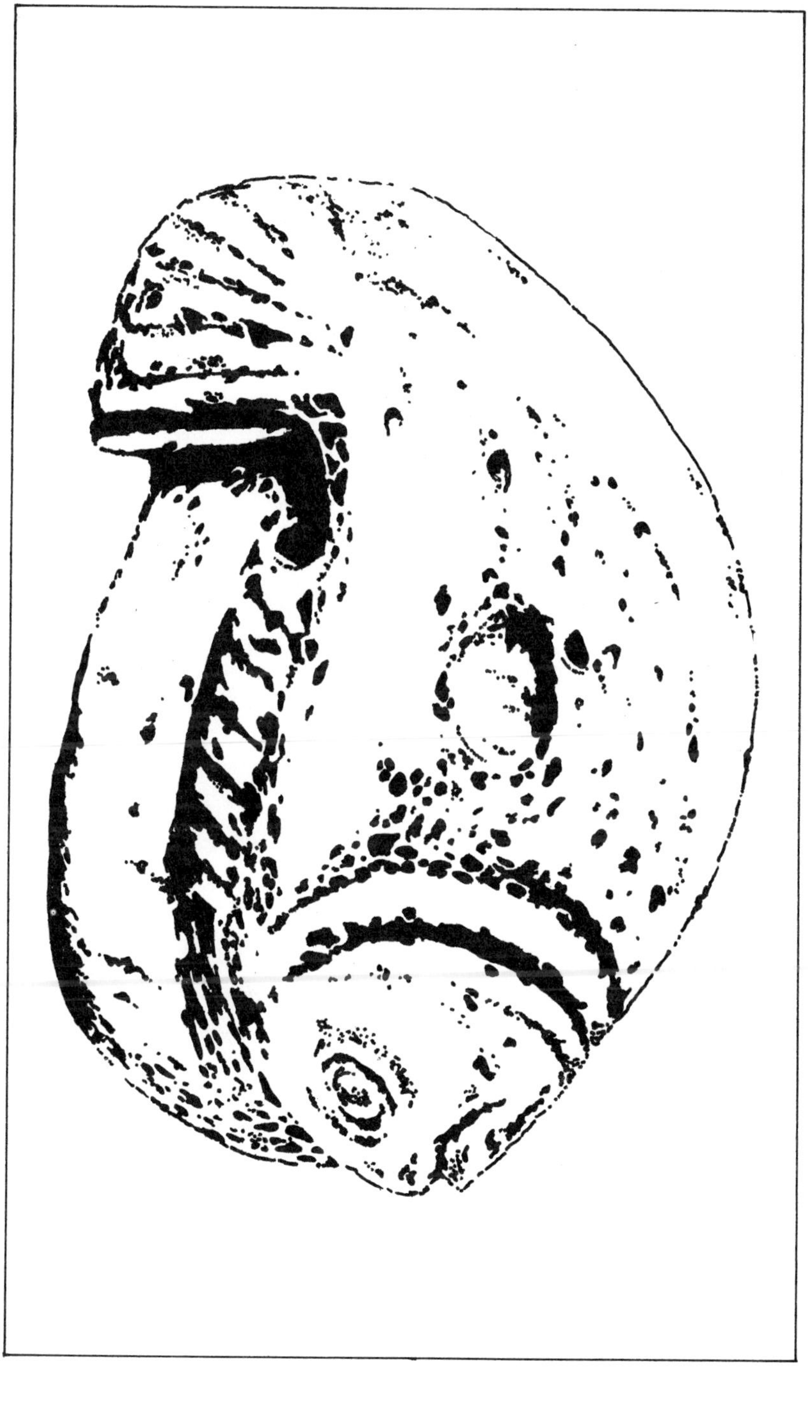

9 THE DEVELOPMENT OF TOURISM

> Peripheral cultures only retain their air of antiquity and their ethnic individuality by virtue of their isolation from the dominant and expanding cultures of the metropoles. This is especially true of the remote island cultures of . . . the South Pacific . . . By the building of an airport capable of taking jets, the antique, the ethnic and the pristine . . . are immediately threatened.
>
> Louis Turner, John Ash

Romantic Western images such as the above tend to disregard the fact that "the antique, the ethnic and the pristine" have frequently been impacted upon and often utterly changed long before the arrival of the first jet airplane. The latter, moreover, may be welcomed by the islander as a release from the burden of isolation, as a means of escape, or as the forerunner of economic improvement. What is clear is that tourism is likely to profoundly influence pre-tourist social systems and may exert deleterious physical pressure on small landmasses.[1] The archaeological artifacts of Easter Island, for example, may irretrievably deteriorate under the pressure of a tourist industry which finds its very raison d'etre in their existence.

THE BASIS FOR TOURISM

With the availability of air flights, the growing publicity given to Easter Island after Heyerdahl's expedition of the 1950s rendered some form of tourism inevitable. Because of the biases of the available literature, it is likely that tourists visiting the island will have little interest in the landscape, and probably little more in the present residents. Landscape features are mentioned only in passing in most available books, and vestiges of pre-1860 cultural traits are not apparent to the untrained eye. Tourist knowledge will lean heavily towards archaeology, and archaeological sites, particularly Orongo, Rano Raraku, and a number of exceptional *ahu* such as Vinapu, will be the most prominent attractions for the visitor. In addition, the generalized South Pacific image is likely to have suggested palm-fringed beaches to many tourists, who will find this phenomenon on Easter Island only at Anakena (Figure 1,9).

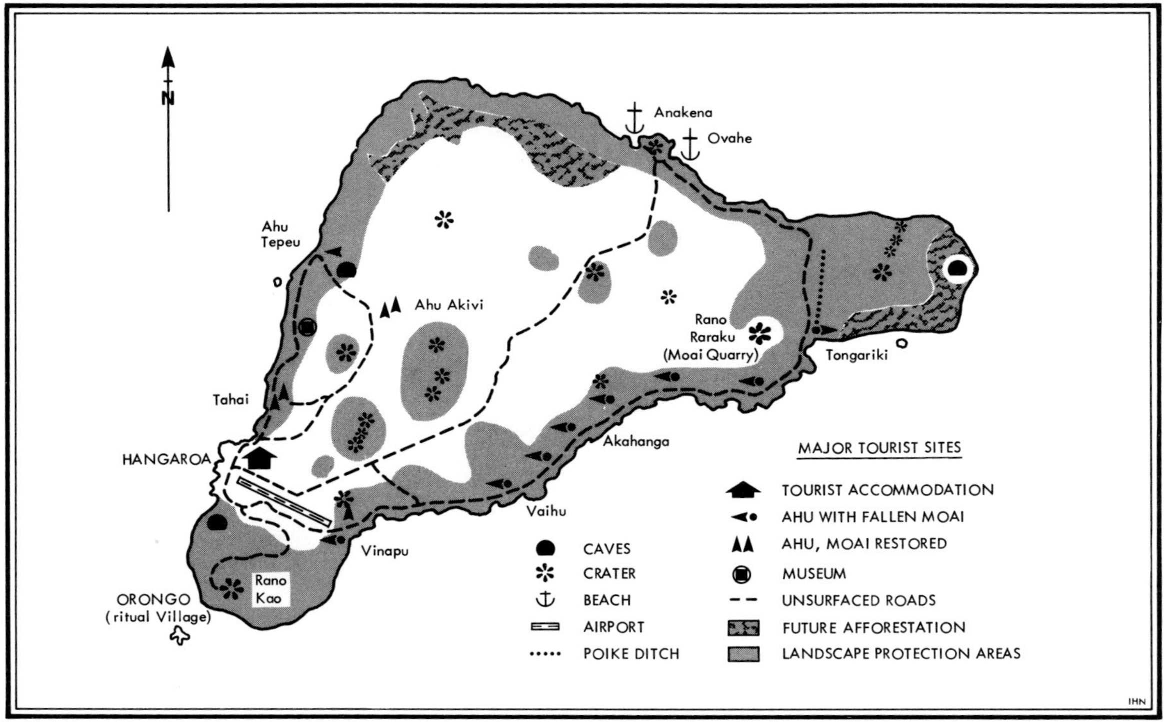

FIGURE 1,9 Major tourist sites.

Archaeological Restoration

After the middle of the nineteenth century, no *moai* stood upright upon an *ahu*. Although ruins and the decayed remnants of civilizations have a strong fascination for many Western tourists, an appreciation of the megalithic achievements of the prehistoric Easter Islanders has been enhanced by the restoration of several traditional ceremonial centres. Restoration has been extremely limited in scope, and has been undertaken by archaeologists for the purposes of preserving crumbling structures, testing theories concerning construction methods, and the faithful renewal of previous structures both as an end in itself and as an opportunity for further study.

Most restoration efforts have taken place since the Norwegian Expedition of 1955. This work indicates a welcome change of attitude toward the island on the part of the outside world, for until the 1960s Easter Island was systematically pillaged of all small artifacts by Europeans, Americans, and Chileans. Only a few *moai* were carried off, but wooden *rongo-rongo* tablets bearing the Easter Island script, painted wall tablets from the Orongo houses, small wood and stone images, weapons, clothing, skulls, and other artifacts now reside in foreign museums and inaccessible private collections in Chile and elsewhere. The meagre display in the island's new museum testifies to the cultural impoverishment which has resulted from the ransacking of the island over the last century.

One of the several small *moai* presently to be seen in central Hangaroa was erected as early as 1939. A further *moai* was re-erected by islanders and Norwegian archaeologists at Anakena in 1955. Figueroa and Mulloy, respectively Chilean and American archaeologists who accompanied the Norwegian Expedition, have been responsible for much of the post-1955 restoration. With the cooperation of the University of Chile and the Fulbright Commission, seven *moai* were set upright at the inland ceremonial centre of Ahu Akivi in 1960. Considerable effort was involved in the restoration of a ceremonial complex and village at Tahai, immediately north of Hangaroa, where traditional stone houses, boat-shaped house foundations, coastal slipways, *ahus*, ceremonial areas, and several erect *moai* may be seen. The only statue complete with red topknot was erected at Tahai with the aid of French funds in 1968. Other important *ahu* restorations include Huri a Urenga, Hanga Kio'e, and most recently, Ahu Naunau (1978).

Restoration has proceeded under the aegis of Chilean government agencies, which have been concerned not only with artifact preservation but also with the creation of tourist attractions.[2] A discussion of Easter Island art, for example, suggested that "this strange, disconcerting, and mysterious culture" would become "a major source of income" for Chile.[3] UNESCO consultants and Chilean commissions have suggested a major restoration

PLATE 40
Moai on launching-pad, Rano Raraku

PLATE 41
Restoration of ahu and seven moai, Ahu Akivi

programme with the object of making the island a "cultural, artistic, and touristic centre."[4]

In the 1970s, the major focus of restoration work was the cult village of Orongo, which was in danger of decomposing into amorphous rubble because of artifact looting, vandalism, the mining of the flat basalt slabs for construction material, erosion, animal depredations, and increased visitor access.[5] As the Orongo stone houses were built with precise counterweighting, the removal of even a few vital slabs can precipitate widespread collapse. Restoration began in July 1974, supported by Chilean government agencies, FACh, American private funds, and significantly, a major American tour operator and LAN, monopolist of island air services.

Beach Destruction

Tourists expecting lush vegetation and other components of the South Pacific image may be disappointed to find a rounded, treeless, windswept, savannah landscape. The image of a golden sand beach is an integral part of the South Seas myth. But Easter Island, because of its lithology and lack of major coral formations, has never enjoyed significant beach development.

In 1955 only four accessible coralline sand beach areas existed. A small beach, Pea, served Hangaroa, and three larger stretches occurred on the north coast at Anakena, Ovahe, and La Pérouse Bay. Modernization, radically increasing demands for construction sand, led to the mining of these beaches. By 1960 the Hangaroa beach had all but disappeared. In 1966 a rock crusher was installed at Mataveri for public works use, but none of its products were supplied to the general public, who continued to mine beaches; the small beach at La Pérouse was destroyed by a mere six months of sand extraction in 1972.[6]

Beach destruction on this scale is a myopic act for a population which increasingly depends upon tourism. The two remaining beaches are important tourist attractions. Ovahe, a small cove floored with roseate sand, is of extraordinary beauty. Nearby Anakena, the island's only sizeable beach, its graceful curve backed by a coconut palm forest planted in 1961, is the only locale which gives concrete expression to the tourist's South Pacific image. Beach destruction has not only reduced tourist potential but has also incensed many residents. Further, sand extraction has directly damaged several archaeological sites at Anakena. Stronger wave erosion consequent upon the almost total beach loss at Hangaroa and La Pérouse has resulted in increased damage to Ahu Tautira and Ahu Nune.

Little attempt was made to regulate sand extraction until 1967, when the municipality tried to restrict beach mining to Ovahe.[7] Beaches, however, are controlled by the Ministry of Defence. Sand extraction has continued, and beach litter at Ovahe has become offensive.[8] No use of the existing rock crusher has been made to produce sand from the abundant volcanic rock of the Hangaroa quarries. It is possible that this sand, if installed in the small bays of the Hangaroa coast, would form sizeable beaches at the point of maximum access for tourist and resident alike. So far, no attempt has been made to reconstitute the beaches so wantonly destroyed.

The Tourist Circuit

Easter Island is an attractive tourist location not only because of its archaeological riches, but also because a cursory view of these attractions may be obtained in as little as one or two days (Figures 1,9-3,9). As organized in the mid-1970s, excursions by vehicle south of Hangaroa typically include the "Cannibal Cave", with refurbished wall paintings, the Rano Kao crater, Orongo, with its restored stone houses, sea and crater views, and groups of important petroglyphs, and the Inca-like *ahu* at Vinapu. North and east of Hangaroa visitors are shown the Punapau crater, source of the red *moai* topknots, several erect *moai*, including the major restoration at Ahu Akivi, the restored ceremonial centre at Tahai, lava tube caves, and an enormous *ahu* and boat-shaped house foundation at Ahu Tepeu.

Excursions around the island include *ahus* at Vinapu, Vaihu, and elsewhere, but the major attractions are at the southwest corner of the island. Here are found the Poike Ditch, scene of intertribal wars, the *moai* quarry at Rano Raraku, where several expeditions have revealed interesting *moai* variants, and the Tongariki *ahu*, from which 45,000 kilogramme (100,000 pound) statues were carried up to 90 metres (100 yards) inland in 1960 by a tsunami (Chapter 5). Following the road north and westwards, the tourist reaches the beaches of Ovahe and Anakena, and then returns to Hangaroa via the interior road. Excursions to other sites usually require prior negotiation, and are often best made on horseback.

THE DEVELOPMENT OF TOURISM

Members of the many European and American South Pacific expeditions may be considered the island's first modern tourists. Their members were concerned to view the strange sites, and to carry off any removable booty. The later, scientific, expeditions were matched by a few tourists and curiosity seekers who managed to secure berths on the annual CEDIP or Navy vessel.

FIGURE 2,9 Poike and Tongariki from Rano Raraku, a major tourist site, as seen by Routledge in 1916 (redrawn).

FIGURE 3,9 Anakena Bay, an important historic and tourist site, as seen by Routledge in 1916 (redrawn).

Antecedents of Tourism

Official recognition of the island's tourist potential was slow to emerge, largely because of accessibility problems. Bryan, however, with his experience of Hawaii, was led to make the following aside while commenting upon Easter Island's temperature regime in 1920:

> Such favorable temperatures for bodily comfort are rare in the world and go far towards making Pascua an ideal resort. The beautiful bathing beach at Anakena and the prevailing agreeable temperature coupled with the extensive unique ethological (sic) ruins, if developed and advertized, would certainly make the Island an ideal recreation ground for the Southern Pacific, vieing in attractiveness with the famous Waikiki . . .[9]

CEDIP, to whom the report was addressed, did not implement this rather premature recommendation.

Chilean government interest in the island as a tourist centre emerged in the 1930s, in response to the realization that the island was rapidly being stripped of its unique artifacts (Chapter 8). Although CEDIP had agreed to preserve archaeological sites, their despoliation continued into the Navy period (Chapter 4).[10] The first steps towards official recognition of the island's heritage were taken in 1935 when Easter Island was declared a National Park and the cutting of *toromiro* forbidden. The latter was a vain gesture, as the tree was by that time almost extinct.[11] Further, the loss of artifacts to the "audacious and scandalous" Franco-Belgian Expedition of Métraux provoked Chilean patriots to seek measures to prevent further removals.[12] All expeditions would hereafter require a license and, officially, no artifact could be removed from the island.[13] The island was declared a Historic Monument in 1935, and an inventory of artifacts was begun.[14]

The continued use of the island as a sheepranch, however, effectively prevented the proper preservation of both trees and monuments. It was not until 1968 that the island was regionalized, and two separate parks instituted (Figure 4,9). No considerable effort was made to conserve or renovate landscape features until late in the period of naval administration; the early recommendations of both Chilean and international historic monument agencies were not fully implemented.[15] Erosion continued almost uncontrolled, notably on the slopes of volcanic cones and around Vaitea. The only erosion control measures attempted consisted of afforestation, rather than the recommended grassland regeneration, and the trees used

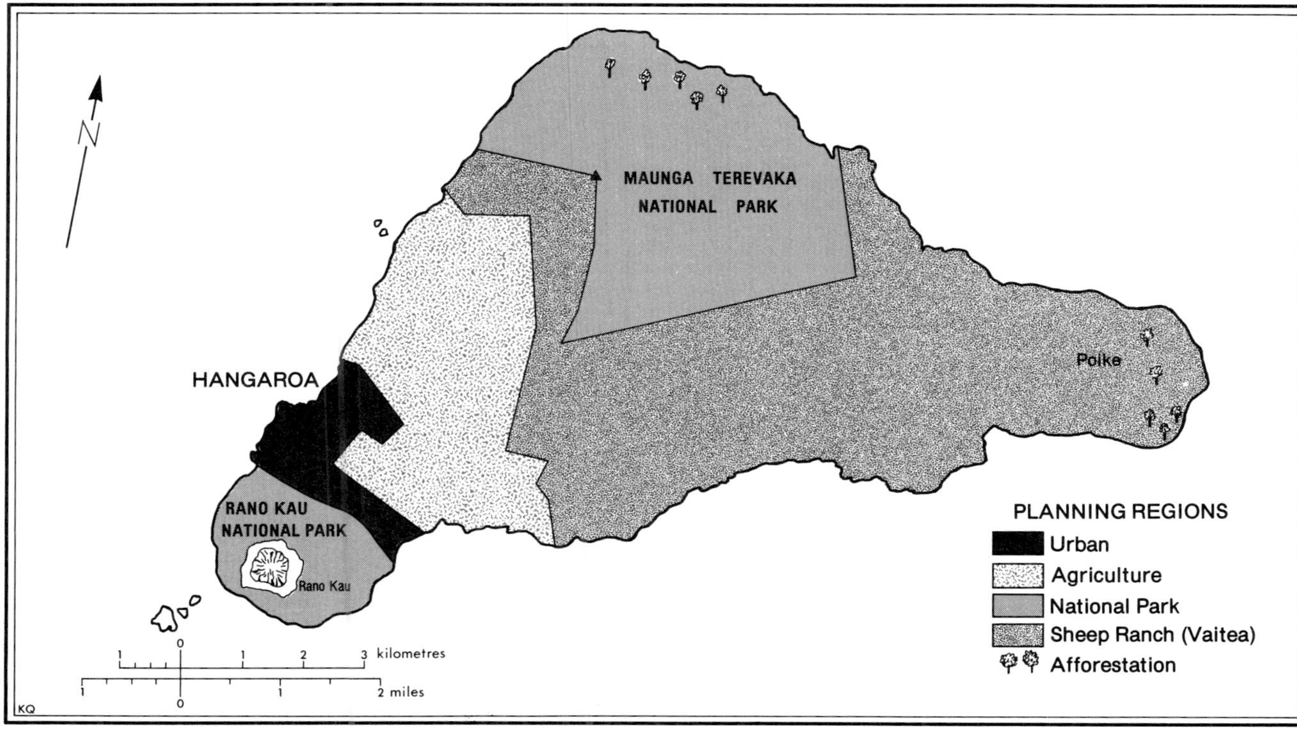

FIGURE 4,9 Easter Island planning regions, 1971 (redrawn from Odeplan, *Plan Sexenal*, 1973).

were largely exotics planted in straight lines, again contravening all recommendations. No attempt was made to plant trees which would provide wood suitable for the carving industry. In sum, according to the National Economic Plan of 1972, the operation of the national parks from 1935 to 1970 in no way conformed to the officially-recognized concept of a Chilean national park.[16] This report recommended a special status for the island, involving rural land use zoning, the restriction of afforestation, and the preservation of the character of the existing landscape.

After the designation of the island as a national park and historic monument, government interest flagged for a generation. Writers of the 1940s felt that afforestation with tropical fruit trees, while of commercial value, would also improve the island's image as a tourist resort.[17] But even in the early 1960s the occasional visitor by sea still complained of the total lack of accommodation for travellers; visiting dignitaries were compelled to lodge in the hospital.[18] Only with modernization and airport construction in the late 1960s did a tourist industry become feasible. It is significant that the first commercial flights to Easter Island in 1967 were largely filled with North American tourists, archaeologists, and travel agents.[19] To accommodate these first tourists LAN, the state airline, and HONSA, the state hotel corporation, collaborated in the provision of tents and food supplies from the mainland.[20]

Tourist promotion was aided by publicity campaigns in the United States and by the publication of leaflets in Spanish and English. It was also felt that the growth of tourism in Tahiti during the 1960s would have significant spillover effects on Easter Island.[21] An American tourist agency specializing in excursions to remote locations was the first to promote package tours, operating five two-week tours in each of 1968 and 1969. Several American, French, and other foreign agencies developed special links with Easter Island in the 1970s, and LAN has promoted both Easter Island and combined Easter Island-Galápagos tours. It was hoped that tourism, in conjunction with the new South Pacific air route, would not only revive the island's economy but would also reaffirm Chile's geopolitical position in Oceania.[22]

The Tourist Infrastructure

After the problem of access to a region rich in touristic interest has been solved, the nascent tourist industry must rapidly provide accommodation, food supplies, and transportation to individual tourist attractions. In major cities much existing infrastructure can be used, but remote locations are faced with the problem of creating a totally new system, the components of which are usually not available locally. In the case of food supplies the bulk of tourist consumption, especially in the hotel, is imported, local agriculture not having yet responded to the challenge.

Motor vehicles were not extensively used on Easter Island until after World War II; their numbers increased rapidly with the naval administration, with modernization, and with the United States presence in the late 1960s. The growth of tourism led to the importation, in 1971 alone, of at least six vehicles and a small 17-seat bus. Multipurpose vehicles such as jeeps, station wagons, and microbuses are used; ordinary automobiles are rare. By 1971 at least 15 vehicles were available for the transportation of tourists (Table 1,9). Of these, 10 had been acquired since 1965. Approximately 150 tourists can be moved at any one time, a capacity which becomes restrictive only when a major cruise ship arrives. Other vehicles are also occasionally used, and almost unlimited numbers of horses appear to be available for hire. Self-drive rentals, except for horses, are difficult to arrange, as tourists are expected to take guided tours at so much per head.

Accommodation remained spartan during the late 1960s. In 1967 HONSA erected a group of tents, sufficient for 40 persons, with facilities centralized in a wooden *casino*. The tents, unfortunately located close to the end of the Mataveri runway, were relocated closer to Hangaroa in 1971 when HONSA imported a prefabricated 120-bed hotel via Miami. Tents were still rented, although very occasionally, until the mid-1970s.

After the mid-1960s island residents began a rapid programme of house rearrangement, extension, and construction. While HONSA's hotel capacity has remained static at 120 beds, the number of beds provided by the Rapanui has risen dramatically.[23] In 1971 only 70 such beds were officially registered, with space for a further 30 in progress.[24] By 1975 islanders offered almost 300 beds, including a new 20-bed hotel, and were able to accommodate almost the entire passenger complement of an Australia-Chile charter airplane which was compelled to make an unexpected landing at Mataveri (Table 2,9).

Accommodation quality varies widely (Table 3,9). In the HONSA hotel, the tourist is assured of a private bathroom, running hot water, and the use of a telephone. Progressing towards Class 4, baths became communal, telephones rare, and hot water scarce. Prices, of course, vary with quality, but also within each class.

TOURIST TRAFFIC 1967-76

Tourists wishing to visit Easter Island may arrive either by cruise ship or, more commonly, by regularly-scheduled air flight.

TABLE 1,9 Vehicles used in Tourism 1971

	Number of Vehicles	Number of 1971 make	Seating Capacity
Indigenous tourist transportation cooperative	9	5	110
Individuals, sometimes working cooperatively	5	3	33
HONSA	1	0	11
All Vehicles	15	8	154

SOURCE: Governor's records.

TABLE 2,9 Tourist Beds Registered as Available 1971-4

	Number of Beds		
Year	HONSA	Islanders	Total
1971	120	70	190
1972	120	approx. 80	200
1973	120	92	212
1974	120	259	379

SOURCE: ODEPLAN: *Plan de Desarrollo del Departamento de Isla de Pacua* (1972); records of Governor and Municipality.

TABLE 3,9 Accommodation Quality 1974

Accommodation Class	Number of Establishments	Mean Number of Beds per Establishment	Mean Number of Baths per 2 Beds	Mean Number of Baths per Establishment	Percentage of Establishments With Telephone	Percentage of Establishments With Running Hot Water
1	1	120.00	1.00	60.00	100	100
2	11	9.55	0.84	4.00	64	82
3	15	5.47	0.51	1.40	80	67
4	14	5.14	0.56	1.43	57	14
Total/Mean	41	9.24	0.71	3.29	68	54

SOURCE: Records of Governor and Municipality.

Visitors by Ship

All visitors arrived by ship before 1967. Although EMPREMAR sends cargo vessels annually from Chile, other ships call only rarely at Easter Island. In the two-year period 1972-3, for example, only one dozen vessels arrived (Table 4,9). Oceanographic vessels rarely had a complement of 100 scientists and crew, whereas cruise vessels carried from 200 to over 1,000 passengers alone. Cargo vessels were not generally delivering cargo to the island, but were making sporadic calls such as the emergency off-loading of critically sick crew members.

The possibility that the island would be unable to absorb the impact of a 1,000-passenger liner is remote, for the passengers of the larger cruise ships are overwhelmingly elderly (Table 5,9). A 50 percent random sample of the passenger lists of two of the four cruise ships calling in the 1972-3 period indicated that at least one-third of the passengers were over 70 years of age and almost all were above 40 years. Elderly passengers are often unable to accept the long journey to shore in an open launch, a rough landing at Hangaroa, and a day's journey on unsurfaced roads. Nevertheless, the 150-seat capacity of the island's transportation fleet is severely strained by larger vessels, and repeat tours must be arranged in rapid succession as cruise liners rarely stay more than one or two nights.

Visitors by Air

Visitors by ship descend upon the island at irregular intervals, strain transportation facilities to the limit, rarely stay more than one day, and never require accommodation. In contrast, air passengers form the backbone of the Easter Island tourist economy. Whereas a mere 444 air passengers reached Easter Island in 1967, by 1971 over 10,000 passengers annually travelled the route between Tahiti and Santiago. Major increases followed the prolongation of the route to Papeete in 1968, and the use of Boeing 707 aircraft from 1970. Indeed, the leap in passenger statistics from 1,851 in 1969 to 8,192 in 1970 is of the order of 350 percent. These gross figures include direct travel between Santiago and Papeete, however, and the proportion of the total passengers who spend one night or more on Easter Island is somewhat less than half.

Figures for 1972-5 indicate that the number of annual commercial air passenger arrivals at Mataveri fluctuates markedly around a mean of 4,300, of which approximately one quarter are non-Chileans (Table 6,9). Although the general trend is upward, particularly for the minor source (Tahiti), both foreign and mainlander arrivals fell markedly after the 1973 coup. As over

TABLE 4,9 Non-Chilean Vessels 1972-3

Origin	Cargo	Cruise	Scientific	All Vessels
American	1	3	2	6
French	0	1	1	2
U.S.S.R.	0	0	1	1
Other	3	0	0	3

SOURCE: Governor's records.

TABLE 5,9 Age Structure of Cruise Ship Passengers 1972-4

	Percentage of all Passengers	
Age Group	Vessel 1	Vessel 2
over 70	54.5	33.7
41 - 70	45.0	57.0
21 - 40	0.5	9.3
under 21	0.0	0.0

SOURCE: Governor's records.

TABLE 6,9 Air Passenger Arrivals 1972-5

	From Santiago			From Tahiti			Both Sources	
Year	Chileans**	Aliens	Total	Chileans**	Aliens	Total	Aliens	Total
1972	2,971	701	3,672	29	105	134	806	3,806
1973	4,641	752	5,393	77	164	241	916	5,634
1974	1,597	889	2,486	89	181	270	1,070	2,756
1975*	3,122	1,530	4,652	44	304	348	1,834	5,000

* Estimate based on first 6 months.
** Figures for Chileans include both mainlanders and islanders.

SOURCE: LAN manifests annotated by International Police.

90 percent of all arrivals originate in Santiago, post-coup economic problems and a general decline in Chilean tourism strongly affected Easter Island.

These gross figures include not only tourists, although most aliens fall into this category, but also returning residents, government officials, scientific workers, and temporary construction workers or others with skills not to be found on Easter Island. Without lengthy name-by-name analysis, it is impossible to assess the nature of the dichotomy between Chilean tourists and island residents. Santiago-Papeete traffic includes a major Easter Island component. Many of these travellers, whether resident or tourist, fly only between Mataveri and Santiago; they are largely Chilean. On the Papeete-Santiago route less than 10 percent of all passengers make a stopover at Easter Island. These are overwhelmingly aliens, but also include Rapanui returning from visits to relatives in Tahiti.

Tourist Origins

Analysis of tourist origins based on the available data must unfortunately exclude anything more than a cursory assessment of cruise ship passengers and Chilean tourists arriving by air. From the available vessel passenger lists it appears that cruise passengers are largely of United States nationality. The MS *Sagafjord*, for example, which visited Easter Island on 24 March

1974, carried 400 passengers of whom 380 were Americans and 15 Canadians, largely professionals, housewives, or retired persons. Chilean air arrivals include officials, Rapanui, mainlander residents, and temporary workers, as well as tourists. During 1972-3 several large groups of Chilean tourists, often parties of trade unionists, visited the island as part of the Allende government's educational programme. These package tours terminated in September 1973.

All aliens recorded on LAN manifests, however, are registered by the *carabinero* force in their capacity as International Police. Annotations to the manifests, which give name, date of arrival and point of embarkation, include nationality and intended place of residence on the island. Unfortunately, these data are collected inconsistently, contain gaps, and are handwritten; a complete and accurate time series cannot therefore be derived. Nevertheless, some general characteristics of non-Chilean arrivals by air can be discerned.

South America, including Mexico and the Caribbean, receives only 19 percent of the world's tourists.[25] Easter Island lies well beyond the acknowledged "tourist peripheries", and is unlikely to participate in mass tourism during the 1980s.[26] Remoteness from the major tourist origin nations in Europe and North America ensures that the island can be visited neither easily nor cheaply. However, given the strong air connections between Chile and North America, United States citizens might be expected to dominate tourism on Easter Island, followed perhaps by French citizens via Tahiti. New air links with Tahiti and Fiji, and from Tahiti to Japan, would argue for considerable numbers of Australian, British, and Japanese visitors. Tourist statistics on the world scale indicate that 75 percent of all international tourist trips are made by the citizens of 12 nations (United States, West Germany, France, Britain, Canada, Belgium, Netherlands, Italy, Switzerland, Sweden, Denmark, and Austria). The United States and West Germany alone account for approximately 40 percent of the world's total tourist arrivals.[27]

For Easter Island, the 10 most important source countries were isolated for each year of the period 1972-5 (Table 7,9). The total range of national origins is very wide, embracing approximately 50 countries. Much of this spread was occasioned by delegates to the UNCTAD IV Conference held in Santiago in 1972. Ten nations, however, annually account for almost 90 percent of all arrivals; France and the United States annually provide over 40 percent of the island's foreign tourists. With West Germany, these three nations originate at least 50 percent of all arrivals, conforming strongly to world tourist patterns, although the role of France is strengthened because of the proximity of French Polynesia.[28] It is noteworthy, however, that the proportion of all alien arrivals accounted for by these three nations fell from

TABLE 7,9 National Origins of Alien Visitors 1972-5

	Percentage of All Alien Visitors			
	1972	1973	1974	1975*
France	28.2	28.6	28.5	20.0
United States	27.1	16.2	18.3	22.0
West Germany	12.5	12.7	14.4	8.0
Spain	4.3	—	—	1.9
Switzerland	3.7	1.9	1.7	1.4
Britain	3.6	3.3	4.6	2.4
Italy	2.5	7.0	—	—
Australia	2.1	3.6	3.5	4.8
Brazil	1.9	—	3.5	3.8
Sweden	1.7	—	—	—
Argentina	—	8.4	7.1	26.9
Japan	—	2.6	6.7	1.7
South Africa	—	2.1	—	—
Canada	—	—	2.3	—
Others	12.4	13.6	9.4	7.1
	100.0	100.0	100.0	100.0

* Estimate based on first 6 months.

SOURCE: LAN manifests annotated by International Police.

over two-thirds in 1972 to barely half in 1975, largely because of the emergence of Argentina as a major tourist origin.

Other countries rarely provide even five percent of Easter Island's foreign tourists. Of the 14 nations considered in Table 7,9, only Australia, Britain, and Switzerland have consistently appeared in the top ten alongside France, the United States, and West Germany. Of these three minor originators, only Australia indicates a steady proportional growth. The island's location is responsible for the appearance of Argentina, Australia, Brazil, and Japan, and cultural linkages for the appearance of Spain.

Although over 90 percent of all Easter Island arrivals originate in Santiago, the Papeete-Easter Island route is dominated by aliens (Table 6,9). Over 80 percent of all aliens arrive via Santiago, however, with only Australia and Britain showing a significant countertrend (Table 8,9). It is possible that British arrivals via Tahiti include Australian residents travelling on British passports (Figure 5,9).

Seasonality

During the 26 month period 1972-4, foreign air arrivals averaged 77.6 per month, 22.8 percent of the mean monthly total of 339.7 arrivals by air from both directions (Table 9,9). A heavy influx of arrivals is experienced in the southern hemisphere summer, 42.5 percent of all arrivals occurring in the four months from December to March. Alien arrivals exhibited greater seasonality, ranging from a low in November (3.7 percent of annual alien arrivals) to a high in August (14 percent). The alien concentration upon the Easter Island winter season, with 25.4 percent of all arrivals in July and August alone, reconfirms their origins in northern hemisphere midlatitude nations. A second, lower, peak for aliens coincides with the overall December-March peak (36.8 percent of all alien arrivals). As alien tourists carry hard currencies, their July-August peak provides a welcome counterweight to the Chilean emphasis on December-March. Climatically, of course, Easter Island poses little problem at any season (Chapter 5).

Accommodation and Length of Stay

Two major types of airborne tourists visit Easter Island. Group tours, overwhelmingly American or French, often include Easter Island as one part of an extended tour and therefore rarely remain for more than one week. They are almost invariably accommodated in the HONSA hotel. Independent travellers, in contrast, exhibit a much wider range in terms of

TABLE 8,9 Alien Arrivals by Flight Origin 1972-5

	Percentage of All Arrivals Originating in Santiago			
	1972	1973	1974	1975*
France	93.8	88.2	90.8	68.9
United States	90.8	89.2	91.3	92.6
West Germany	84.2	66.4	82.5	86.3
Spain	100.0	—	—	100.0
Switzerland	90.0	70.6	52.6	92.3
Britain	34.5	46.7	53.0	72.7
Italy	100.0	92.2	—	—
Australia	41.2	30.3	27.0	52.2
Brazil	86.7	—	92.1	91.4
Sweden	92.6	—	—	—
Argentina	—	98.4	84.2	94.3
Japan	—	70.8	75.0	81.2
South Africa	—	100.0	—	—
Canada	—	—	76.0	—
Others	80.0	85.7	88.8	66.2
All Aliens	87.0	82.1	83.0	83.4

* Estimate based on first 6 months.

SOURCE: LAN manifests annotated by International Police.

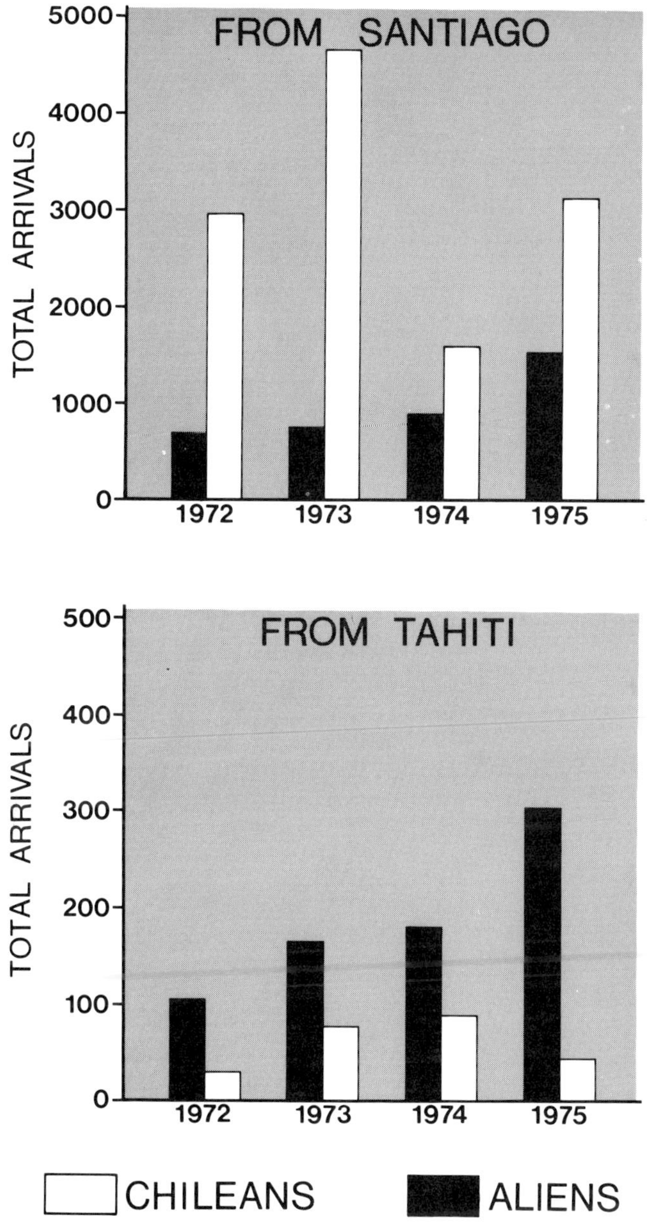

FIGURE 5,9 Tourist arrivals by air 1972-5
(data source: International Police, Hangaroa).

TABLE 9,9 Accumulated Monthly Alien Arrivals 1972-4

Month	Number of Aliens	Number of Arrivals	Aliens as a Percentage of Arrivals	Aliens Percentage per Month	Arrivals: Percentage per Month
January	268	1,478	18.1	9.6	12.1
February	241	1,301	18.5	8.6	10.6
March	260	1,278	20.3	9.3	10.5
April	202	947	21.3	7.2	7.8
May	177	1,139	15.5	6.3	9.3
June	115	730	15.8	4.1	6.0
July	315	901	35.0	11.4	7.4
August	388	1,051	36.9	14.0	8.6
September	205	873	23.5	7.3	7.1
October	258	688	37.5	9.2	5.6
November	102	701	14.6	3.7	5.7
December	262	1,141	23.0	9.3	9.3
TOTALS	2,795	12,228	—	100.0	100.0

SOURCE: LAN manifests annotated by International Police.

both length of stay and accommodation used. On arrival at Mataveri airport, independent travellers are greeted not only by artifact vendors but also by guesthouse proprietors seeking prospective clients.

Although the consistency of police annotations of LAN manifests with regard to place of accommodation varies greatly from year to year, a fairly complete time series is available for the 12-month period April 1974 to March 1975 (Table 10,9). Overnights (number of visitors x nights spent on island) peak in December-March and again in July-August. Islander guesthouses attract a slightly larger proportion of all visitors (58.2 percent) in the major peak (December-March), when Argentine visitors appear in signifi-

TABLE 10,9 Alien Overnights by Accommodation Type 1974-5

Month	Overnights Spent: At HONSA Hotel	Overnights Spent: In Islander guest houses	Total Overnights	Percentage to Islanders	Remarks
April	16	93	109	85.3	incomplete
May	367	152	519	29.3	
June	86	3	89	3.4	incomplete
July	432	461	893	51.6	
August	535	335	870	38.5	
September	305	5	310	1.6	incomplete
October	198	201	399	50.4	
November	129	285	414	68.8	
December	373	310	683	45.4	
January	716	1,768	2,484	71.2	
February	520	364	884	41.2	
March	322	241	563	42.8	
Totals/Mean	3,999	4,218	8,217	51.3	

SOURCE: LAN manifests annotated by International Police.

cant numbers. In contrast, the government hotel attains a slim lead (54.9 percent) in the minor July-August peak, when alien visitors may account for over one-third of all visitors.

Overnight data are valuable as a crude indicator of the dichotomization of hard currency cash flows into Easter Island. If HONSA indeed supplies 48.7 percent of the alien accommodation demand, then its significantly higher prices will ensure its receiving perhaps two-thirds of the island's dollar income from accommodation and food supply. (The island has no significant food outlets outside hotel and guesthouses, and tariffs invariably include meals.) Personal observation, however, suggests that the islander share of overnights is somewhat greater than half. They receive much of the Chilean tourist influx, whereas the hotel is hampered here by a significant inflow of officials who receive free accommodation. Further, Rapanui incomes are enhanced through their control of ground transportation and the artifact-carving industry.

The HONSA Hotel

No detailed analysis of tourist expenditures or even of tourist overnights spent in guesthouses is yet possible; few of the latter keep accurate records. In contrast, the government hotel has made daily records since its opening in September 1971.

Tourist group travel is important in filling hotel beds. The meagre data available suggest that groups may account for about 50 percent of all hotel arrivals (Table 11,9). During the short period June-November 1975 a total of 30 group tours arrived, of which 13 were American, 9 French, 2 Japanese, 2 Chilean, and the remainder German, Belgian, Italian, and Argentine. European groups were significantly larger than United States or Latin American groups, though none included more than 30 persons. Unfortunately, group tours tend to coincide temporally, so that a period when the hotel may have over 50 guests is often followed by intervals when the number of guests falls below 10. Group tours are likely to increase in importance as the island becomes better known to travel agents.

Because of the hotel's dependence on irregularly-scheduled group tours, strong fluctuations in occupancy rates are inevitable (Figure 6,9). Monthly occupancy rates are uniformly low, the absolute peak being less than 60 percent occupancy. During the 4-year period from September 1971 to August 1975 a total of approximately 170,000 overnights were possible. Only 36,411 were recorded, however, giving a mean daily occupancy rate of only 21.4 percent. Hotels normally required rates of at least two-thirds to show adequate profit.

Seasonal fluctuations cannot be adequately assessed, as they have been strongly deformed by large-scale secular trends. Most notably, occupancy during the hotel's second year of operation (1972-73) rose to considerably more than double the rate of business experienced in the inaugural year. The third year of operation, however, was opened by the coup of 11 September 1973, after which guest numbers fell by almost half, continuing to decline in 1974-5. The high occupancy rates of over 30 percent which were continuously recorded from January to October 1973 were due in part to Chilean group tours which have since been drastically curtailed.

TABLE 11,9 Tourist Groups in Hotel Hangaroa, June-November 1975

Month	All Arrivals	Arrivals in Groups	Group guests as a Percentage of all Arrivals
June	172	42	24.4
July	315	185	58.7
August	164	66	40.2
September	217	53	24.4
October	344	204	59.3
November	499	296	59.3

SOURCE: HONSA records.

TABLE 12,9 Origins of Hotel Guests 1974-5

Origin	Arrivals	Overnights	Mean Overnights per Visitor	Percentage of All Overnights
Chile	1,109	5,684	5.1	46.4
Europe	790	2,309	2.9	18.9
North America	522	2,174	4.2	17.8
Latin America	228	1,346	5.9	11.0
Asia	153	562	3.7	4.6
Oceania	59	163	2.8	1.3
Africa	0	0	0.0	0.0

SOURCE: HONSA records.

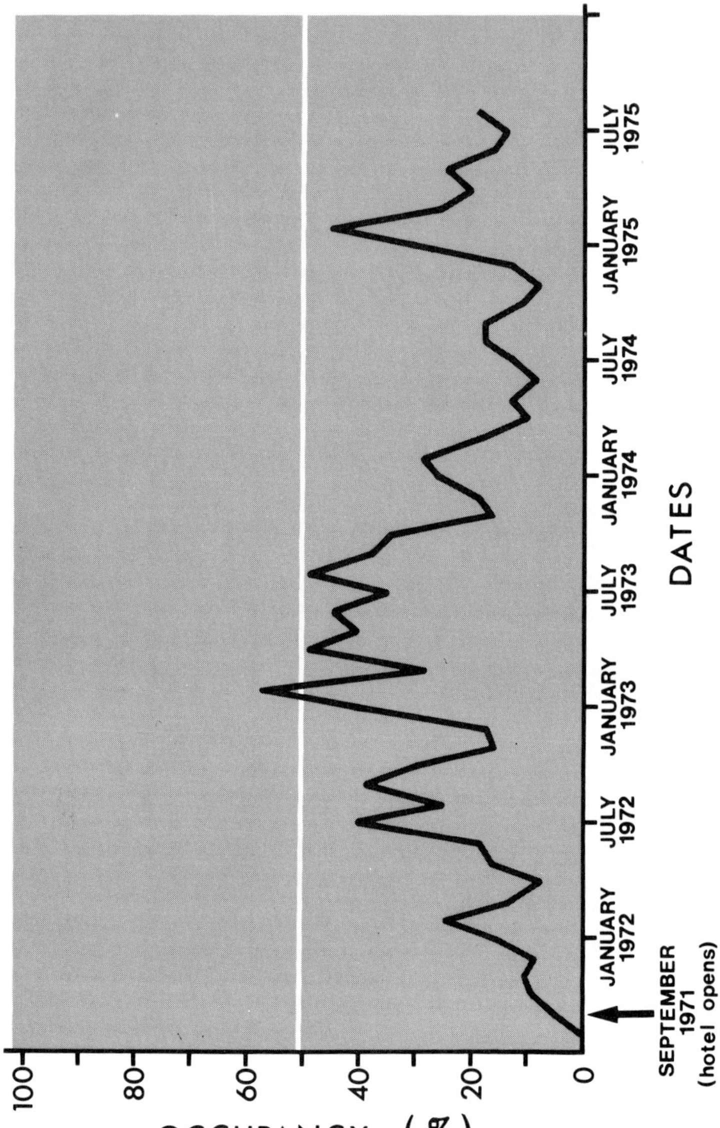

FIGURE 6,9 Hotel Hangaroa occupancy rates 1971-5 (data source: HONSA, Hotel Hangaroa).

Origins of Hotel Guests

From January 1974 HONSA recorded details of guest origins in terms of an arbitrary set of world regions (Table 12,9). During 19 months of 1974-5, Chileans accounted for almost half of all overnights spent in the hotel. With Latin Americans in general, they recorded the lengthiest stays, averaging over five nights each. Because of cost and a limited number of obvious tourist attractions, alien visitors, many of whom are in transit across the Pacific, average only 2-4 days each. This short stay is possible whether the traveller returns to his originating point or whether he is in transit westbound (giving a 3½ day stopover) or eastbound (2½ days). As the same air schedules are used by guesthouse visitors, Easter Island is clearly a short-stay tourist generator, comparable with many major cities or national monuments.

Cost, physical isolation, and deficiencies of the physical environment will effectively prevent Easter Island from developing the long-stay, beach-oriented mass tourism envisaged by Bryan in 1920. Too many intervening opportunities are available for Europeans, North Americans, Australians, and Asians. For Chileans, the beaches and casino of Viña del Mar are far closer. Retirement is also of little importance. Although the island has received its share of youthful "dropouts" from both Chile and North America, only a single American retiree had arrived by 1975.

PLATE 42 Rapanui, Chileans, North Americans at airport ▶

10 THE EFFECTS OF MODERNIZATION

> There is the . . . question of whether "modernisation", as currently practised . . . is actually producing agreeable results . . . For it is not a question of choosing between "modern growth" and "traditional stagnation". It is a question of finding the right path of development, the Middle Way . . .
>
> E.F. Schumacher, *Buddhist Economics*

Since 1860 Easter Island has been depopulated by slavers, more than decimated by disease, treated as a geopolitical pawn, dominated by a succession of foreign entrepreneurs, neglected by Chile, and turned over first to sheep and then to tourists. Throughout this book the emphasis on external forces and their impacts upon the island has been stressed. The sheepmasters were powerful and the islanders weak; the sheep were many, the Rapanui few. When the first sheep company began to operate in earnest after 1871 the native population was well below 200, and when the last of the sheepmasters left in 1953 the total island population was still only about 800, including mainlanders (Figure 3,1). During the latter part of the nineteenth century the indigenous population failed to reach 200, and had not reached 300 by the 1920s (Table 4,7). In contrast, the territory which had once supported perhaps 4,000 indigenes was devoted, throughout this period, to a flock of sheep which reached over 50,000 in number.

Yet one would like to know more of the means by which the few remaining islanders made shift to survive the aftermath of the first external impact. Unfortunately, no precise data exist and the question requires the detailed attention of an historical anthropologist.[1] It is clear, however, that although the Rapanui population was severely demoralized after 1862, their material demands were low. After such a population crash the will to survive may have been weak, but the means for survival, in this case arable land, was abundant. Moreover, it is probable that, having lost their chiefly class, the Rapanui population looked to the alien sheepmasters as a substitute, and thus were more ready to accept alien control. As in most company state situations, the proletariat becomes dependent upon the company and, recognizing this, develops a love-hate relationship with the entrepreneur. Reports that the indigenes were starving, had little shelter, and few clothes, reflect not only this new dependence on a niggardly or ill-provided company agent, but also the projection of Chilean bourgeois standards upon a Polynesian people whose needs were very few.

Despite alleged oppression by the sheep companies, until the 1950s there were rarely sufficient Europeans on Easter Island to support a regime of continuous oppression, unless aided by certain sectors of the native population. That such aid was given is evidenced by the company police, company workers, company-related Polynesian families resident at Mataveri and Moeroa, and by miscegenation between Scottish managers and Rapanui women. This division among the indigenes, which was never deep during the company years, was nevertheless the forerunner of the social divisions which exist among contemporary islanders. During the company regime the company wall remained permeable for both man and beast. Company meat could be stolen on the hoof, and, in time-honoured Polynesian tradition, what was stolen from the company was shared among or appropriated by other Rapanui.

Miscegenation provided a biological base for the survival of a racial subgroup which the Chileans of the 1880s thought to be on the verge of extinction. More important, however, was Polynesian cultural resilience and the ability of an impacted population to come to terms with an alien power. It is not uncommon for colonized peoples to inhabit two social worlds, the outsiders' and their own. Until the early twentieth century indigenous lifestyles continued in the Hangaroa area, with some modifications in terms of housing, dress, and food items. Most of the materials used, however, and in particular the staple foods consumed, were still derived from traditional horticulture. In the early years the CEDIP agent himself was obliged to use antiquated equipment, and there was little to spare for the indigenous population.

When called upon to work for the company, however, as at shearing time, the Rapanui were able to change social worlds and act in the manner expected by the company manager. At such times imported goods would provide a welcome change from the monotony of local horticulture with its sweet potato staple. Yet when a deep sense of injustice was felt, the Rapanui were not loathe to challenge company power, their exploits including several murders and insurrections.

It was chiefly with the company-induced improvements of the 1920s, and the impact of Chilean functionaries in the 1930s, that the Rapanui became aware of their rather restricted opportunities and their poverty. These feelings were supported by more frequent visits from non-company vessels, which stimulated demands for material goods and a general feeling of relative deprivation. Challenges to the company, including strikes, were sometimes supported by resident mainlanders. Above all, improved contact with the outside world rekindled the long-thwarted desire to leave the island. The few islanders who had visited Chile, often army and navy recruits, brought back information which had never before been available to this isolated people. It was such a returnee who, during the intense modernization period of the 1960s, was to lead the indigenous demand for the relaxation of a naval control which in many ways was as authoritarian as that of the company it had succeeded. Although we can only speculate about the reactions of the Rapanui to the initial external impact and the years of company power, it is possible to provide much more detailed information concerning the ongoing modernization phase which began in the early 1960s.

THE EFFECTS OF RAPID MODERNIZATION

The American presence, civil government, the influx of Chilean administrators, and scheduled air services operated synergistically to profoundly affect the political, social, and economic life of Easter Island after 1965. It is as yet too early to assess the long term effects of such rapid modernization; any meaningful assessment would require a separate sociological study. Some immediate changes can be seen, however, in the areas of population, occupational, and social structure, and the generation of protest and discontent.

Population Structure

Between 1952 and 1970 the population of Easter Island rose from approximately 800 to over 1,600 (Figure 3,1), a feat of doubling which cannot be accounted for by natural increase alone. To accommodate this increase, the decade 1960-70 saw the doubling of the housing stock from 178 to 367; at least 50 of the new dwelling units were for mainlander inmigrants. Although a significant number of Rapanui, probably between one-third and one-quarter, have left for the mainland since the mid-1960s, by the late 1970s the island population was approaching 2,000, of which approximately one quarter were *continentales* (mainlanders).

By 1952 the population, still almost wholly Polynesian, had filled out and somewhat normalized the rather accidented pyramid of 1918 (Figure 1,10). Using Drapkin's very basic categorization, however, it can be seen that the islander pyramids of 1918 and 1952 show a fair constancy of form throughout the 34-year period, although major anomalies, such as the pronounced underrepresentation of elderly males, had been much reduced by mid-century (Figure 2,10). The proportional basal narrowing of the

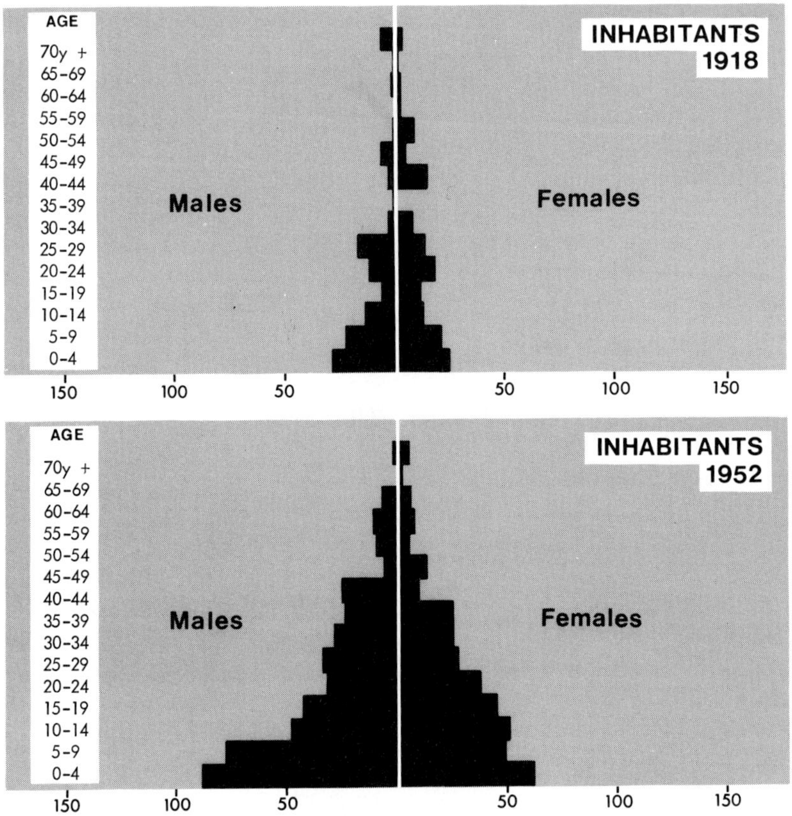

FIGURE 1,10 Population pyramids, 1918 and 1952 (sources: Bienvenido de Estella, 1918, and 1952 Census of Chile).

islander pyramid for 1970 (Figure 3,10) may indicate the beginning of a secular downtrend in natality after several generations of rapid natural increase.[2]

Comparison of the 1970 pyramids for islanders and mainlanders reveals fundamental but not unexpected differences between indigenous and inmigrant demographic structures (Figure 3,10). A relative absence of male islanders of ages 15-19 indicates that males rather than females are selected for mainland schooling and military service. Less than 2 per cent of the population is over 65 years of age, possibly the result of inadequate medical attention and poor living conditions. Despite these irregularities, the 1970 Islander pyramid indicates a balanced population undergoing fairly rapid increase.

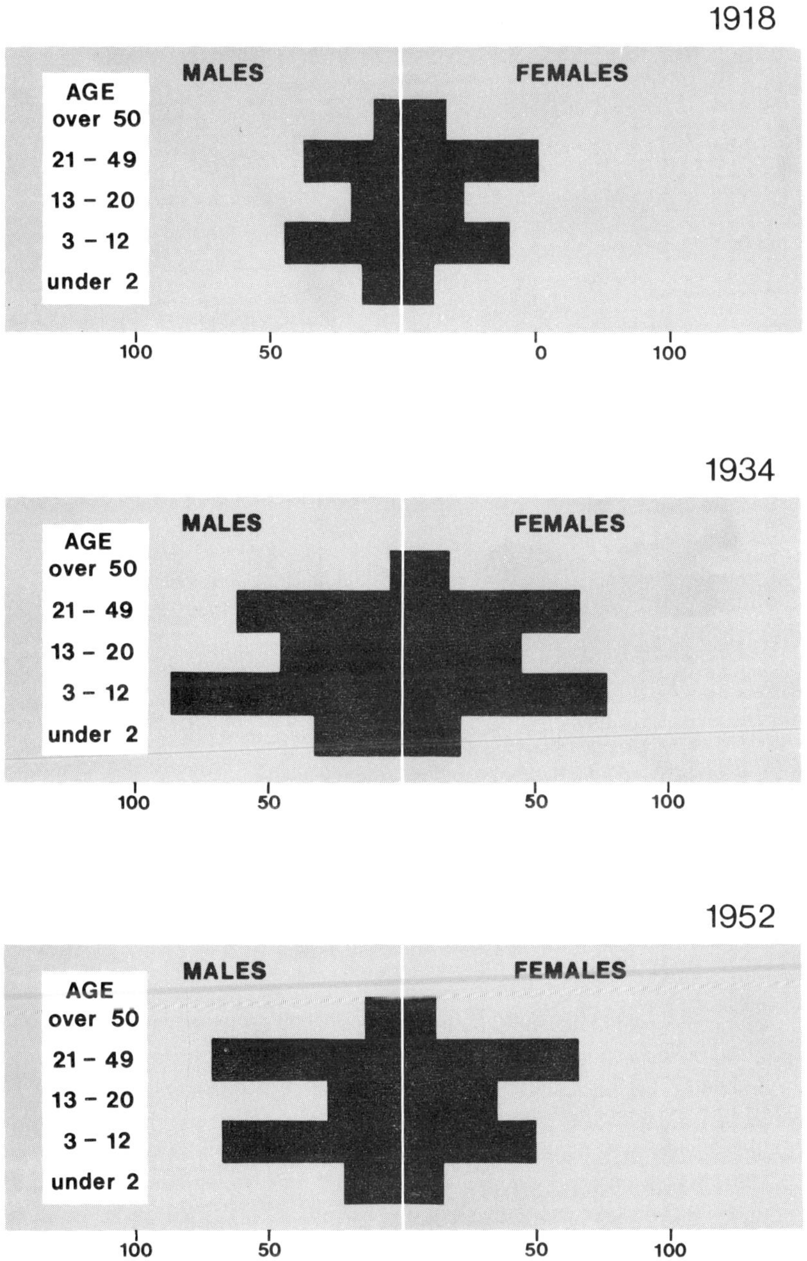

FIGURE 2,10 Population pyramids, 1918, 1934, and 1952
(sources: as for Figure 1,10 with data transformed; Drapkin, 1935).

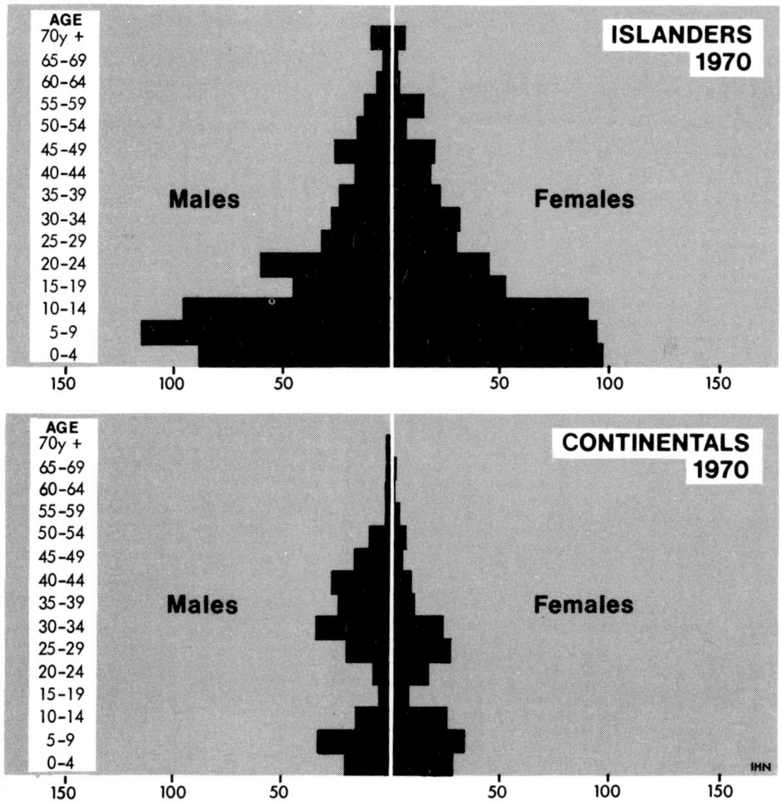

FIGURE 3,10 Population pyramids of islanders and mainlanders, 1970 (source: 1970 Census of Chile).

In sharp contrast, the 1970 Mainlander pyramid resembles the ill-balanced population structures of resource frontier communities.[3] Both the elderly (60 plus) and adolescent to young adult (15-24) groups are grossly under-represented, while the young (under 15) are also relatively few in number. Over 64 percent of continental males and 51 percent of mainlander females fall into the 20-64 age category. Indeed, in the 30-34 age range the island contains more mainlander than islander males. The Mainlander pyramid is typical of many immigrant settlements in remote areas, with a significant proportion of unattached males, and of married males between ages 25 and 50 with their younger wives and small children. As adolescent mainlanders invariably leave the island for schooling, and as many adults are on the island only on tours of duty, the Mainlander pyramid's skew towards middle-age and maleness may not readily be eradicated. Had the 67 American servicemen on the island in 1970 been added to the non-Polynesian pyramid, this skewness would have been even more pronounced.

Occupational Structure

Easter Island is plagued by the ghosts of unrealised economic improvement plans. The vision of the island as Chile's tropical plantation, which dominated much mainland thinking between 1888 and 1920 (Chapters 2-7), was revived in the 1940s during the agitation leading to the cancellation of CEDIP's lease. Marin, for example, felt that the island could be an important source of bananas, pineapples, and other tropical products.[4] During the early 1950s tropical fruit production and meat and fish processing were proposed once more, although there were occasional dissenting views.[5] CORFO made several feasibility studies.[6] A coconut plantation was begun at Anakena in 1961.[7] In essence, however, the agrarian economy of the island has continued to be dominated by sheepranching. Since the onset of Chilean control, however, sheep numbers have declined and failure to burn regularly has reduced pasture quality and increased fly numbers.

Although CORFO set up the Vaitea station as an experimental farm, and some afforestation has been attempted on Rano Kao and Poike, little has been done to fulfil the vision of Easter Island as tropical plantation.[8] Water supply problems, the low organic content of the soil, the abundance of pests, the high cost of fertilizers, and labour difficulties are cited as drawbacks. Water supply problems also render a *charqui-* or fish-processing plant unlikely. Perhaps the most useful task for the experimental station would be the renovation of pasture quality through the introduction of better grass types.[9]

Ferdon's plea in 1955 for an overall plan for the island was answered in 1972 by the Allende government's 318-page *Plan de Desarrollo del Departamento de Isla de Pascua* (Easter Island Development Plan).[10] This plan sought to develop agricultural, fishing, and tourist industry cooperatives, several of which were organized in 1972. Full implementation, however, was prevented by the military coup of 1973. The succeeding government has developed a *Plan de Manejo* (1976), to deal with the national park areas, and a comprehensive plan which calls for the development of fishing and agriculture in the service of tourism and self-sufficiency. However, with the inauguration of air services from Chile and Tahiti attention was drawn from agriculture towards tourism (Chapter 9).

One major result of the failure of agrarian projects, of the growth of tourism, and of rapid modernization has been a radical shift in occupational structure. During the CEDIP era, the company provided few regular jobs. As late as 1943 CEDIP's operations required a permanent staff of 2 administrators, 8 shepherds and guards, and 6 labourers, although up to 70 persons were employed in shearing and embarking the wool clip of 73 tons.[11] The permanent Rapanui employees represented a mere four percent of the Polynesian population. By 1965, after 13 years of military rule, there were 50 salaried Chileans in a total mainlander population of 140, although only 97 of almost 1,000 islanders had permanent employment with the CORFO *fundo* (52), ECA (27), FACh (14), the Navy (2) and the governor (2). These are almost certainly inflated figures.[12] In the early 1960s Flores estimated that 70 islanders, or six percent of the population, had government employment, while only a further 20 percent could be considered agriculturalists. The remainder were substantially unemployed or were dependents.[13] By 1969 the workforce had remained at 26 percent of the Rapanui population, but a strong shift from self-employment in agriculture to wage-labour had become apparent.[14] By 1973, under the Allende government, about two-thirds of the Rapanui males were employed by the Chilean Public Services.

As frequently occurs in modernizing economies on isolated islands, many islanders have several jobs.[15] Most families own, or have access to, an agricultural land parcel of five hectares (12 acres), and many own horses and let rooms to tourists. As employment on Easter Island is highly flexible, any attempt to analyze occupation structure must consider secondary as well as primary occupations (Table 1,10). For example, although self-employed agriculture had become unimportant as a primary pursuit by 1969, there were at least 117 registered owners of agricultural parcels. The 34 fishermen were almost matched by 31 persons who stated fishing to be a secondary occupation. Many males are involved to varying degrees in stone and wood carving. Construction, usually a part-time or family occupation, was grossly inflated in 1969 by hotel building; both before and after 1969 airport construction work absorbed many unskilled workers who would otherwise have been regarded as unemployed or as agriculturalists. If these construction workers are added to the 13.5 percent of the potential workforce without jobs, a considerable pool of underemployed labour is apparent. On the other hand, shearing and embarkation still provided seasonal work for some. Moreover, the figures omit reference to the tourist industry, which by the early 1970s was becoming an important secondary and even primary occupation. It is clear, at least, that the construction workers and carvers of 1969 were oriented towards the tourist market.

As the term is used in industrialized societies, the majority of the Rapanui are unskilled workers. Considerable skill and attention, however, is re-

TABLE 1,10 Primary Occupations of Islanders in 1969

Activity	Self-Employed	Skilled Labour	Unskilled Labour	Total
Agriculture, personal	9			9
Agriculture, CORFO			26	26
Fishing	34			34
Carving artifacts	17			17
Construction			24	24
Commerce	5			5
Armed Forces		35		35
Public Services		10	64	74
"Private Sector"		1	19	20
Unemployed	3		35	38
TOTAL	68	46	168	282

SOURCE: Adapted from ODEPLAN: *Plan de Desarrollo del Departamento de Isla de Pascua* (1972), p. 45.

quired for carving, fishing, and food production. As in most small, remote islands which have no pretensions to autarky or economic profitability, the majority of the potential workforce is engaged in tertiary occupations (48.9 percent). Primary production (agriculture and fishing) occupies a further 25 percent, with 6 percent in secondary production (artisan carving). The remaining 7.1 percent of the "private sector" are also mainly involved in services, with an orientation towards tourism.

The rapid decline of agriculture as a major occupation during the 1960s is reflected in the abandonment of former agricultural land (Table 2,10). ODEPLAN's agricultural planning region (Figure 4,9) comprises over 80 percent abandoned land. Moreover, of the 637.5 hectares (1,575 acres) designated as "in use", only 130 hectares (320 acres) were actually under some form of production when surveyed in 1971. With full use of modern techniques on the better soils of the area (Figure 2,5), ODEPLAN estimates that about 350 hectares (865 acres) would be sufficient to support the entire Easter Island population.[16] On the other hand, Table 2,10 does not take into consideration the *huerta*-like townscape of "urban" Hangaroa, which has a population density of only six persons per hectare (2.4 persons per acre). Fruit and vegetables for family consumption are produced in some quantity within the town itself. Since 1967, however, both mainlanders and Rapanui have begun to import packaged food, including even bread and chicken, by air freight from Chile and Tahiti.

Social Structure

The Polynesian was neither an economic nor a social individualist. Traditionally, any windfall gains would be shared with the community. Thus there was little incentive for Polynesian people to strive for personal economic success before the arrival of Western entrepreneurs.[17] This ethos remained permanent in Easter Island until the 1950s, because of isolation coupled with the company's commercial monopoly. Working for the company occupied a very few of the male population, and growing maize for CEDIP never became a full-scale cash cropping operation. Consequently, until the early 1950s, the chief social divide on Easter Island was the deep gulf separating CEDIP administrators and the Polynesian population. When the Navy replaced CEDIP an improvement in living standards occurred for those who secured government employ.[18] Modernization since 1965, however, and in particular the rapidly changing occupational structure, has exacerbated traditional divisions within island society and created new ones.

Islanders with permanent jobs, or who take in tourists on a regular basis, have become fully absorbed into the money economy which gradually replaced barter and payment in kind during the twentieth century. Many Rapanui have become partially involved in the new economic system through temporary construction jobs. Those who infrequently take paid employment, are unemployed, or regard agriculture as a major occupation, however, frequently remain on the periphery of the cash economy. The engrossing of lucrative employment opportunities by certain energetic

TABLE 2,10 Easter Island Land Use 1970

	Type	Category		Hectares
1.	Urban	a)	Hangaroa town	260
		b)	airport (Mataveri)	230
2.	Agricultural	a)	in use	637
		b)	abandoned	2,888
3.	Pastoral	Vaitea *fundo*		7,858
4.	National Park	a)	Maunga Terevaka	3,605
		b)	Rano Kao	1,150
	TOTAL			16,628

SOURCE: Adapted from ODEPLAN: *Plan de Desarrollo del Departamento de Isla de Pascua* (1972), p. 61.

or well-placed families has led to the emergence of a nascent Rapanui middle class and "generated the beginnings of social disintegration."[19] In particular, the extended family has shown a tendency to disintegrate into its nuclear components, especially among the young islanders, the better-educated, and those involved in salaried or entrepreneurial activities. Incipient social divisions, however, are still considerably modified by kinship relations and the sharing of wealth.

Housing quality directly reflects these growing divisions. The houses of the nascent middle class resemble the Chilean bourgeois ideal, which itself reflects North American and European preferences. Lounge suites, coffee tables, tiled floors, hot water systems, telephones, televisions and other electrical gadgets, and displays of books, records, pictures, and photographs characterize these dwellings. Their owners are likely to have regular employment, to be involved in several subsidiary enterprises, including letting rooms to tourists, to have children at high school or university, and to own at least a share in a vehicle. Some are already building second houses for the tourist trade.

PLATE 43
Going to church

PLATE 44
After the service

At the opposite end of the spectrum are Rapanui whose houses remain sparsely furnished and in a state of disrepair. A house may contain merely one or two beds, a table, several chairs, and a chest of drawers. These people are more likely to live in crowded conditions, to speak poorer Spanish, and to be less well educated. As they often have no permanent jobs, and their houses appeal only to the hardiest tourists, they are unable to generate the level of cash inflow enjoyed by the fully modernized sector of the population. Most of the Rapanui population falls between these two extremes. It is likely, however, that income disparities and social divisions will continue to grow as the groups which have wholeheartedly entered the cash economy proceed more rapidly up the socio-economic spiral.

Mainlanders constitute a separate group, although considerable intermarriage has occurred. All are permanent, salaried employees, none own land, and almost all live in government housing of standard quality. They are not a homogeneous group, but comprise major divisions, as between military and civilian personnel. The demands of this group for living standards approximating to those of urban Chile have resulted in an increased level of imports and a general rise in prices. As with the Americans before them, the higher living standards of the Chileans have increased feelings of relative deprivation among the Rapanui. Because of favoured treatment at the hands of the relatively wealthy Americans, islanders often look unfavourably upon the mainlander population.

Protest and Discontent

Modernization, by increasing wants, invariably promotes discontent. After 1965 the islander's awareness of the outside world was enormously enhanced, and both Chileans and Americans presented new lifestyle models. However, Chilean attempts to impose rapid modernization upon the island were not found wholly acceptable by the permanent residents.

During December 1966, for example, disputes arose regarding the use of land for new streets, street widening, and the siting of civil installations. Agitation resulted in clashes between Rapanui and *carabineros*.[20] In 1967 protest arose on the grounds that development plans disregarded traditional island values and that consultation with the Rapanui had been, at best, perfunctory.[21] The modernization process of the mid-1960s appears to have been a case of planning for people, rather than with them.[22] Islanders were unable to perceive the value of the first public works projects, which consisted of runway construction and the erection of housing for *continentales*.

Protest was led by the leader of the 1964-5 "revolution", who was opposed by some Rapanui and branded a communist in the pay of the French by other residents.[23] Nevertheless, he received the greatest voter support in the first municipal elections of April 1967, indicating that the "ill-feeling which exists in Easter Island" was more widespread than had been realised.[24] Some islanders still felt that they were treated paternistically by Chile; said one:

> I don't accept that we should be treated as simple "island folk." The very pronunciation of these words revolts me.[25]

Paternalist feelings, however, are difficult to eradicate.[26]

Mainlander residents are probably more concerned with the problems of coping with life in isolation than with their relations with the Rapanui. In 1965 the Frei government awarded mainlanders in government employment a special salary adjustment of 200 percent to compensate for isolation and difficult living conditions. When this was reduced to 50 percent in 1974 by the military *junta*, mainlander discontent dramatically increased.[27] The attention of the authorities was directed to the poor shipping services, irregular airline schedules, lack of mainland radio and television reception, inadequate telephone, telegraph and postal systems, and poor personal contacts with mainland Chile. Deteriorating housing, inadequate medical and educational facilities, and lack of recreational opportunities exacerbated *islitis*, a "cabin fever" neurosis common among urban dwellers transferred to remote communities. A major issue was high living costs, especially in relation to air and sea freightage. Higher freight charges were reflected as much in the difficulties attendant upon maintaining an adequate diet as in the forty or so incomplete houses scattered throughout Hangaroa. On the whole, the mainlanders felt, they were called upon to make considerable sacrifices when asked to serve on "La isla mas isla del mundo."[28]

During the period 1974-6 some attempts were made to ameliorate this situation. Television relay and a new hospital were among the necessary and unnecessary improvements. A new plan for island development was prepared. This plan, recognizing current island realities as well as the needs of Chile as a whole, emphasizes the promotion of tourism. Preference is, however, given to Chilean tourism, to "selective" tourism, and to the development of agriculture and fishing to meet both tourist and local needs.

PROBLEMS AND EFFECTS OF TOURISM

The sudden development of tourism is likely to have a profound effect upon the economy, society, and landscape of a small, remote island. No data are yet available regarding resident incomes from tourism, although the impact of this source of revenue is clearly visible in terms of consumer goods purchasing, travel to the mainland, and house construction. No surveys have yet attempted to elicit attitudinal data from islanders, mainlanders, or tourists, although the Rapanui are clearly split on the issue of rapid tourist development. At the time of writing the Easter Island tourist industry had existed for little more than a decade. Some initial generalizations can, however, be made.

Employment

As the hotel, and indeed, many guesthouse proprietors, still import the bulk of all supplies from the Chilean mainland, no great impact on island agriculture has occurred. This circumstance derives from visitor attitudes to island produce, its low quality and lack of variety, and male islanders' reluctance to reengage in agricultural occupations. At present, fish, shellfish, and fruit are provided locally by individual suppliers. Guesthouse operation, however, has created an important employment opportunity for Rapanui women, both as proprietors and assistants. Direct employment opportunities for Rapanui males have occurred in transportation, carving, and other service operations.

Some statistics are available for hotel employment (Table 3,10). At almost one person per room the 1973 employment level was somewhat inflated, and has since been reduced. In relation to occupancy, employment ratios remain high. With an average occupancy rate of 21.4 percent, representing approximately 25 guests per day, the guest:staff ratio remained 1:1.5 even in 1974. However, an employment rate of one man-year per room, as found in Antiguan hotels, has not been achieved in Easter Island. Further, as in most small islands of the Third World, tourism has generated islander employment opportunities mainly at the lower occupational levels (Table 4,10). Mainlanders overwhelmingly occupy professional and clerical posts, and are almost all *empleados* (skilled salaried employees). In contrast, islanders are chiefly unskilled *obreros* (labourers). Mainlanders dominate kitchen and restaurant, whereas islanders are employed in the laundry, in general maintenance, in room service, and as night watchmen. Whereas 69.2 percent of mainlander hotel workers are male, 54.5 percent of the islanders are female. Only the training of islanders in hotel management skills will alter this situation.

Until detailed surveys can be accomplished, it is impossible to quantify the multiplier effect of tourism in Easter Island. The tourist industry has clearly encouraged carving and transportation, but has had little effect on

TABLE 3,10 Employment in Hotel Hangaroa 1972-5

Year	Mainlanders	Islanders	Total
1972	26	25	51
1973	24	33	57
1974	N/A	N/A	N/A
1975	20	19	39

SOURCE: HONSA records.

agriculture.[29] Social costs, again unquantifiable, have been incurred in the areas of relative deprivation, the disruption of long-established lifestyles, and the growth of social divisions among islanders. Indeed, according to Chilean planners, tourism has "severely distorted the internal economy" of the island.[30]

Landscape Deterioration

Easter Island has suffered a long history of despoliation, losing artifacts to visiting ships, to the Salmons, to scientific expeditions, and even to missionaries such as Bienvenido de Estella. The landscape changes wrought by the sheepmasters have already been delineated (Chapters 6, 7).

Since the inauguration of the tourist industry, landscape deterioration has increased at a rapid rate. Litter is beginning to appear at all major tourist sites. The re-erected *moai* of Ahu Akivi are severely etched by graffiti, although some of these appear to be of resident origin. Beach destruction, noted earlier, is a wholly resident-created problem, though in part generated by tourism. Chilean agencies have been guilty of violating landscape aesthetics; in particular, the gleaming fuel storage tanks at the airport are visible from as far away as Poike. Belonging to the state petroleum agency, ENAP, and inappropriately sited close to the much-visited *ahu* of Vinapu, this eyesore is known locally as Enapu.

TABLE 4,10 Employment by Skill Level, Hotel Hangaroa 1972

Origin	*Empleados*	*Obreros*	Professional and Clerical	Skilled	Unskilled
Mainlander	10	16	7	10	9
Islander	3	22	1	2	22

SOURCE: HONSA records.

Perhaps the greatest deterioration has occurred at Orongo on the Rano Kao crater rim. Lying between a precipitous sea cliff and the inner crater wall, Orongo occupies an extremely dangerous site. To gain access, visitors have clambered upon the roofs of the traditional stone houses, damaging these already unstable structures. Heavy visitor use has promoted erosion, and in certain areas shod feet have already worn away nearly one third of the petroglyphic relief.[31] On the recommendation of Mulloy, who restored Orongo during 1975-6, the site has been fenced to exclude animals and vehicles, paths have been created, and a guard posted. Should visitor numbers substantially increase, more stringent measures will be necessary to protect both the delicate site from the visitors and the visitors from the dangerous site.

Tourist Perceptions

Unstructured interviews with tourists indicate that Easter Island is regarded generally as an open-air museum. Major problems encountered by tourists include the lack of standardization of accommodation, prices, and service in island guesthouses, the high cost of the HONSA hotel, and occasional indifferent or neglectful treatment. These problems were also defined by informed Chilean sources, which suggest that conditions are generally below the standard expected by international tourists.[32]

Tourists rapidly become aware that the most-frequented portion of the coastline, from Hotel Hangaroa to Tahai, is also the most polluted by solid waste of varying kinds. This zone, the only area travelled on foot by most tourists, is also the site of the slaughterhouse. Poor road conditions are also mentioned. Some tourists complain that guided tours are too cursory and often unpunctual, that guides lack information about many sites, and that few guides adequately speak languages other than Spanish and Rapanui. The inadequacy of local beaches also provokes comment. An occasional, but vehemently expressed, complaint concerns LAN's air schedule between Mataveri and Santiago. It is not uncommon for flights to be cancelled or overbooked, leaving the hapless tourist stranded on the island for several days, and in some cases for more than one week.

THE FUTURE OF EASTER ISLAND

From the metropolitan point of view, Pacific islands are losing their primary productive value and becoming increasingly regarded as tourist destinations and strategic bases for communications and defence.[33] Chilean authorities envisage Easter Island as performing both roles.

The revival of geopolitical concepts in Chile in the 1970s has reaffirmed the position of Easter Island in strategic thinking. Growing acceptability of a 320-kilometre (200-mile) economic limit for territorial waters has provoked Chilean interest in the Pacific Ocean as a future resource base. The enactment of Supreme Decree No. 346 on 5 June 1974 officially named the waters off Chile as the "Sea of Chile", and confirmed the nation's maritime avocation. From this point of view Easter Island becomes a valuable psychological symbol of a possible Chilean sphere of influence in Oceania (Figure 4,10).

More pragmatically, Chile's urgent need for hard currencies had, by 1976, promoted plans for major investments in the tourist industry throughout Chile.[34] As a unique resource, Easter Island is likely to be dedicated to tourism for the forseeable future.[35] This decision has been based on the ultimate realization that the island is unlikely ever to produce commercial exports other than wool, given freight costs and the amount of investment required. On the other hand, modest agrarian improvement could reduce the island's need to import foodstuffs on the present scale. It is perfectly conceivable that beef, mutton, milk, poultry, fish, shellfish, fruits, and vegetables could be produced in sufficient quantities to supply residents and tourists alike.

It is unlikely that earlier plans for a major international airport at Anakena will be implemented in the near future. The island will continue to rely on planes of the Boeing 707 category, with a maximum capacity of 150 passengers. By 1975, however, proposals had already been made for the construction of hotels and guesthouses outside Hangaroa, notably at Anakena and near Rano Raraku.

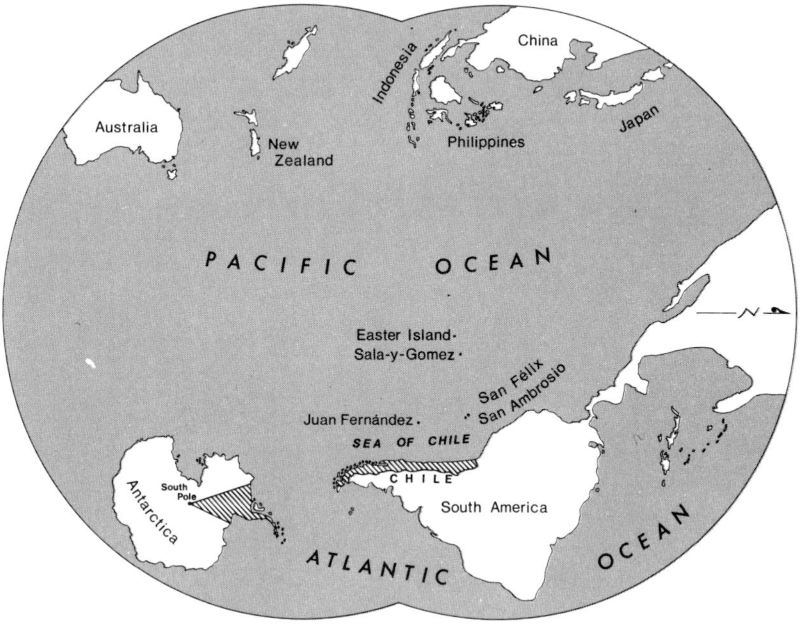

FIGURE 4,10 Chile's geopolitical perception of the Pacific in the 1970s. Note the transposition of land masses (source: Orrego Vicuña, 1975).

There is no doubt that Easter Island could absorb a higher level of tourist inflow. In comparison with more accessible tourist islands, the island has not yet reached saturation point, as measured by crude visitor densities (Table 5,10). Montserrat, smaller than Easter Island but with three times its visitor volume, was still starting up its tourist industry in 1972 and was not regarded as tourist-saturated. In contrast, even the casual visitor to Antigua or Barbados is struck by the overwhelming dominance of tourism, which has led to the overutilization of limited physical space, has imbalanced the local economy, and has accentuated sociocultural friction.[36]

Other measures, however, indicate that Easter Island, because of its very low resident population, is a rather fragile entity (Table 6,10). Tourist arrivals per 1,000 population equal the Hawaii rate, and the peak monthly level is already half that of the Bahamas and considerably more than the Jamaica rate, even if only aliens are included. Anti-tourist sentiment is already important in these islands. If tourist inflow into Easter Island radically increases above the present level, it will prove difficult to retain the present rural quality and casual atmosphere. Building outside Hangaroa will especially change the existing ambience of the *campo* which, with its strong

TABLE 5,10 Visitor Densities in Small Tourist Islands 1972

Island	Size in Square miles	Tourist Arrivals	Visitor Density (Arrivals/sq.mi.)
Montserrat	38	18,000	473
EASTER ISLAND (1973)	64	5,634*	88
Antigua	108	147,000	1,361
Grenada	133	67,000	504
St. Vincent	150	34,000	227
St. Kitts/Nevis	155	22,000	142
Barbados	166	250,000	1,506

* All arrivals by air.

SOURCE: J. Lundgren, in R.P. Momsen (ed.), *Geographical Analysis for Development in Latin America and the Caribbean* (1973), p. 13.

winds, waving grasses, lone sheep, silent megaliths, broken *moai*, and utter absence of people, still supports the air of mystery which is one of the island's major assets in the world tourist market.

Further, rapid expansion of tourism would probably radically alter the nature of the control of the tourist industry at the local level. In the late 1970s at least half the alien visitors used accommodation provided by islanders, and the latter also controlled carving and transportation. Lack of standardization may have as many benefits as drawbacks for the adventurous traveller. Package tourism, however, results in the standardization of accommodation and other services, the tight scheduling of tours, and a resulting decline in the depth of the tourist experience. With mass tourism, the inefficient, casual, and often friendly attitudes of the first tourist decade may give way to the efficiency, indifference, and exploitation of established tourist resorts.

TABLE 6,10 Indicators of Tourist Pressure

Island	Population per sq. mile	Tourist Arrivals per sq. mile	Tourist Overnights per sq. mile	Tourist Arrivals per 1,000 population	Peak Monthly Tourists/ Island population
Bahamas (1972)	31	319	1,786	10,250	70.1%
Hawaii (1972)	119	325	3,256	2,728	N/A
Jamaica (1972)	451	112	884	248	»1%
EASTER ISLAND* All Arrivals (1975)	31	78	—	2,500	31.8%
EASTER ISLAND* Alien Arrivals (1975)	31	29	128	917	11.3%

* Estimating 5,000 arrivals, 2,000 population, 1,834 alien arrivals by air, 636 arrivals (225 aliens) in February 1975.

Package tourism, moreover, requires extensive publicity abroad and strong connections with European and North American travel agencies. These are more readily achieved by mainlander travel agencies based in Santiago. One of these entered the Easter island market in 1975, importing its own vehicles into the island. If the ten years of haphazard tourist development, 1967-76, give way to an increasing reliance on package tours paid for in the country of origin, it is likely that mainlander operators and the HONSA hotel will receive a growing proportion of the trade. The

Rapanui, lacking organization, experience, and off-island connections, and competing intensely among themselves, are in no position to reduce this erosion of their existing share of the tourist trade.

More generally, plans which base Easter Island's economic development on tourism involve a major dilemma for policy makers. The desire to make Easter Island, for the first time in its history, an asset to the Chilean economy, may be difficult to achieve in conjunction with the expressed goal of preserving the island as a unique, open-air archaeological museum. The latter is quite compatible with the "adventure-holiday" type of tourist, where much personal effort is required and high standards are not expected. Easter Island, however, as a high-cost tourist goal, is more likely to attract visitors who demand high standards of hotel service, comfortable tours on paved roads, and easy access to archaeological sites.

The experience of the Acropolis, the Colisseum, and the Lascaux caves suggests that the preservation of such unique monuments is incompatible with mass tourism. Restricted tourist access, combined with the conservation work of UNESCO, as in the Galápagos archipelago, would be a more appropriate mode for Easter Island tourist development. Highly-capitalized attempts to cater to the high levels of demand of the mass tourist market will destroy the existing quality of the tourist experience, will exacerbate existing problems, will reduce the economic role of the islander, and may result in the rapid deterioration of the very artifacts that the tourists come so very far to see.

ENVOI

If, as predicted, a mainlander-organized system of package tourism becomes the dominant factor in the Easter Island economy, the islanders' last opportunity to control their way of life will have disappeared. In terms of traditional concepts of development and modernization, where development is equated with economic growth and modernization with spreading the benefits of Westernization, Easter Island is indeed undergoing both development and modernization.[37] But this unilinear mode of progression, as developed by Western theoreticians, is perhaps inappropriate for the Polynesian setting.[38] A more satisfactory definition of development for the Third World is that of Caldwell, who emphasizes "the drive for self-reliance to the utmost degree."[39] In this sense the Rapanui may have been modernized in the last one hundred years, but they have, at the same time, been *underdeveloped*.[40] The change from cultural autonomy in 1850 to an existence as wage-labourers or state welfare recipients in the alien-dominated economy of the year 2000 can hardly be viewed without misgivings.

Given the contemporary, possibly temporary, rejection of agriculture by the Rapanui, no other mode of life appears possible unless the Chilean government is able to generate a cash-crop farming economy related to the servicing of tourism. Such a programme is doubtful of success, because of the attitudes of both Rapanui and Chileans. As late as 1963 Dr. Ricardo Cruz-Coke, a Chilean physician, felt able to describe the Rapanui as "the most idle human group on the face of the earth".[41] Moreover, in such an isolated location, far from major world air routes, tourism is at best a risk-laden economic base. Emigration to the mainland may be an alternative solution to the demographic and social pressures of Easter Island. Before the development of tourism in 1967, the 1960s emigration rate was over 8 percent, with over 22 percent in the 20-29 age group.[42] The Westernization processes of the 1960s have generated new demands which cannot be satisfied by the local economy. It is likely, therefore, that many Rapanui, especially the young, will continue to emigrate to the Chilean mainland or beyond either in a direct search for work and educational opportunities or through inter-marriage with Chileans and foreigners.

In 1911 the determinist geographer Ellen Churchill Semple felt able to write, of Easter Island:

> The island today shows only abandoned fields, the silent monuments of . . . stone, and the shrunken remnant of a deteriorated people.[43]

Seventy years later, the "shrunken remnant" has vigorously multiplied and successfully adapted to new modes of life, but the abandoned fields remain, and graffiti accrete upon the silent monuments of stone.

PLATE 45 At Rano Raraku ▶

Oh Isla de Pascua, no me atrapes,
hay demasiada luz, estás muy lejos,
y cuánta piedra y agua:
too much for me! Nos vamos!

Pablo Neruda
La Rosa Separada (1973)

PLATE 46 Rat (Kon-Tiki Museet artifact 1716) ▶

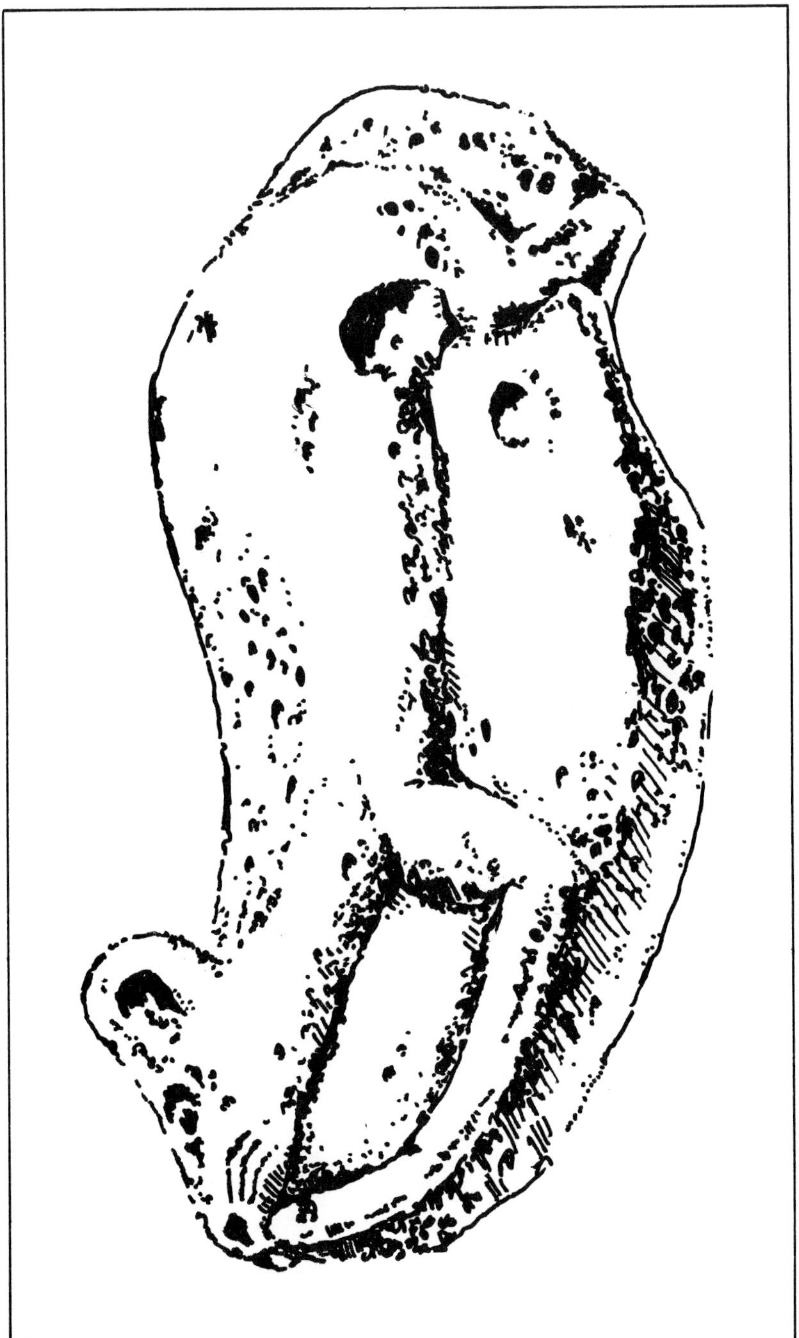

NOTES AND REFERENCES

A number of abbreviated forms have been used throughout the references:

Actas, —	*Libro de Actas de la Municipalidad de Hangaroa, Isla de Pascua*. (Municipal minute book, Hangaroa, Easter Island).
Documentos, LE —	*Documentos de la Isla de Pascua Pertenecientes al Señor Enrique Merlet*, Valparaiso. An archive of forty items, arranged and numbered by the author, presently located at the Compañia de Inversiones "La Escosesa" Limitada, Calle MacIver 142, Santiago, Chile. Items are typewritten or handwritten in Spanish, French, and English, and cover the period 1868-1939. Some of the items are to be found also in Vergara (see below). A detailed list is to be found in Reference Appendix I.
El Mercurio, —	Major Santiago daily newspaper. (*El Mercurio de Valparaiso* is cited in full throughout).
La Unión, —	Major Valparaiso newspaper in early twentieth century. (*La Unión de Santiago* is cited in full throughout).
Vergara, Appendix —	Victor M. Vergara de la P., *La Isla de Pascua: Dominación y Dominio*. Memoria de Preuba para optar al grado de Licenciado en la Facultad de Ciencias Jurídicas y Sociales de la Universidad de Chile, 1939 (Santiago, Chile: Instituto de Geografía Militar, 1939). A thesis on the administrative history of Easter Island. Pages 11-83 constitute the text, of which pp. 39-79 constitute a legal history of the island from the 1860s until the mid-1930s. Pages 85-254 comprise 61 appendices, consisting of reproductions of documents relating to Easter Island, some of which are found also in the Documentos (see above). A detailed list is to be found in Reference Appendix II.

REFERENCE APPENDIX I

Arabic numerals are used to refer to the 40 items comprising the Documentos, *op. cit.*, archive. As items have been arranged chronologically by the author, this numbering system differs from that in partial use, probably by Merlet, on the documents themselves. Original titles are given where available. Short descriptions are provided where necessary.

1 "Acte de Société Brander Dutrou-Bornier, 30 October 1871, extracted (16 April 1918) from the minutes of M. Gustave Vincent, notary, of Papeete, Ile Tahiti." Handwritten.

2 "Certificats de Vente." A series of handwritten copies of Easter Island land purchases made by Dutrou-Bornier (1868-73) and registered in Papeete in 1880.

3 "Plan de la Proprieté du Sieur Dutrou-Bornier comprenant les terres de Hanga Piko, Mataveri, et Rano Kao, mesurant ensembles sept cent six hectares 1/2 (706½)." Handwritten.

4 "Expedition d'un arrêt du Tribunal Superieur de Papeete, Chambre Civil, du 8 mai 1884; Dame Valentine Foulon, Veuve Dutrou-Bornier c/Dame Darsie et Consorts. Greffe des Tribunaux de Papeete, Ile Tahiti." Extracted 2 May 1918. Handwritten.

5 "Expedition d'un Jugement d'adjudication du Tribunal de Premier instance de Papeete, Chambre de Criées, du 24 Juin 1884; Vente de l'exploitation de l'Ile de Pâques Brander Dutrou-Bornier. Greffe des Tribunaux de Papeete, Ile Tahiti." Extracted 2 May 1918. Handwritten.

6 Two copies of parts of items 4 and 5, plus "Cahiers de Charges, 31 January 1881." Handwritten.

7 Copy of sale contract between M. Tati Salmon of Tahiti and M. Policarpo Toro of Chile, 7 August 1888; notary Auguste Goupil, Chilean Consul in Papeete, Tahiti. In Spanish. Typed.

8 "Cesión de Derechos, Don Policarpo Toro a Don Juan H. Mora, Valparaiso, Chile." (26 November 1892).

9 Handwritten document giving judgement of Court of Bordeaux, France, 4 August 1893, on Brander Dutrou-Bornier case.

10 The Goupil Packet. Compiled by M. Goupil of Papeete, this packet contains handwritten copies of:

LE 10/i: Letter, Auguste Goupil, Papeete, to M. Merlet, Valparaiso, 27 June 1902. In French.

LE 10/ii: Agreement of Sale between M. John Brander, Proprietor, living on Easter Island, but presently in Papeete, and M. Policarpo Toro H., Captain, of Valparaiso, but presently in Papeete, 21 August 1888, before A. Goupil. In French.

LE 10/iii: Letter, John Brander, of Papeete, to A. Goupil, of Papeete, 22 June 1895. In English.

LE 10/iv: Letter, A. Goupil, of Papeete, to John Brander, of Papeete, 22 June 1895. In French.

LE 10/v: Letter, John Brander, of Papeete, to A. Goupil, of Papeete, 22 June 1895. In English.

LE 10/vi: Letter, A. Goupil, of Papeete, to John Brander, of Papeete, 24 June 1895. In French.

LE 10/vii: Letter, A. Goupil, of Papeete, to Policarpo Toro, of Colina, near Santiago, Chile, 24 June 1895. In English.

11 Partial set of Goupil Packet, item 10.

12 Contract between the Directory of the Treasury, Chile, and Enrique Merlet of Valparaiso, in Santiago, 3 September 1895. In Spanish.

13 Confirmation of Brander's title to lands on Easter Island, made by George Darsie and Tetuanuireiaiteraiatea Salmon, or Darsie, in Anstruther, Fife, 2 May 1896. In English. Handwritten.

14 Copy of letter, John Brander, of Papará, Tahiti to __________ Schlubach, Chile, 13 February 1897. In English. Handwritten.

15 Company Statutes of "Sociedad Compañía Esplotadora de la Isla de Pascua." Valparaiso, 20 July 1903. In Spanish.

16 "Estatutos de la Compañía Esplotadora de la Isla de Pascua." Valparaiso, 20 July 1903. Handwritten original of item 15.

17 "Compraventa D. Enrique Merlet y Otro a Compañía Esplotadora de la Isla de Pascua." Valparaiso, 13 November 1903.

18 Two Chilean newspaper clippings:

LE 18/i: "Los Sucesos de la Isla de Pascua parte del Comandante de la *Baquedano*," by Luis Gomez Carreño, "Dirección General de la Armada de Chile," 12 January 1905.

LE 18/ii: "Informe Sobre la Isla de Pascua agregado del parte del comandante del *Baquedano*," by Horacio Cooper, "subdelegado marítimo de la Isla de Pascua." No date; c. January 1905.

19 "Contrato de Cuenta Corriente Prenda y Fianza Williamson Balfour & Cia. a Cia. Explotadora de la Isla de Pascua," 13 June 1908. Typed resumé, omitting clauses 3-10, of item 20.

20 "Contrato de Cuenta Corriente prenda y fianza Williamson Balfour Compañía a Compañía Explotadora de la Isla de Pascua." February 15 1908.

21 Letter, Dr. Ernesto A. Hubner, Valparaiso, to don Enrique A. Rodriguez, Minister, Government of Chile, 28 March 1911. In Spanish.

22 "Informe de Doctor Knoche Sobre una Visita a la Isla de Pascua, Abril de 1911."

23 "Informe de Pedro Adams, Osorno." Handwritten copy of report of Pedro Adams on Easter Island agriculture, 10 September 1914.

24 Copy of decree of 26 April 1916 declaring Easter Island part of the Department of Valparaiso and designating it for colonization under the Ministry of Colonization. In Spanish.

25 "Prórroga Merlet, Enrique." Santiago, 21 June 1916. (Extension of Merlet's 1895 contract for an indefinite term).

26 "Aclaración." Explanation of limits of Merlet and Government lands on Easter Island; Valparaiso, 27 September 1916.

27 Copy of decree by President Sanfuentes declaring Merlet's 3 September 1895 lease of the Government lands on Easter Island to have expired. Santiago, 7 November 1916. In Spanish.

28 Notes of Humberto Molina Luco, lawyer, concerning Enrique Merlet's attempt to register Easter Island land claims. Valparaiso, 2 November 1916. In Spanish.

29 Letter, "de Capitaine Joseph Dillinger ex commandant du voilier Francais 'Jean' a Monsieur Williamson." Undated, 1916. In French.

30 Letter, Percy H. Edmunds, of Easter Island/Valparaiso, to Compañía Esplotadora de la Isla de Pascua, Valparaiso, 22 November 1916. In English.

31 Letter, Frank T. Green, to Messrs. The Easter Island Co., c/o Williamson Balfour and Co., Valparaiso, 23 November 1916. In English.

32 Letter, M. Lucien Sisogne. Papeete, Tahiti, to Balfour Guthrie & Co. of San Francisco, May 3 1918. In English.

33 Letter, Balfour, Guthrie & Co., San Francisco, to Messrs. Williamson, Balfour & Co., Valparaiso, 22 May 1918. In English.

34 Two typed copies of Dutrou-Bornier's land titles, see item 2. In French.

35 "Report on the Water Supply and Possible Agricultural and General Development of the Island of Pascua by WILLIAM ALANSON BRYAN B.Sc. etc., Professor Zoology and Geology, Biological Engineer, 1920."

36 "Informe Sobre Concesión de la Isla de Pascua, Santiago, 26 de Agosto de 1927." Report by Alfonso Bulnes to the Controller-General.

37 Report on the Easter Island Concession by the Consejo de Defensa Fiscal, 14 March 1929. In Spanish.

38 "Conclusiones de un informe," by "Luis Felipe Martinez, Jefe de la Sección Concesiones, Consejo de Defensa Fiscal," 19 March 1929.

39 Decree of President Ibañez and C.O. Frödden, Naval Ministry, ending the Temperamento Provisorio, 19 April 1929. In Spanish.

40 "Map of Easter Island." Undated, hand-drawn map, about 1" to 1 mile.

REFERENCE APPENDIX II

Roman numerals are used to refer to the 61 appendices to be found in Vergara, *op. cit.* Vergara's original titles are given.

I Memoria sobre la Isla de Pascua, de don Policarpo Toro Hurtado, en su visita en la Corbeta "Abtao". Noviembre de 1886.

II Carta de don Policarpo Toro a Mr. John Brander, 20 de Septiembre de 1887.

III Carta de Mr. John Brander a don Policarpo Toro.

IV Carta de Mr. John Brander a don Policarpo Toro.

V Decreto de 26 de Septiembre de 1887 (sin numero), que autoriza celebración un contrato de promesa de venta con Mr. John Brander.

VI Comunicación del Consul chileno en Tahiti dirigida al Ministro de Relaciones de Chile, 25 de Febrero de 1887.

VII Parte de don Policarpo Toro al señor Ministro de Hacienda don Agustín Edwards, 24 de Febrero de 1884.

VIII Carta del R.P. Félix Jaffuel de los SS. CC. al autor de esta Memoria con transcripción de cartas de Mons. Jaussen y de Mons. Verdier, sobre la Isla de Pascua.

IX Informe de don Osvaldo Rengifo y Jorge Hunneus, sobre la ocupación chilena de Pascua.

X Instrucciones del Ministro Dávila Larrain a don Policarpo Toro, sobre adquisición de propiedades de particulares en la Isla.

XI Comunicación al Comandante General de Marina, en que don Policarpo Toro da cuenta de la ocupación chilena de la Isla de Pascua.

XII Acta de Cesión de la Soberanía de la Isla, suscrita por los Jefes indígenas.

XIII Acta de Proclamación de la Soberanía de Chile, en el acto de la "Toma de Posesión".

XIV Compra-venta de terrenos hecha por el R.P. Roussel a varios indígenas, Nov. 30, 1887.

XV Compra-venta: Gaspar Zumbohn a Pierre Mau, Rapa-Nui, Diciembre 2 de 1869.

XVI Compra-venta: Dutron-Bornier o Tokí André y otros 10 de Noviembre de 1880.

XVII Compra-venta: Dutron-Bornier a Koreta Puakurunga y otros, Isla de Pascua, 9 de Mayo 1873.

XVIII Adjudicación a Mr. John Brander (Resolución Tribunal Alzada de Papeete, 24 de Junio 1884).

XIX Sentencia de la Corte de Burdeos, 20 de Junio de 1893.

XX Compra-venta: Tatí Salmon a Monseñor Tepano Jaussen, Papeete 30 de Noviembre de 1887.

XXI Compra-venta: Policarpo Toro a Tatí Salmon y otro; Papeete, 2 de Enero de 1888.

XXII Compra-venta: Policarpo Toro a Monseñor Verdier; Papeete, 8 de Agosto de 1888. Documentos relacionados con la cancelación del precio de esta compra.

XXIII Compromiso de Compra-venta: Policarpo Toro a Mr. John Brander y otro; Papeete, 23 Agosto 1888.

XXIV Arriendo: Policarpo Toro a Mr. John Brander; Papeete, 21 de Agosto de 1888.

XXV Inventario: Policarpo Toro con Mr. John Brander, Valparaiso, Septiembre 7 de 1889.

XXVI Promesa de venta: John Brander a Enrique Merlet; Valparaiso, 25 de Mayo de 1895.

XXVII Declaración: Enrique Merlet a Juan Brander; Valparaiso, 27 de Enero de 1896.

XXVIII Compra-venta: Juan Brander e Enrique Merlet; Valparaiso, 31 de Agosto de 1897.

XXIX Arrendamiento: Fisco a Enrique Merlet; Santiago, 3 de Septiembre de 1895.

XXX Compañía Explotadora de la Isla de Pascua (Escritura Social); Valparaiso, 20 de Julio de 1903.

XXXI Compra-venta: Enrique Merlet y otro a Compañía Explotadora de la Isla de Pascua.

XXXII Prórroga arrendamiento Fisco a Merlet; Santiago, a 21 de Junio de 1916.

XXXIII Aclaración: Enrique Merlet; Valparaiso, 27 de Septiembre de 1916.

XXXIV Expediente completo, Juicio Oposición Inscripción de Dominio, Caratulado "Fisco con Merlet", 2.° Juzgado de Letras de Valparaiso (1916).

XXXV Decreto 1291, de 7 de Noviembre de 1916, declarando caducado el arrendamiento a Merlet.

XXXVI "Temperamento Provisorio" (Oficio N.° 34, de 5 de Mayo de 1917, del Ministerio de Relaciones Exteriores, que entregó neuvamente la Isla de Pascua a la Compañía Explotadora).

XXXVII Decreto 946, de 19 de Abril de 1929, pone término al "Temperamento Provisorio" y ordena inscribir la Isla como propiedad fiscal.

XXXVIII Decreto N.° 942, 12 de Julio de 1933, constituye la Comisión Consultiva de la Isla de Pascua.

XXXIX Decreto N.° 1045, 29 de Julio de 1933, nombra Asesor de la Comisión Consultiva al Auditor Naval Fernando Reyes Ugarte.

XL Oficio N.° 1, de 30 de Agosto de 1933 y Memorandum de la Comisión Consultiva, en que se pide al Supremo Gobierno de cumplimiento al Decreto N.° 946.

XLI Inscripcion de fs. 2.400, N.°2424, del Registro de Propiedades del Conservador de Bienes Raices de Valparaiso, a nombre del Fisco de Chile.

XLII Solicited de Arrendamiento, presentada por la Compañía Explotadora, 12 de Abril 1935.

XLIII Informe de la Comisión Consultiva, 5 de Febrero de 1936.

XLIV Extracto Informe N.°8, de 29 de Octubre de 1935, del Auditor Fernando Reyes U.

XLV Contrato de Arrendamiento de la Isla de Pascua a la Compañía Explotadora (Santiago, 19 de Marzo de 1936, Notaría Cruz).

XLVI Modificaciones al Contrato de Arrendamiento (Santiago, 3 de Julio de 1937, Notaría Cruz).

XLVII Protocolización Decreto N.° 196, autorizando cesion arrendamiento a Sociedad Anónima.

XLVIII Decreto N.° 3986, 3 de Noviembre de 1937, autorizando existencia y aprobando estatutos Sociedad Anonima "Compañía Explotadora de la Isla de Pascua".

XLIX Protocolización certificado legalización "Compañía Explotadora de la Isla de Pascua".

L Decreto N.° 1512, 21 de Octubre 1938, declara transferido el arrendamiento de la Isla a la nueva Sociedad Anónima.

LI Decreto N.° 1561, 31 de Octubre de 1938, que introduce leves modificaciones al Contrato de Arrendamiento.

LII Acta suscrita el 1.° de Diciembre de 1938, ante el Ministro de Defensa Nacional, en que se da cuenta y pone término a las labores de la Comisión Consultiva.

LIII Decreto N.° 1826, de 23 de Diciembre de 1938, reconoce y pone término a las labores de la Comisión Consultiva.

LIV Decreto N.° 444, 26 de Abril 1916, destina la Isla a la colonización y la declara Subdelegación del Departamento de Valparaiso.

LV Ley N.° 3220, 29 Enero 1927, coloco la Isla de Pascua bajo el control y dependencia de la Marina.

LVI Decreto Ordinario N.° 85, de la Comandancia en Jefe de la Armada, 28 de Abril de 1936, que nombra Comisión redactora del Reglamento Interno de Vida y Trabajo en la Isla de Pascua.

LVII Reglamento de Régimen Interno de Vida y Trabajo en la Isla de Pascua.

LVIII Decreto N.° 103, 16 de Enero de 1935, declarando Parque Nacional la Isla de Pascua.

LIX Oficio de 8 de Julio de 1935, del Consejo de Monumentos Nacionales al Sr. Ministro de Educación.

LX Decreto N.° 4536, 23 de Julio de 1938, declarando a la Isla de Pascua Monumento Histórico.

LXI Inventario de especies de gran valor etno-arqueológicas que encierra la Isla de Pascua.

INTRODUCTION

1. Easter Island's "mysteries" are emphasized in the titles of the following. Spanish (Chilean): BIENVENIDO DE ESTELLA, R.P., *Los Misterios de la Isla de Pascua*. Santiago, Chile: Cervantes, 1920; CAMPBELL, R., *El Misterioso Mundo de Rapanui*. Buenos Aires: Francisco de Aguirre, 1973. English: DOS PASSOS, J., *Easter Island: Island of Enigmas*. Garden City, N.Y.: Doubleday, 1971; HEYERDAHL, T., *Aku-Aku: The Secret of Easter Island*. London: Allen and Unwin, 1958; MACMILLAN BROWN, J., *The Riddle of the Pacific*. London: T. Fisher Unwin, 1924; ROUTLEDGE, Mrs. Scoresby, *The Mystery of Easter Island: The Story of an Expedition*. London: Sifton, Praed, 1919. French: CASTEX, L., *Les Secrets de l'Ile de Pâques*. Paris: Hachette, 1966; CHAUVET, S., *L'Ile de Pâques et ses Mysteres*. Paris: Tel, 1935; MAZIERE, F., *Fantastique Ile de Pâques*. Paris: Laffont, 1965 (English edition: *Mysteries of Easter Island*); SCHWARZ, J-M., *The Mysteries of Easter Island*, English edition. New York: Avon, 1975.

2. Ten titles are listed in note 1, above. Titles which emphasize the island's remoteness include the following. ENGLERT, S., *Island at the Center of the World: New Light on Easter Island*. New York: Scribners, 1970; FERDON, E.N., *One Man's Log*. London: Allen and Unwin, 1966; FLORES, J., *Te Pito Te Henua*. Santiago, Chile: Orbe, 1965; FONCK, O., *Rapa Nui: El Ultimo Refugio* (El Origen de Los Pascua). Santiago, Chile: Zig-Zag, 1974; REID, H.E., *A World Away: A Canadian Adventure on Easter Island*. Sydney: Angus and Robertson, 1967. Problems of the island's prehistoric culture are emphasized in the following. Spanish (Chilean): ENGLERT, S., *La Tierra de Hotu Matu'a: Historia, Etnología y Lengua de la Isla de Pascua*. Padre las Casas, Chile: San Francisco, 1948. English: CASEY, R.J., *Easter Island: Home of the Scornful Gods*. London: Elkin Mathews and Marrott, 1942; WOLFF, W., *Island of Death: A New Key to Easter Island's Culture through an ethno-psychological study*. New York: J.J. Augustin, 1948. French: LAVACHERY, J., *Ile de Pâques*. Paris: Grasset, 1935; METRAUX, A., *Easter Island: A Stone Age Civilization of the Pacific*. London: Deutsch, 1957.

3. FERDON, E.N. and HEYERDAHL, T., eds., *Archaeology of Easter Island*. Santa Fe, N.M.: School of American Research and Museum of New Mexico Monograph 24, part 1, 1961.

4. HEYERDAHL, T., *The Art of Easter Island*. London: Allen and Unwin, 1976. See also LAVACHERY, H., *Les Pétroglyphes de l'Ile de Pâques*. Antwerp, 1939.

5. METRAUX, A., *Ethnology of Easter Island*. Honolulu: Bernice P. Bishop Museum Bulletin 160 (1940), reprinted 1971.

6. CAMPBELL, R., *La Herencia Musical de Rapanui: Etnomusicología de la Isla de Pascua*. Santiago, Chile: Andres Bello, 1971.

7. CHURCHILL, W., *Easter Island: The Rapanui Speech and the Peopling of Southeast Polynesia*. Washington, D.C.: Carnegie Institution Publication 174, 1912.

8. NOGRADY, G.L., *Microbiology of Easter Island*. Montreal: G.L. Nógrády, 1974.

9. VERGARA, M. de la P., V., *La Isla de Pascua: Dominación y Dominio* (Memorio de Prueba, Universidad de Chile). Santiago, Chile: Instituto Geográfico Militar, 1939.

10. ENGLERT, 1948, *op. cit.*

11. AYRES, W.S., *The Cultural Context of Easter Island Religious Structures*. Unpublished Ph.D. dissertation, Department of Anthropology, Tulane University, 1973; McCOY, P.C., *Easter Island Settlement Patterns in the late Prehistoric and Proto-historic Periods*. Unpublished Ph.D. dissertation, Department of Anthropology, Washington State University, 1973.

12. Modernization generally refers to the process whereby a relatively closed traditional society becomes transformed through contacts with modern societies. Traditional folkways become recessive, Western ways of life gradually become dominant. As used in this book, modernization is regarded as a very broad term which subsumes "development" and also includes landscape change. A vast literature on modernization and development exists; it would be

inappropriate to discuss the concepts in detail here. For an introduction to these complex concepts see BROOKFIELD, H.C., *Interdependent Development*. London: Methuen, 1975; DE SOUZA, A.R. and PORTER, P.W., *The Underdevelopment and Modernization of the Third World*. Washington, D.C.: Association of American Geographers Resource Paper 28, 1974; LERNER, D., *The Passing of Traditional Society: Modernization in the Middle East*. New York: Free Press, 1958; MYINT, H., *The Economics of Developing Countries*. London: Hutchinson, 1964; SZENTES, T., *The Political Economy of Underdevelopment*. Budapest: Akademiai Kiado, 1971.

13. Actas, 17 January 1969.

14. SEPULVEDA WHITTLE, T.B., "Dominación Chilena en la Isla de Pascua," *Revista de Marina* 51 (1936), 564-78, 677-90.

15. Personal communication, Antonio Tepano, December 1975.

CHAPTER 1

1. MOOREHEAD, A., *The Fatal Impact: An Account of the Invasion of the South Pacific 1767-1840*. Harmondsworth: Penguin, 1968, p. 79; COOK, J., *The Explorations of Captain James Cook in the Pacific*. New York: Dover, 1971.

2. MOOREHEAD, *op. cit.*, p. 14.

3. *Ibid.*, *passim*.

4. WEBB, W.P., *The Great Frontier*. Boston: Houghton Mifflin, 1952.

5. OLIVER, D.L., *The Pacific Islands*. New York: Natural History Library, 1961; LIND, A.W., *Hawaii*. London: Oxford University Press, 1969.

6. MOOREHEAD, *op. cit.*, p. 96.

7. OLIVER, *op. cit.*, p. 121.

8. *Ibid.*, p. 112.

9. MOOREHEAD, *op. cit.*, p. 65.

10. *Ibid.*, p. 117.

11. HEYERDAHL, 1952, *op. cit.*

12. ENGLERT, S., *La Tierra de Hotu Matu'a: Historia, Etnología y Lengua de la Isla de Pascua*. Padre las Casas, Chile: Editorial San Francisco, 1948.

13. COOK, J., *Voyages*. London: Heron, (BARROW, J., ed., 1860), p. 163.

14. METRAUX, A., *Ethnology of Easter Island*. Honolulu: Bernice P. Bishop Museum Bulletin 160 (1940), 1971, pp. 39-40.

15. *Ibid.*, p. 41.

16. *Ibid.*, p. 42.

17. OLIVER, *op. cit.*, p. 128.

18. METRAUX, *op. cit.*, p. 42; BROWN, J.M., *The Riddle of the Pacific*. London: T. Fisher Unwin, 1924, pp. 298-9.

19. METRAUX, *op. cit.*, p. 43. Other authorities cite larger figures, e.g. VERGARA, V.M., *La Isla de Pascua: Dominación y Dominio*. Santiago: Universidad de Chile, 1939, has 1500 (p. 23), and *La Unión* (Valparaiso) of 30 November 1888 has 1200-1500.

20. METRAUX, *op. cit.*, p. 43.

21. *Ibid.*, p. 44; VERGARA, *op. cit.*, pp. 23-5; *El Mercurio* (Valparaiso) 19 February 1889; BALLESTEROS, J., "Isla de Pascua" (1872), pp. 73-147 in SILVA, L.I., *La Isla de Pascua*. Santiago: Biblioteca Geográfica e Histórica Chilena, Vol. 1, 1903; MACHOWSKI, J., *Island of Secrets*. Hale: London, 1975, p. 105.

22. METRAUX, *op. cit.*, pp. 44-5.

23. In the literature the first part of Dutrou-Bornier's surname is variously spelled Dutrou, Dutron, Dutroux, Dutrouz, and Du Tron.

24. VERGARA, *op. cit.*, p. 25.

25. Transcriptions of letters of Mons. Jaussen and Mons. Verdier in VERGARA, Appendix VIII. MACHOWSKI, *op. cit.*, p. 110.

26. VERGARA, Appendix XIV.

27. *La Unión* 19 February 1889, 8, 9 September 1916.

28. BIENVENIDO DE ESTELLA, R.P., *Los Misterios de la Isla de Pascua*. Santiago: Cervantes, 1920, p. 115.

29. Transcriptions of letters of Mons. Jaussen and Mons. Verdier, in VERGARA, Appendix VIII.

30. *Ibid.*

31. *Ibid.*

32. *Ibid.*; METRAUX, *op. cit.*, p. 46.

33. Documentos, LE 1.

34. Documentos, LE 6, 9.

35. SALMON, Ernest, *Alexandre Salmon 1820-1866 et sa femme Arii-taimai 1821-1897: Deux figures de Tahiti a l'epoque du Protectorat*. Paris: Musée de l'Homme, Publications de la Société des Océanistes 11, 1964.

36. Documentos, LE 4, 5, 6, 9.

CHAPTER 2

1. OSBOURNE, L., "A Son of Empire," pp. 321-31 in BOWMAN, J.S., ed., *A Book of Islands*. Garden City, N.Y.: Doubleday, 1971.

2. VERGARA, Appendix XII.

3. VERGARA, Appendix XIII.

4. VERGARA, Appendix XI.

5. THORNTON, A.P., "Overseas Empires," pp. 215-38 in BRIGGS, A., ed., *The Nineteenth Century*. London: Thames and Hudson, 1970, p. 216.

6. RASKIN, J., *The Mythology of Imperialism*. New York: Random House, 1971.

7. OSBOURNE, *op. cit.*, p. 322.

8. OLIVER, D.L., *The Pacific Islands*. New York: Natural History Library, 1961, p. 139.

9. PIKE, F.B., *Chile and the United States 1880-1962: The Emergence of Chile's Social Crisis and the Challenge to United States Diplomacy*. Notre Dame, Indiana: University of Notre Dame Press, 1963, p. 31.

10. *Ibid.*, p. 2.

11. TALBOTT, R.D., *A History of the Chilean Boundaries*. Ames, Iowa: Iowa State University Press, 1974.

12. RATZEL, F., *Anthropogeographie*. Stuttgart, 1882, 1891.

13. PINOCHET UGARTE, A., *Geopolítica*, second edition. Santiago, Chile: Andres Bello, 1974, p. 214.

14. PIKE, *op. cit.*, p. 61 note 73.

15. *Ibid.*, p. 33.

16. *Ibid.*, p. 36.

17. BROOKFIELD, H., *Interdependent Development*. London: Methuen, 1975.

18. ORREGO VICUÑA, F., *El Océano Pacifico*. Santiago, Chile: Gabriela Mistral, 1975, p. 20.

19. *Ibid.*, p. 37.

20. VERGARA, Appendix I.

21. *La Unión* 6 November 1916.

22. DELANO, A., *A Narrative of Voyages and Travels in the Northern and Southern Hemispheres*. Boston 1817, quoted in CHURCHILL, W., *Easter Island: The Rapanui Speech and the Peopling of Southeast Polynesia*. Washington, D.C.: Carnegie Institution, 1912, p. 310.

23. *El Mercurio* 19 February 1889.

24. *El Independiente* 17, 24 November and 15, 22, 29 December 1872.

25. PHILIPPI, R.A., "Jeografía: La Isla de Pascua i sus habitantes," *Anales de la Universidad de Chile* 43 (1873), 365-434, p. 376.

26. *La Unión* 6 November 1916.

27. VERGARA, Appendix I.

28. DELANO, in CHURCHILL, *op. cit.*, p. 309.

29. ROUTLEDGE, Mrs. Scoresby, *The Mystery of Easter Island: The Story of An Expedition*. London: Sifton, Praed, 1919, p. 157.

30. LOPEZ, J.E., "Esploración de las Islas Esporadicas al Occidente de la Costa de Chile," *Anuario Hidrográfico de la Marina de Chile* 2 (1876), 63-84.

31. CASEY, R.J., *Easter Island: Home of the Scornful Gods*. London: Elkin Mathews and Marrot, 1932, p. 292.

32. VERGARA, Appendix I.

33. *La Unión* 1 July 1888.

34. *Ibid.*, 1 July 1888.

35. *Ibid.*, 8 March 1889.

36. *Ibid.*, 1 July 1888.

37. *Ibid.*, 6 November 1916.

38. VICUÑA MACKENNA, B., "El Reparto del Pacífico: la posesión de la Isla de Pascua," *Revista de Marina* 1 (1885), 65-68.

39. LOPEZ, *op. cit.*, pp. 82-3.

40. *La Unión* 1 July 1888.

41. *Ibid.*, 30 September 1888.

42. VERGARA, Appendix I.

43. *El Mercurio de Valparaiso*, 28 May 1887.

44. PIKE, *op. cit.*, p. 36.

45. *El Mercurio de Valparaiso*, 28 May 1887.

46. *Gaceta de Lima* 42, 7 October - 26 November 1770, and 44, 27 January - 30 May 1771; VERGARA, *op. cit.*, pp. 19-20.

47. VERGARA, Appendix I.

48. *La Unión*, 7 December 1888.

49. *Chilean Times*, 30 June 1888.

50. COOK, H., 1971, *op. cit.*, p. 155.

51. VERGARA, V.M., *La Isla de Pascua: Dominación y Dominio*. Santiago: Universidad de Chile, 1939. A similar, contemporary apologia is to be found in SEPULVEDA WHITTLE, T.B., "Domina-

ción Chilena en la Isla de Pascua," *Revista de Marina* 51 (1936), 564-78.

52. VERGARA, Appendix I.

53. *Ibid.*

54. *La Unión* 6 November 1916.

55. *Ibid.*, 5 April, 1 and 24 July, 19 August, 1887.

56. *El Mercurio de Valparaiso* 27 May 1887.

57. VERGARA, Appendix VI.

58. VERGARA, Appendix VII.

59. CASTEX, *op. cit.*, pp. 115-17; VERGARA, *op. cit.*, p. 37; CHURCHILL, *op. cit.*, p. 317.

60. Bornier had apparently had some undefined official status as French representative and had made several attempts to interest France in the island. See CHURCHILL, *op. cit.*, p. 317; VAN HOOREBEECK, A., "Le Roi de l'Ile de Pâques," *L'Eventail* (Brussels), 7 November 1975, pp. 22-3.

61. VERGARA, Appendix I.

62. VERGARA, Appendix XX.

63. VERGARA, Appendix II.

64. VERGARA, Appendix III.

65. VERGARA, Appendix V.

66. VERGARA, Appendix XXI.

67. VERGARA, Appendix XXIII.

68. VERGARA, Appendix XXI; Documentos, LE 7.

69. VERGARA, Appendix XXII.

70. VERGARA, Appendix XXIII.

71. VERGARA, Appendix XXIV.

72. VERGARA, Appendix IX.

73. *Ibid.*

74. *La Unión* 4, 11, 12 July 1888.

75. *La Unión* 29 June 1888.

76. *Ibid.*, 30 September 1888; *El Mercurio de Valparaiso* 19.

77. February 1889; SEPULVEDA WHITTLE, *op. cit.*

78. *La Tribuna* 21 November 1888; *El Mercurio de Valparaiso* 19 February 1889.

CHAPTER 3

1. SOJA, E.W., *The Political Organization of Space*. Washington, D.C.: Association of American Geographers Resource Paper No. 8, 1971.

2. PORTEOUS, J.D., "The Corporation as Frontier Developer," *B.C. Geographical Series*, 17 (1973), 79-88.

3. PORTEOUS, J.D., "The Company State: A Chilean Case Study," *Canadian Geographer* 17 (1973), 113-26.

4. *Ibid.*; PORTEOUS, J.D., "Urban Transplantation in Chile," *Geographical Review* 62 (1972), 455-78; PORTEOUS, J.D., "Social Class in Atacama Company Towns," *Annals of the Association of American Geographers* 64 (1974), 409-17.

5. PORTEOUS, J.D., 1973, *Canadian Geographer, op. cit.*

6. LATCHAM, R.A., *Chuquicamata: Estado Yankee*. Santiago, Chile: Nascimento, 1926.

7. PORTEOUS, J.D., 1972, *op. cit.*

8. PORTEOUS, J.D., 1973, *Canadian Geographer, op. cit.*

9. *El Mercurio de Valparaiso* 28 May 1887. Bananas can be produced in Arica, Chile's northernmost town.

10. *La Unión* 30 September, 25 November, 7 December, 1888.

11. *Ibid.*, 30 September 1888.

12. *Ibid.*, quotation by J. Eden of captain of the naval vessel *O'Higgins*.

13. *Ibid.*, 19 February 1889.

14. *Ibid.*, 30 September 1888.

15. VERGARA, Appendix X.

16. *La Unión* 13 July 1888.

17. *Ibid.*, 25 September 1888.

18. *Ibid.*, 21 August 1889.

19. *Ibid.*, 17 August 1889.

20. *Ibid.*, 21 August 1889.

21. Documentos, LE 8.

22. *El Heraldo* 9 December 1892.

23. *Ibid.*, 10 December 1892.

24. *La Unión* 21 August 1889.

25. Documentos, LE 8.

26. *El Mercurio* 11 November 1916.

27. *Ibid.*

28. VERGARA, Appendix XXVI.

29. Documentos, LE 10/iii.

30. Documentos, LE 10/iv.

31. Documentos, LE 10/v.

32. Documentos, LE 10/vi.

33. Documentos, LE 10/vii.

34. VERGARA, *op. cit.*, p. 44.

35. Documentos, LE 12; VERGARA, Appendix XXIX.

36. VERGARA, Appendix XXVII.

37. Documentos, LE 13.

38. VERGARA, Appendix XXVIII.

39. VERGARA, Appendix XIV.

40. VERGARA, Appendix XV.

41. Documentos, LE 5.

42. Documentos, LE 2, 5; VERGARA, Appendices XVI, XVII.

43. PORTEOUS, J.D., "The Island Parish of Jura," *Scottish Geographical Magazine* 84 (1968), 56-65; UHLIG, H., "Die Ländliche Kulturlandschaft der Hebriden und der Westschottischen Hochlande," *Erdkunde* 13 (1959), 22-46.

44. Documentos, LE 9.

45. Documentos, LE 5, 6.

46. Documentos, LE 5.

47. VERGARA, Appendix XXV.

48. VERGARA, Appendix XXVI.

49. *Ibid.*

50. Documentos, LE 14.

51. VERGARA, Appendix XXVIII.

52. VERGARA, Appendix IX.

CHAPTER 4

1. HUNT, W., *Heirs of Great Adventure: The History of Balfour, Williamson and Company Limited*. London: Balfour, Williamson & Co. Ltd., 1951 (Vol. 1), 1960 (Vol. 2), I p. 15.

2. *Ibid.*, I p. 122.

3. *Ibid.*, I p. 78.

4. Documentos, LE 14.

5. *Ibid.*

6. Personal communication; interview with Gerald Cooper and Reginald Stockins, Compañía de Inversiones "La Escocesa" Ltda., Santiago, Chile, 25 April 1974.

7. Documentos, LE 21.

8. Documentos, LE 10/i.

9. *El Mercurio* 11 November 1916.

10. HUNT, *op. cit.*, II p. 20.

11. Documentos, LE 15; VERGARA, Appendix XXX.

12. Documentos, LE 16.

13. HUNT, *op. cit.*, II p. 21.

14. Documentos, LE 15, 16; VERGARA, Appendix XXX.

15. Documentos, LE 17; VERGARA, Appendix XXXI.

16. Documentos, LE 19.

17. *Ibid.*

18. Documentos, LE 36.

19. Documentos, LE 18/ii.

20. BRIONES, R., *Glosario de Colonización*, 3rd. edition. Santiago, Chile: Majía, 1902, pp. 519-27; *La Unión* 13 June 1914.

21. *La Unión* 13 June 1914.

22. *La Unión de Santiago* 13 June 1914.

23. VIVES SOLAR, J.I., "Una Revolución en la Isla de Pascua en 1914," *Pacifico Magazine* 10 (1917), 655-64.

24. Documentos, LE 25; VERGARA, Appendix XXXII.

25. Documentos, LE 24; VERGARA, Appendix LIV.

26. Documentos, LE 26; VERGARA, Appendix XXXIII.

27. *El Heraldo* 7 October 1916.

28. Documentos, LE 28; VERGARA, Appendix XXXIV.

29. EDWARDS, R., *La Isla de Pascua*. Santiago, Chile: San José, 1918; *La Unión* 12 March 1916.

30. One of the most prolific was BIENVENIDO DE ESTELLA, R.P., who produced: i) "Ocho Meses entre los Canacas Pasuences," *La Revista Católica* 19 (1919), 182-191; ii) "Isla de Pascua," *Publicaciones del Museo de Etnología y Antropología de Chile* 2 (1920), 45-118; iii) *Los Misterios de la Isla de Pascua*. Santiago, Chile: Cervantes, 1920; iv) *Mis Viajes a Pascua*. Santiago, Chile: Cervantes, 1921, in all of which he severely castigated the company.

31. *La Unión* 16 March 1916.

32. *Ibid.*, 19, 22 July, 29 September 1916.

33. *Ibid.*, 18 November 1916.

34. *Ibid.*, 26 October 1916.

35. *La Unión de Santiago* 13 June 1914.

36. *La Unión* 12 May 1916.

37. *Ibid.*, 2 September 1916.

38. All Bishop Edwards' charges, with additions, were repeated in BIENVENIDO DE ESTELLA, 1920, *Los Misterios, op. cit.*

39. *La Unión de Santiago* 13 June 1914.

40. *La Unión* 18 November 1916.

41. *Ibid.*

42. *Ibid.*

43. *La Unión* 12 November 1916.

44. *Ibid.*

45. *La Unión* 17 November 1916.

46. *Ibid.*, 2 September 1916.

47. *Ibid.*, 12 November 1916.

48. *Ibid.*, 27 November 1916.

49. *Ibid.*, 1 December 1916.

50. *Ibid.*, 20 November 1916.

51. BIENVENIDO DE ESTELLA, 1919, *op. cit.*; VIVES SOLAR, J.I., review of ESTELLA, 1920, *Los Misterios*, in *El Mercurio* 14 November 1920.

52. BIENVENIDO DE ESTELLA, 1919, *op. cit.*

53. BIENVENIDO DE ESTELLA, 1920, "Isla de Pascua," *op. cit.*

54. Edmunds was CEDIP's island manager; Green had supported CEDIP during the 1914 revolt; Dillinger, marooned, had been fed, clothed, and housed by the company during his enforced stay on Easter Island.

55. Documentos, LE 30.

56. *La Unión* 2 September 1916.

57. *Ibid.*, 8 November 1916.

58. *Ibid.*, 12 November 1916.

59. EDWARDS, *op. cit.*, p. 25.

60. ROCUANT, D.E., *La Isla de Pascua: Estudio de los Titulos de Dominio, de las Derechos y de los Contratos de Don Enrique Merlet y de la Compañía Explotadora de la Isla de Pascua.* Valparaiso, Chile: Universo, 1916.

61. *Ibid.*, p. 2.

62. *Ibid.*, p. 37.

63. *La Unión* 8 November 1916.

64. *Ibid.*, 12, 17 November 1916.

65. *Ibid.*, 10 November 1916.

66. *La Opinión* 18 November 1916; *La Unión* 19 November 1916.

67. *La Unión* 19 November 1916.

68. Documentos, LE 27; VERGARA, Appendix XXXV.

69. Documentos, LE 36.

70. VERGARA, Appendix XXXVI.

71. VIVES SOLAR, 1917, *op. cit.*; R.M.G., "La Isla de Pascua," *Zig Zag* 20 March 1920.

72. Documentos, LE 39; VERGARA, Appendix XXXVII.

73. VERGARA, Appendices XXXVIII, XL.

74. VERGARA, Appendix XLI.

75. VERGARA, *op. cit.*, pp. 52-66.

76. VERGARA, Appendix XLII.

77. VERGARA, Appendices LVI, LVII.

78. HUNT, *op. cit.*, II p. 159.

79. *Ibid.*, p. 241.

80. Personal communication, as Chapter 4, reference 6.

81. *El Mercurio* 29 December 1951.

82. *Ibid.*, 10 January 1952.

83. *Ibid.*, 29 January 1952.

84. *Ibid.*, 13 January 1952; BARAHONA, A., "Actividades de la Sociedad 'Amigos de la Isla de Pascua' de Santiago," *Geochile* 1 (1951), 39-40. The whole of the first issue of *Geochile*, the organ of the Chilean Geographical Society, was devoted to Easter Island (December 1951).

85. *El Mercurio* 13 January 1952.

86. *El Mercurio* 29 January 1952.

87. *El Diario Oficial* 5 October 1953.

CHAPTER 5

1. ROUTLEDGE, Mrs. Scoresby, *The Mystery of Easter Island*. London: Sifton, Praed, 1919.

2. MACMILLAN BROWN, J., *The Riddle of the Pacific*. London: T. Fisher Unwin, 1924.

3. VON DANIKEN, E., *Chariots of the Gods*. New York: Bantam, 1971.

4. BANDY, M.C., "Geology and Petrology of Easter Island," *Bulletin of the Geological Society of America* 48 (1937), 1589-1610; CHUBB, L.J., *Geology of Galapagos, Cocos, and Easter Island*. Honolulu: Bernice P. Bishop Museum Bulletin 110, 1933.

5. MAZIERE, F., *Mysteries of Easter Island*. London: Collins, 1969, p. 41.

6. *Ibid.*, p. 218. See also ENGLERT, 1948, *op. cit.*, p. 46.

7. BANDY, *op. cit.*, pp. 1592-6.

8. Based largely on BANDY, *op. cit.*, and CHUBB, *op. cit.*

9. GULICK, in SKOTTSBERG, C., ed., *The Natural History of Juan Fernandez and Easter Island*. Uppsala, Sweden: Almqvist and Wiksell, 1920-56, I, p. 423. SKOTTSBERG's Volume I contains an extensive description of the island's "Geography, Geology, and Origin of Island Life."

10. BANDY, *op. cit.*, pp. 1591-2.

11. Documentos, LE 35, p. 4.

12. THOMSON, in DOS PASSOS, J., *Easter Island*. Garden City, N.Y.: Doubleday, 1971, p. 107.

13. WOLFF, W., *Island of Death*. New York: Augustin, 1948, p. 13.

14. Further climatic details are to be found in HEYERDAHL, T., ed., *Archaeology of Easter Island*. Santa Fe, N.M.: School of Ameri-

can Research and Museum of New Mexico Monograph 24, 1961; SKOTTSBERG, *op. cit.*

15. SKOTTSBERG, *op. cit.*, I, p. 6.

16. DIAZ VIAL, C., "Reconnaissance Soil Survey of Isla de Pascua (Easter Island), Chile," *Proceedings, Seventh Pacific Science Congress* 6 (1953), 113-16.

17. WATTS, D., "Ecosystems of Small Islands: Some Theoretical Considerations," pp. 3-10 in MOMSEN, R.P., ed., *Geographical Analysis for Development in Latin America and the Caribbean*. Chapel Hill, N.C.: CLAG, 1975.

18. SKOTTSBERG, *op. cit.*, Vol. II.

19. SKOTTSBERG, *op. cit.*, II, p. 426.

20. MACMILLAN BROWN, *op. cit.*, p. 146.

21. SKOTTSBERG, *op. cit.*, I, p. 7.

22. *Ibid.*

23. *Ibid.*

24. HEYERDAHL, *op. cit.*

25. SKOTTSBERG, *op. cit.*, Vol. III.

26. *Ibid.*

27. MACMILLAN BROWN, *op. cit.*, p. 28.

28. METRAUX, A., *Ethnology of Easter Island*. Honolulu: Bernice P. Bishop Museum Bulletin 160, 1971, p. 67.

29. WILHELM, O.E., and HULOT, A.L., "Pesca y peces de la Isla de Pascua," *Boletín de la Sociedad de Biología de Concepción* 32 (1957), 139-55.

30. WILHELM, O.E., "Las gallinas de la Isla de Pascua," *Boletín de la Sociedad de Biología de Concepción*, 32 (1957), 133-37.

CHAPTER 6

1. SHAPIRO, H.L., "The Physical Relationships of the Easter Islanders," pp. 24-7 in METRAUX, A., *Ethnology of Easter Island*. Honolulu: Bernice P. Bishop Museum Bulletin 160, 1971.

2. SUGGS, R.C., *The Island Civilizations of Polynesia*. New York: New American Library, 1960, p. 23.

3. LEVISON, M., WARD, R.G., and WEBB, J.W., *The Settlement of Polynesia: a computer simulation*. Minneapolis: University of Minnesota Press, 1973.

4. SUGGS, *op. cit.*, p. 118; METRAUX, *op. cit.*

5. METEI, *Preliminary Report of the Medical Expedition to Easter Island* (METEI), Montreal (mimeo.), 1965, p. 153.

6. METRAUX, *op. cit.*, *passim.*

7. OLIVER, *op. cit.*, p. 198.

8. McCOY, P., *Easter Island Settlement Patterns in the late Prehistoric and Protohistoric periods*. Unpublished Ph.D. thesis, Washington State University, 1973.

9. METRAUX, *op. cit.*, p. 152.

10. FUENTES, F., "Reseña Botanica sobre la Isla de Pascua," *Boletín de la Museo Nacional de Chile* 5 (1913), 320-37.

11. CASEY, *op. cit.*, pp. 247-8.

12. Documentos, LE 35, p. 36.

13. THOMSON, W.J., quoted in DOS PASSOS, J., *Easter Island: Island of Enigmas*. Garden City, N.Y.: Doubleday, 1971, pp. 96-121.

14. ROUTLEDGE, *op. cit.*, p. 137.

15. METRAUX, *op. cit.*, pp. 128-9.

16. ROUTLEDGE, *op. cit.*, p. 265.

17. METRAUX, *op. cit.*, p. 120.

18. *Ibid.*, p. 129; BIENVENIDO DE ESTELLA, 1920, *Los Misterios*, *op. cit.*, p. 132.

19. Documentos, LE 14.

20. VERGARA, Appendix VIII.

21. Documentos, LE 5, 6; VERGARA, Appendices IV, XXV.

22. VERGARA, Appendix IV.

23. *Ibid.*

24. PHILIPPI, *op. cit.*, DOS PASSOS, *op. cit.*, p. 80.

25. BIENVENIDO DE ESTELLA, 1920, *Los Misterios*, *op. cit.*, p. 142.

26. *Ibid.*, pp. 182-4.

27. PREBBLE, J., *The Highland Clearances*. Harmondsworth: Penguin, 1969, p. 13.

28. YOUNGSON, A.J., *After the Forty-five: The Economic Impact on the Scottish Highlands*. Edinburgh: Edinburgh University Press, 1973, p. 170.

29. WALKER, J., *Economic History of the Hebrides and Highlands of Scotland*. Edinburgh, 1812, p. 407.

30. MILLS, D., and PARRY, M.L., "A Scottish Agricultural Revolution?," *Area* 8 (1976), 237-39.

31. PREBBLE, *op. cit.*, p. 29.

32. *Ibid.*, p. 27.

33. YOUNGSON, *op. cit.*, p. 173.

34. OLIVER, *op. cit.*, pp. 280-81.

CHAPTER 7

1. Documentos, LE 6.

2. Documentos, LE 1; VERGARA, Appendix VIII.

3. Documentos, LE 6.

4. *Ibid.*

5. Documentos, LE 5, 6.

6. Documentos, LE 28.

7. VERGARA, Appendix XXV.

8. *Ibid.*

9. Documentos, LE 22.

10. Documentos, LE 23.

11. Documentos, LE 35.

12. Anon., "Datos sobre la Isla de Pascua," *Geochile* 1 (1951), 13-14.

13. Documentos, LE 1.

14. Documentos, LE 6.

15. VERGARA, Appendix III, IV.

16. *Ibid.*

17. VERGARA, Appendix XXV.

18. Documentos, LE 35.

19. *Ibid.*

20. Documentos, LE 23.

21. Documentos, LE 35.

22. *Ibid.*, p. 2.

23. *Ibid.*, p. 3.

24. *Ibid.*, p. 10.

25. *Ibid.*, p. 13.

26. *Ibid.*, p. 15.

27. ROUTLEDGE, *op. cit.*, p. 125.

28. Documentos, LE 35, p. 16.

29. *Ibid.*, p. 20.

30. *Ibid.*, p. 22.

31. *Ibid.*, p. 24.

32. *Ibid.*, p. 38.

33. HUNT, *op. cit.*, II p. 161.

34. ZOSIMO VALENZUELA, P., *La Isla de Pascua*. Santiago, Chile: San José, 1912, p. 6; Documentos, LE 22, p. 8.

35. HEYERDAHL, T., "General Discussion," pp. 493-526 in FERDON, E.N., and HEYERDAHL, T., eds., *Archaeology of Easter Island*. Santa Fe, New Mexico: Monographs of the School of American Research and the Museum of New Mexico No. 24, 1961.

36. METRAUX, *op. cit.*, p. 13.

37. PALMER, J.L., "Davis or Easter Island," *Proceedings of the Liverpool Literary and Philosophical Society* 29 (1875), 275-97.

38. COOKE, G.H., "Te Pito te Henua," *U.S. National Museum Report* (1899), 689-723, p. 705.

39. METRAUX, *op. cit.*, p. 16.

40. *Ibid.*, p. 17. For details of its fate, see HEYERDAHL, T., "Historical Summary," pp. 127-31 in PICKER, F., *Rapa Nui: Easter Island*. New York: Two Continents Publishing Group/Paddington Press, 1974.

41. Documentos, LE 22, pp. 7-8.

42. METRAUX, *op. cit.*, p. 153.

43. Documentos, LE 35, p. 18.

44. METRAUX, *op. cit.*, p. 151.

45. TUAN, Y-F., *Topophilia*. Englewood Cliffs, N.J.: Prentice-Hall, 1974.

46. Documentos, LE 35, p. 16.

47. METRAUX, *op. cit.*, p. 151.

48. *Ibid.*, p. 129.

49. MULLOY, W., *Investigation and Restoration of the Ceremonial Center of Orongo, Easter Island*, part I. New York: Easter Island Committee, International Fund for Monuments Inc., Bulletin 4, 1975.

50. MAZIERE, F., *Mysteries of Easter Island*. London: Collins, 1969.

51. ROUTLEDGE, *op. cit.*, p. 125.

52. Personal communications, Leon Tuki Hey, 1974-5.

53. ROUTLEDGE, *op. cit.*, p. 135-6.

54. Documentos, LE 35, p. 13.

55. HUNT, *op. cit.*, II p. 224.

56. METRAUX, *op. cit.*, p. 47.

57. Documentos, LE 22, p. 9.

58. METRAUX, *op. cit.*, p. 152.

59. CASEY, *op. cit.*, p. 247.

60. *Ibid.*, p. 249.

61. Documentos, LE 18/ii; *El Heraldo* 17 January 1905.

62. Anon., *op. cit.*, p. 13.

63. BIENVENIDO DE ESTELLA, 1920, *Los Misterios*, *op. cit.*, pp. 185-6.

64. OLIVER, *op. cit.*, p. 280.

65. Documentos, LE 35, p. 39.

66. METRAUX, *op. cit.*, pp. 14, 20-22.

67. *El Heraldo* 17 January 1905.

68. Documentos, LE 22, p. 12; BIENVENIDO DE ESTELLA, 1919, *op. cit.*

69. METRAUX, *op. cit.*, p. 23.

CHAPTER 8

1. ROUTLEDGE, *op. cit.*, p. 142.

2. *Ibid.*, pp. 142-3.

3. *Ibid.*, p. 148.

4. METRAUX, *op. cit.*, p. 49.

5. RAMIREZ, J.T., *Navegando a Rapa-Nui*. Padre Las Casas, Chile: San Francisco, 1935, pp. 77-8.

6. CASEY, *op. cit.*, p. 118.

7. *Ibid.*, pp. 248-49.

8. MARIN, R., *Pascua: La Isla Lejana y Misteriosa*. Chile, 1945 (?), p. 151.

9. FLORES, J., *Te Pito Te Henua*. Santiago, Chile: Orbe, 1965, pp. 44-5.

10. CASEY, *op. cit.*, pp. 118-9, 243.

11. *Ibid.*, pp. 246-7.

12. *Ibid.*, p. 291.

13. FERDON, E.N., *One Man's Log*. London: George Allen and Unwin, 1966, p. 70.

14. CASEY, *op. cit.*, p. 258.

15. Personal communication, Gerald Cooper, see Chapter 4, note 6.

16. FERDON, *op. cit.*, p. 71.

17. OLIVER, *op. cit.*, pp. 333, 342-5.

18. METRAUX, *op. cit.*, p. 47.

19. FLORES, *op. cit.*, p. 63.

20. See VERGARA, *op. cit.*, 79-83; FLORES, *op. cit.*, pp. 44, 139; CASTEX, *op. cit.*, pp. 136-8; CAMPBELL, R., *El Misterioso Mundo de Rapanui*. Buenos Aires, Argentina: Francisco de Aguirre, 1973, p. 35.

21. BARAHONA, A., *op. cit.*, p. 40; MERINO REYES, L., *Rumbo a Oceania*. Santiago, Chile: Zig-Zag, 1955.

22. CAMPBELL, *op. cit.*, p. 35.

23. MERINO, *op. cit.*, p. 35.

24. ENGLERT, quoted in MERINO, *op. cit.*, p. 69.

25. OLIVER, *op. cit.*, pp. 396, 416.

26. MAZIERE, *op. cit.*, pp. 144, 187.

27. *Ibid.*, p. 168.

28. *Ibid.*, pp. 23-4.

29. *Ibid.*

30. MERINO, *op. cit.*, p. 120.

31. METEI, *op. cit.*

32. REID, H.E., *A World Away: A Canadian Adventure on Easter Island*. Sydney: Angus and Robertson, 1967, pp. 37, 151-2.

33. *Ibid.*, p. 128.

34. BROOKS, R., "Social Planning in Columbia," *Journal of the American Institute of Planners* 37 (1971), 373-79; PORTEOUS, 1974, *op. cit.*

35. FERDON, *op. cit.*, p. 72.

36. PORTEOUS, 1972, 1973, 1973, 1974, *op. cit.*

37. Personal communications, several Easter Island residents.

38. REID, *op. cit.*, p. 37.

39. *Ibid.*, p. 42.

40. *Ibid.*, p. 51.

41. *El Mercurio* 11 January 1965.

42. Actas, 16 March 1966, 21 May 1967.

43. Actas, 8 August 1967.

44. *El Mercurio* 25 January 1967.

45. *Ibid.*, 24 January 1967.

46. To the extent of intermarriage, as early as 1967.

47. *El Mercurio* 25 January 1967.

48. Actas, *passim*.

49. REID, *op. cit.*, p. 25.

50. LOPEZ, *op. cit.*, p. 80.

51. Indications of early 1960s air route proposals are to be found in CASTEX, *op. cit.*, p. 25; FERDON, *op. cit.*, p. 75; FLORES, *op. cit.*, p. 58; MAZIERE, *op. cit.*, p. 169; REID, *op. cit.*, p. 14.

52. OLIVER, *op. cit.*, pp. 145-6.

53. PARRAGUE SINGER, R., "Primer Vuelo a La Isla de Pascua," *Geochile* 1 (1951), 6-9.

54. REID, *op. cit.*, p. 145.

55. *El Mercurio* 28 February 1965, 23 April 1967.

56. *Ibid.*, 29 January 1952.

57. *Ibid.*, 20 April 1965.

58. *Ibid.*, 7 February, 7 March, 1967.

59. *Ibid.*, 6 April, 1967.

60. Odeplan, *Plan de Desarrollo del Departamento de Isla de Pascua 1971-76*. Santiago, Chile: Oficina de Planificación Nacional, Plan de la Economia Nacional Series I no. 15, 1972, p. 52.

61. *Ibid.*, pp. 51-3.

62. *Ibid.*, pp. 25, 34.

63. *El Mercurio* 12, 27 January, 1 February, 9 March, 1967.

64. *Ibid.*, 7 February 1967.

65. COOK, J., 1971, *op. cit.*, p. 155.

66. ROUTLEDGE, *op. cit.*, p. 137.

67. CAMUS GUNDIAN, D., "Biografía humana en la Isla de Pascua," *Geochile* 1 (1951), 24-38.

68. VIVES SOLAR, J.I., *Te Poki Rapanui (El Niño Pascuense)*. Santiago, Chile: Cervantes, 1923.

69. DRAPKIN, I., *Contribution to the Demographic Study of Easter Island*. Honolulu: Bernice P. Bishop Museum Occasional Papers, Vol. 11, no. 12, 1935.

70. BARAHONA, *op. cit.*

71. REID, *op. cit.*, pp. 58-71; METEI, *op. cit.*

72. ZOSIMO, *op. cit.*

73. REID, *op. cit.*, p. 66.

74. FERDON, *op. cit.*, p. 73.

75. Odeplan, *op. cit.*, pp. 47-8.

76. Thatching continues in use in the 1980s, mainly on tourist-oriented buildings.

77. Documentos, LE 35, p. 38.

78. BIENVENIDO DE ESTELLA, 1920, *Los Misterios, op. cit.*, X.

79. BIENVENIDO, 1920, "Isla de Pascua;" 1921; *op. cit.*

80. CASEY, *op. cit.*, p. 114.

81. Documentos, LE 22, p. 10; ZOSIMO, *op. cit.*; ROUTLEDGE, *op. cit.*, p. 141; Documentos, LE 35, p. 38.

82. REID, *op. cit.*, p. 113.

83. CAMUS GUNDIAN, *op. cit.*, p. 26.

84. *El Mercurio* 7 March 1967.

85. BIENVENIDO DE ESTELLA, 1920, *Los Misterios, op. cit.*, X, located 36 (72 per cent) of the island's 50 dwellings at Hangaroa, and 3 (6 per cent) at Mataveri. Smaller nodes included 5 (10 per cent) at Moeroa, the section of Hangaroa closest to Mataveri, 4 (8 per cent) at the leprosarium, north of Hangaroa, and 2 (4 per cent) at Vaihu, for the use of shepherds. With the leprosarium, Hangaroa had 80 per cent of the dwellings in 1920, Mataveri (with Moeroa and Vaihu) having the remaining 20 per cent.

CHAPTER 9

1. TURNER, L., and ASH, J., *The Golden Hordes: International Tourism and the Pleasure Periphery*. London: Constable, 1975.

2. *El Mercurio* 15 March 1965.

3. *Ibid.*, 11 January 1967.

4. *Ibid.*, 16 February 1967.

5. MULLOY, *op. cit.*

6. Odeplan, *op. cit.*, pp. 2-3; RAPU HAOA, S., and FIGUEROA, G., "Desaparicion de las playas de la Isla de Pascua" (mimeo.), Santiago, 1973.

7. Actas, 5 December 1967.

8. Actas, 2 November 1971.

9. Documentos, LE 35, p. 5.

10. MULLOY, *op. cit.*; VERGARA, Appendix LVIII.

11. VERGARA, Appendix LVIII.

12. VERGARA, Appendix LXIX.

13. VERGARA, Appendix LXIX. Many small artifacts were subsequently removed, however, notably by Heyerdahl. See HEYERDAHL, T., *The Art of Easter Island*. London: Allen and Unwin, 1976.

14. VERGARA, Appendices LX, LXI.

15. Odeplan, *op. cit.*, p. 67.

16. *Ibid.*, p. 68.

17. MARIN, *op. cit.*, pp. 150-1.

18. CASTEX, *op. cit.*, p. 28.

19. *El Mercurio* 5 March, 5, 6, 7, 8 April 1967.

20. *Ibid.*, 9 March, 5 April 1967.

21. *Ibid.*, 23 April 1967.

22. *Ibid.*

23. Actas, 7 July 1970.

24. Odeplan, *op. cit.*, p. 59.

25. MATLEY, I., *The Geography of International Tourism*. Washington, D.C.: Association of American Geographers Resource Paper 76-1, p. 1.

26. TURNER and ASH, *op. cit.*

27. MATLEY, *op. cit.*, p. 1.

28. *Ibid.*

CHAPTER 10

1. Since this was first written (1977), the question has been addressed in some detail in McCALL, G., *Reaction to Disaster: Continuity and Change in Rapanui Social Organization*. Unpublished Ph.D. thesis, Australian National University, Canberra, 1977.

2. Odeplan, *op. cit.*, pp. 41, 70.

3. PORTEOUS, J.D., "Quality of Life in British Columbia Company Towns," pp. 332-46 in PRESSMAN, N., ed., *New Communities in Canada: Exploring Planned Environments*. Waterloo, Ontario: University of Waterloo Faculty of Environmental Studies, 1976.

4. MARIN, *op. cit.*, p. 150.

5. *El Mercurio* 29 December 1951, 29 January 1952. For a dissenting view see DIAZ VIAL, C., "Possibilidades Agricolas de la Isla de Pascua," *Geochile* 1 (1951), 16-23.

6. *El Mercurio* 10 January 1952.

7. FLORES, *op. cit.*, p. 55.

8. *El Mercurio* 15 March 1965.

9. FLORES, *op. cit.*, pp. 110-23.

10. FERDON, *op. cit.*, p. 72; Odeplan, *op. cit.*

11. Anon., *op. cit.*, pp. 13-14.

12. REID, *op. cit.*, p. 148.

13. FLORES, *op. cit.*, p. 86.

14. Odeplan, *op. cit.*, p. 43.

15. PORTEOUS, 1968, *op. cit.*

16. Odeplan, *op. cit.*, p. 63.

17. OLIVER, *op. cit.*, pp. 292, 419.

18. REID, *op. cit.*, p. 128.

19. Odeplan, *op. cit.*, p. 32.

20. *El Mercurio* 4, 5 January 1967.

21. *Ibid.*, 12, 21 January 1967.

22. PORTEOUS, J.D., *Environment & Behavior: planning and everyday urban life.* Reading, Mass.: Addison-Wesley, 1977, Chapters 12-14.

23. *El Mercurio* 5 January 1967.

24. *Ibid.*, 27 January, 3 April 1967.

25. *Ibid.*, 8 April 1967.

26. *Ibid.*, 10 April 1967.

27. Personal communications, several *continentales*.

28. *Ibid.*

29. LUNDGREN, J., "Tourist Impact/Island Entrepreneurship in the Caribbean," pp. 12-19 in MOMSEN, R.P., ed., *Geographical Analysis for Development in Latin America and the Caribbean*. Chapel Hill, N.C.: CLAG Publications, 1975.

30. Odeplan, *op. cit.*, p. 40.

31. MULLOY, *op. cit.*, p. 20.

32. Personal communications, several *continentales*.

33. OLIVER, *op. cit.*, pp. 410-12.

34. BERGESEN, V., "Investment Dilemma," *Latin America and Empire Report* 10 (1976), 17-22.

35. ORREGO VICUÑA, *op. cit.*, p. 42; personal communication, A. Arentsen Petersen, Governor of Easter Island, December 1975.

36. LUNDGREN, *op. cit.*, p. 13.

37. DE SOUZA, A.R. and PORTER, P.W., *The Underdevelopment and Modernization of the Third World*. Washington, D.C.: Association of American Geographers Resource Paper 28, 1974.

38. See four works by BROOKFIELD, H.C.: *Melanesia: A Geographical Interpretation of an Island World*. London: Methuen, 1971; "On One Geography and the Third World," *Transactions of the Institute of British Geographers* 56 (1973), 1-20; *The Pacific in Transition: Geographical Perspectives on Adaptation and Change*. London: Arnold, 1973; *Interdependent Development*. London: Methuen, 1975.

39. CALDWELL, M., quoted in CONNELL, J., "The Geography of Development," *Area* 3 (1971), 259-65.

40. For the concept of underdevelopment as a deleterious *process*, rather than an initial *state*, see: FRANK, A.G., *Capitalism and Underdevelopment in Latin America*. New York: Monthly Review Press, 1969; and DE SOUZA and PORTER, *op. cit.*

41. CRUZ-COKE, R., "Ecología humana de la Isla de Pascua," *Revista Medica de Chile* 91 (1963), 773-79.

42. *Ibid.*

43. SEMPLE, E.C., *Influences of Geographical Environment*. New York: Henry Holt, 1911, Chapter XIII.

PLATE 47 Horse (Kon-Tiki Museet artifact 1542) ▶

PLATE 48 Rabbit(?) (Kon-Tiki Museet artifact 1723) ▶

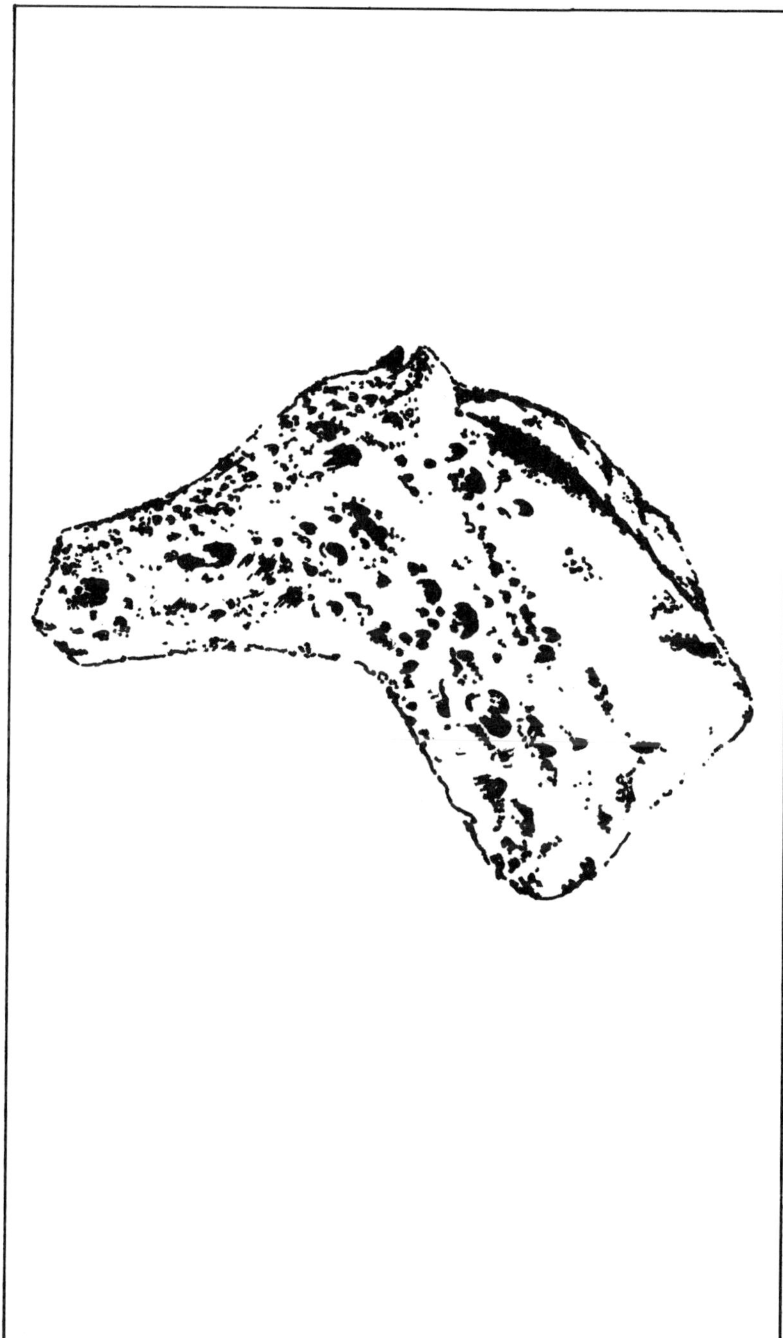

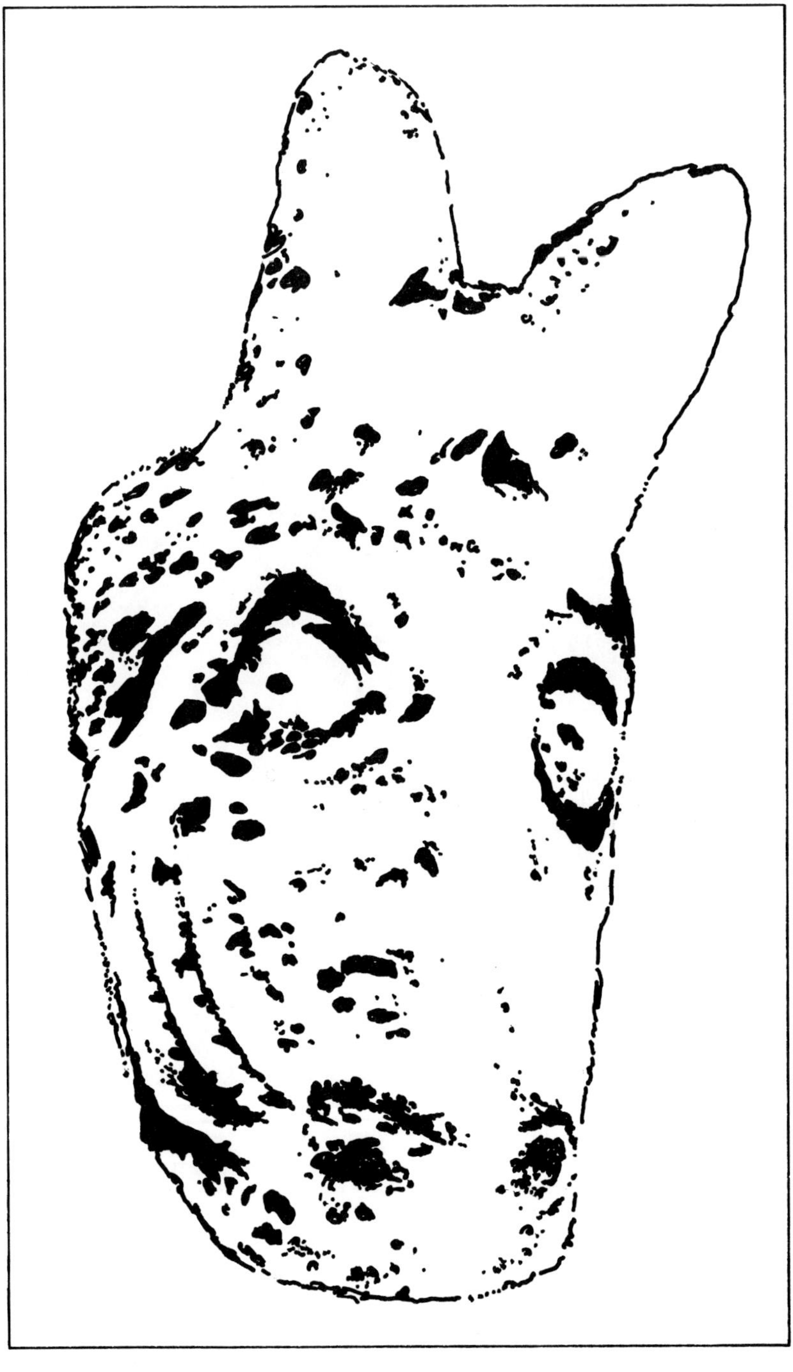

INDEX

PLATE 49 Feline or canine form (Kon-Tiki Museet artifact 1392) ▶

PLATE 50 The Author ▶

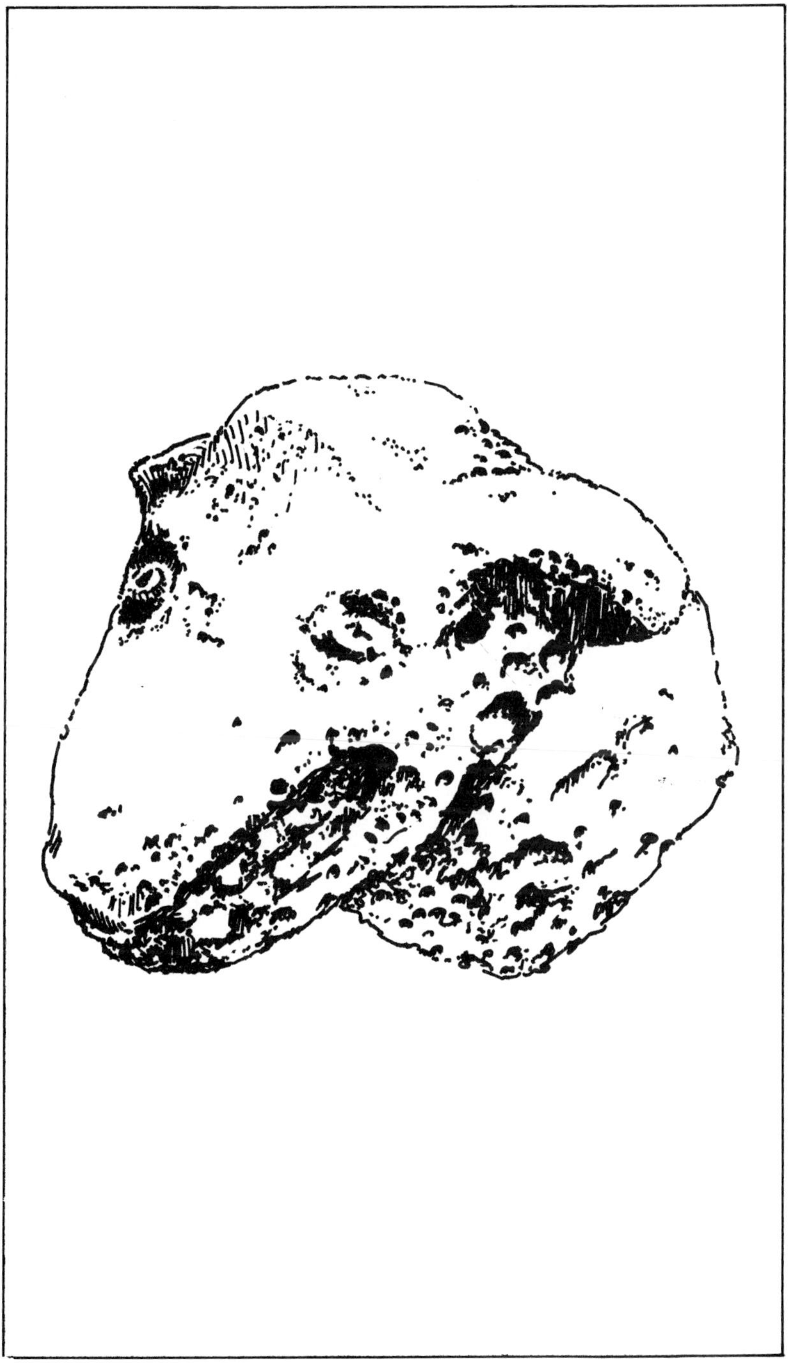

THE AUTHOR

J. Douglas Porteous was born in 1943 in the City of York. An Open Exhibitioner at Jesus College, University of Oxford, he took a first class Honours B.A. and was awarded the Herbertson Memorial Prize for the best honours dissertation of 1965. Among other awards, he received a Dodd Grant for Adventurous Travel (Epirus, 1963).

Having moved from a traditionalist academic environment to the University of Hull, then in the throes of the theoretico-quantitative revolution in Geography, he nevertheless completed his Ph.D. in 1968. The postdoctoral year 1968-9 was spent at the Massachusetts Institute of Technology and Harvard University, where Dr. Porteous was an affiliate of the Joint Center for Urban Studies. During the same year he held a President John F. Kennedy Memorial Scholarship. He joined the University of Victoria in 1969 at age 25, became a Canadian citizen in 1975, and attained the rank of Professor in 1978.

Dr. Porteous' teaching and research interests include: behavioural and humanistic aspects of urban planning; gaming simulation; Latin America; environmental aesthetics; and the history and philosophy of geography. During the last decade he has travelled widely, giving invited lectures from Britain to Bangladesh, delivering papers at professional meetings from Nigeria and New Zealand to the U.S.S.R. and Japan, and doing archival and field research from Chile to Canada.

Dr. Porteous' research and publishing interests are eclectic. Published articles range in subject matter from computer graphics to the social geography of the Hebrides, from English urban history to the spatial behaviour of Chilean beggars, and from territoriality in Canadian teenage gangs to literary geographic analyses of *The Little Prince* and *The Lord of the Rings*. Of his more than sixty publications, perhaps half relate to the social, political, and urban planning aspects of company towns and estates in Chile, Easter Island, Canada, and Britain.

Three earlier books indicate that this breadth of interest has not been achieved at the expense of depth of knowledge. *The Company Town of Goole: an essay in urban genesis* (University of Hull Press, 1969) was followed by *Canal Ports: the urban achievement of the Canal Age* (Academic Press, 1977). In *Environment & Behavior: planning and everyday urban life* (Addison-Wesley, 1977) Dr. Porteous sought to combine behavioural geography, urban sociology, environmental psychology, urban planning, and architecture into a coherent, humane interdiscipline. The current work on Easter Island is an outgrowth of long-term interests in Third World modernization and development and the problems of small, isolated islands.

Current research includes work on autobiogeography, environmental aesthetics, the experience of place, recent developments in geographical thought, and a revolutionary scheme, no doubt doomed to failure, to reorganize universities according to rational and ethical principles. When not travelling the world, Dr. Porteous kayaks, drives an antique lilac Volkswagen, eats *bougatsa*, and pots bullheads.